REVOLUTIONARY SOCIALIST DEVELOPMENT IN THE THIRD WORLD

REVOLUTIONARY SOCIALIST DEVELOPMENT IN THE THIRD WORLD

Editors

**Gordon White, Robin Murray and
Christine White**

*Socialist Development Group,
Institute of Development Studies,
University of Sussex*

A MEMBER OF THE HARVESTER PRESS
PUBLISHING GROUP

First published in Great Britain in 1983 by
WHEATSHEAF BOOKS LTD
A MEMBER OF THE HARVESTER PRESS PUBLISHING GROUP
Publisher: John Spiers
Director of Publications: Edward Elgar
16 Ship Street, Brighton, Sussex

British Library Cataloguing in Publication Data
Revolutionary socialist development in the third world.
  1. Communist countries—Politics and government
  2. Communist countries—Economic policy
  3. Underdeveloped area—Politics and government
  I. White, Gordon   II. Murray, Robin
  III. White, Christine
  330.9171'7   JC475

  ISBN 0-7108-0220-X
  ISBN 0-7108-0225-0 Pbk

Photosetting by Thomson Press (India) Limited, New Delhi
and printed in Great Britain by
Biddles Ltd, Guildford, Surrey

THE HARVESTER PRESS PUBLISHING GROUP
The Harvester Press Publishing Group comprises Harvester Press Limited
(chiefly publishing literature, fiction, philosophy, psychology, science and
trade books), Harvester Press Microform Publications Limited (publishing
in microform unpublished archives, scarce printed sources, and indexes to
these collections) and Wheatsheaf Books Limited (chiefly publishing in
economics, international politics, sociology and related social sciences),
whose books are distributed by The Harvester Press Limited and its
agencies throughout the world.

CONTENTS

In memory of Ruth First, socialist scholar and activist, who dedicated her life to the political and intellectual struggle for socialism in Southern Africa.

EDITORS' PREFACE

This book grows out of work by the Socialist Development Group at the Institute of Development Studies, Sussex University. The group's main aim is to expand the comparative analysis of Third World development which has hitherto been heavily oriented towards various forms of capitalist development. A large percentage of the world's population live in countries which have rejected, more or less comprehensively, capitalist modes of development and adopted various forms of socialist development strategy. The experiences of these countries are very diverse; in its work, the group attempts to comprehend this diversity, to investigate the dynamics characteristic of socialist modes of development, assess their developmental achievements and problems, and generate ideas which may be useful for people involved in socialist movements in North, East and South.[1]

The book contains six case-studies of socialist transformation and development in the Third World, each accompanied by statistical and chronological reference material. Given our particular interest in understanding the dynamics of social transformation, we have concentrated on countries which have adopted a *revolutionary* programme of socialist transition in accordance with Marxist or Marxist-Leninist principles. This does not imply that we regard only these countries as examples of 'genuine' socialism, nor does it imply a lack of interest in the many other forms of non-Marxist evolutionary socialist development current in both North and South. For example, 'social democracy' in its various forms remains a crucial historical phenomenon which is poorly understood; a good deal more work also needs to be done on the specific nature and dynamics of 'intermediate régimes' in the Third World.[2] From an analytical point of view, however, it is more rigorous to examine the revolutionary variant before comparing it with evolutionary alternatives (the most obvious

example being Tanzania).[3] Even with this narrower focus, the
diversity of socialist forms and processes is very wide.

The case-studies fall into two categories. The first two countries – South Yemen and Mozambique – embarked upon the
process of socialist transformation and construction relatively
recently, and are thus unfamiliar to both general and specialist
readers. In both cases, the authors were asked to provide a
general overview of the countries' experience of socialist transition, with particular reference to a set of common issues
which emerged from group discussions at our Institute. The
most important themes were the following: (i) the particular
mode of revolutionary transition to state power, notably the
character of mass mobilisation; (ii) the nature of social, economic and political transformation immediately after the
success of the revolutionary movement; (iii) the basic strategy
of socialist development adopted, and the major constraints
and problems encountered in the process of realising it; (iv) the
nature of the new social formation, notably the character and
role of the state, the general constellation of social classes and
political forces, the nature of the labour process and the quality
of democratic life; (v) a general evaluation of the 'success' of
each particular experience in terms of both socialist and developmental goals.

The next four cases – North Korea, China, Cuba and
Vietnam – are longer established. Their experiences have
received considerable attention, and overall accounts should
be more easily available to our readers. During the past decade,
however, these countries have undergone important shifts in
ideological orientation and development strategy: North
Korea with its economic opening to the West and Japan in the
early 1970s, China after the death of Mao and the arrest of the
Shanghai radical group in late 1976, Cuba after the failure of
the 1970 sugar mobilisation, and Vietnam after the watershed
Sixth Plenum in 1979. The causes and impact of these changes
pose serious analytical problems. In each case, we asked the
authors to describe and explain the shifts, and where possible
draw conclusions about their implications for understanding
the dynamics of established Third World socialist régimes.

Though these questions and themes have provided some
common ground for all six case-studies, each country has its

own key dimensions and each author his/her own points of emphasis – the result is a considerable diversity of approach and argument.

Gordon White
Robin Murray
Christine White

Acknowledgements

Though many people have contributed to the typing of this manuscript, the editors would particularly like to thank Helen Miller, Julia Broomfield and Marguerite Cooke. We would also like to thank Magdalena Reid for preparing the country profiles.

Notes

1 For examples of previous work by members of the Group, see Jack Gray and Gordon White (eds), *China's New Development Strategy*, London, Academic Press, 1982; and Christine White and Gordon White (eds), 'Agriculture, the peasantry and socialist development', *IDS Bulletin* vol. 13, no. 4, 1982 (whole issue).
2 For the idea of 'intermediate régimes', see M. Kalecki, 'Observations on social and economic aspects of intermediate régimes', in his *Essays on Developing Countries*, New Jersey, Humanities Press, 1976, pp. 30–9; K. P. Jameson, 'An intermediate régime in historical context: the case of Guyana', *Development and Change*, vol. 11, 1980, pp. 77–95.
3 James Mittelman has written an interesting comparative study of 'transitional' socialism in Mozambique and 'non-transitional' socialism in Tanzania: *Underdevelopment and the Transition to Socialism: Mozambique and Tanzania*, London, Academic Press, 1981.

Methodological Note Concerning References in the Country Profiles

Letters refer to the source list following the profile; numerals refer to the general bibliography in Appendix A; Roman numerals are note references, listed at the end of the profile. For sources and definitions not specified, see Appendix B.

REVOLUTIONARY SOCIALIST DEVELOPMENT IN THE THIRD WORLD: AN OVERVIEW

Gordon White

The Definitional Dilemma

'Socialism' is a protean concept describing an even more protean reality. The debate about the nature of 'socialist societies' and 'socialist transition' is complex, and I would prefer to avoid entanglement. In a book of this type, however, it is important to be clear at the outset about how one is using the term socialist given the vast amount of ambiguity and contention surrounding it. Though the editors and contributors do not share a common view, one can approach the problem by making a distinction between 'socialist society' as a current reality and as a desired end-state. To varying degrees, the societies analysed in this book share certain basic structural characteristics which may be termed socialist.[1] First, they have broken – in most cases decisively – the autonomous power of private capital over politics, production and distribution, abrogated the dominance of the law of value in its capitalist form, and embarked upon a development path which does not rely on the dynamic of private ownership and entrepreneurship. Second, they have brought about (or are bringing about) certain fundamental transformations – in the economic, political and social realms – which reflect the long-standing aspirations of revolutionary socialist movements everywhere, and the basic principles of the founding fathers of 'scientific socialism': most notably, the nationalisation of industry, socialisation of agriculture, abolition or limitation of markets, and the establishment of a comprehensive planning structure and a politico-ideological system bent on the transition to an ultimate communist society.

On the other hand, many key features of this type of society, as the following case-studies should document vividly, clash with basic socialist values. As an historically-specific type, these 'actually existing socialisms', to use Bahro's term,[2] must be distinguished from a hypothetical 'higher' stage of 'full' socialism marked by an absence of classes and the state, political democracy and conscious control of the social economy by the associated producers. If the latter stage is fully socialist, then the realities of 'actually existing socialisms' fall short of the name.

How then should we describe them? A plethora of terms is available. 'Socialist societies' is too blandly approving, though one tends to lapse into it for reasons of brevity; 'state capitalist' is unconvincingly damning, and 'revisionist' seldom more than a term of abuse.[3] 'Post-capitalist' is historically inaccurate for the cases we are considering, while 'non-capitalist' is too vague; 'transitional societies' begs the question of whether they are in fact in transition to anything. Perhaps more satisfactory would be 'proto-socialist', implying that only certain initial steps have been taken, or 'state socialist' implying that this form of socialism is highly *étati*sed. Whatever label one adopts, however, it is important to avoid two common tendencies: on the one hand, to overestimate the 'socialist' nature of such societies and view 'full' socialism as merely a future extrapolation of current realities; on the other hand, to minimise the difficulties involved in realising socialist goals in current Third World conditions and engage in critiques which are empty because unrealistic. To declare the present as Utopia (as the Kim Il Song régime does with its insistence on North Korea as a 'paradise on earth'), or to damn the present because it falls short of an abstract view of 'real' socialism, both seem equally unreasonable. At the same time, however, the link between actual 'proto-socialist' societies and a future 'fully socialist' ideal is crucial in evaluating the political nature and potential of such societies. The logic of socialist development surely requires that the future should be a guide to action in the present in both theory and reality. Thus proto-socialist societies could be said to be genuinely engaged in 'the transition to socialism' to the extent that efforts are made and institutions designed in such a way as to pre-figure or increasingly to embody the eventual forms of 'full socialism'. Without this dynamic, 'sociaⅼist society' calcifies into a static 'mode of production' which imposes structural and institutional constraints on progressive change.

Context and Constraints

The cases in this volume were chosen and written with three basic purposes in mind. First, we want to probe the problems involved in realising a revolutionary socialist programme in contemporary Third World conditions, both domestic and international, analysing the interaction of socialist theory and praxis in the tortuous process of converting Marx's *obiter dicta* about socialist transformation into coherent programmes and effective institutions. Second, from a more conventional 'development studies' perspective, we wish to evaluate the developmental performance of these six countries in terms of their own aspirations and in the light of developmental performance elsewhere in the Third World. Certain basic problems emerge as characteristic features of socialist development, common to otherwise diverse countries. Third, we wish to develop a deeper understanding of the fundamental dynamics of state socialist societies. Let us address the first of these issues in this section.

It is by now a cliché to state that, in historical terms, revolutionary socialism has 'turned Marx on his head' by succeeding in relatively backward and peripheral contexts. In consequence, rather than being an historical successor to capitalism, socialism has become an historical substitute. Rather than a force for international working-class solidarity among the advanced capitalist nations, it has become a vehicle for radical nationalism in non-industrial societies. Rather than being built on the cultural and economic foundations of advanced capitalism, revolutionary socialism has, in Senghaas's words, become 'the basis and motive of accelerated, delayed development under adverse internal and international conditions'.[4] Rather than basing its political strength on the child of modern industry – the proletariat – revolutionary socialism has relied on classes and strata deemed secondary to the classic socialist project, notably the peasantry and various sections of the petty bourgeoisie.

With the exception of the Soviet Union and (partially) Yugoslavia, successful socialist revolutions have been confined to that socio-politically diffuse yet historically specific entity called the 'Third World': in countries which were peripheral to the centres of world capitalism and subordinated to them through colonialism or various forms of imperialist or 'neo-colonial' control and penetration, and where indigenous capitalism was weakly developed. Thus to understand the basic features and dynamics of Third World socialism, it is crucial to view it as a radical response to both international subordination and dependence on the one hand, and internal backwardness and social oppression on the other. This specific conjuncture, and the aspirations and institutions it has engendered, has left a deep imprint on the face of post-revolutionary societies.

All of the régimes covered in this volume came to power after a period of anti-imperialist, politico-military struggle, either directly against imperial powers (Japan in China and Korea, France in Vietnam, Portugal in Mozambique, Britain in South Yemen) and/or against régimes supported by imperialist powers (United States *vis à vis* the Kuomintang régime in China, and Batista in Cuba). The political origins and class dynamics of these successful revolutions – still a relatively rare historical phenomenon – have been subjected to a good deal of scrutiny by scholars, socialist theorists and political practitioners alike. All of the countries covered here – and particularly the case-studies of Mozambique and South Yemen – make an important contribution to our understanding of the dynamics of revolution. They illustrate the contradictory impact of imperialism as a matrix of revolution: imposing a context of domination and exploitation which produces various forms of radical counteraction, while at the same time incubating the very social forces and political forms which provide the basis of its own overthrow. The more violent the process of decolonisation, it would seem, the more revolutionary the outcome, the radicalising logic of political persecution and military suppression contributing more to the strength of revolutionary politics than a mere sociological head-count of different classes and strata.

South Yemen, and to a considerable extent Mozambique, follow what Fred Halliday calls the 'Cuban path' to revolutionary power, *viz.* the transition from a radical nationalist movement bent on expelling the occupying power to a revolutionary socialist régime bent on internal class transformation. In both cases this transition involved changes in ideological orientation, organisational forms and class alignments. In South Yemen, the National Liberation Front came to represent the small peasant farmers of the hinterland in their guerrilla struggle against local landowners and tribal authorities. In Mozambique, Wield argues, Frelimo came to express more directly the aspirations of the poor peasantry *vis à vis* richer farmers and the conventional authority of chiefs and elders. Both cases illustrate the familiar phenomenon of collaboration between progressive urban working-class or petty bourgeois elements and the poorer sections of the peasantry, a pattern already familiar from the classic revolutionary cases of China, Vietnam and Cuba.

The experience of revolutionary struggle and the social composition of the revolutionary movement exert a powerful influence over the organisational and developmental orientation of the post-revolutionary régime. Institutions and attitudes forged in the heat of politico-military struggle and nurtured in liberated zones, as in Vietnam, Cuba, China and Mozambique, influenced the nature of the new régimes in distinctive ways, particularly in the immediate post-revolutionary period. 'Revolutionary' methods tend to be applied to developmental purposes: for example, the influence of 'Maoism' in China and Vietnam, the Guevaraist period in Cuba, the *grupos dinamizores* in Mozambique. As I shall argue later, this heritage of the period of revolutionary struggle and the problems it encounters in the post-revolutionary era of 'socialist construction' constitute part of the basic dynamics of such societies.

The link between revolutionary socialism and national liberation struggles also help explain basic features of the post-revolutionary scene. Without exception, socialist ideology is merged with a fervent nationalism. This is clearly a positive force in so far as it bolsters national sovereignty against external threats and penetration. Nationalism is also a potent force for mobilising the population for developmental efforts, development being seen, quite reasonably, as a question of redistributing politico-economic power between nations. As Ellman points out, socialism thus becomes a powerful tool used by backward nations to 'catch up' – the Soviet Union being the first successful example.[5] However, nationalism of this intensity sometimes degenerates into chauvinism (Pol Pot's Kampuchea being the most severe example) and exclusionism (for example, in North Korea). The pre- (and post-) revolutionary context of military threat and conflict also contributes to a pervasive militarisation of society, ideologically and institutionally, a heavy security consciousness which tends to retain its strength when the actual level of threat has succeeded. The heavily statist nature of Third World socialist societies both reflects and reinforces these tendencies, a fact which helps to explain the weakness of 'socialist internationalism' and the frequency of wars *between* socialist countries over the past decade.

Turning to the post-revolutionary environment, it has hardly been conducive to a speedy and thorough-going implementation of revolutionary socialist goals. Externally, new socialist countries have faced political hostility and sometimes military aggression from imperialist powers, both capitalist and socialist. Economically, small Third World socialist countries often face the same constraints as many of their non-socialist counterparts: dependence on exports of one or two primary products and vulnerability to the structure and dynamics of international markets. Even where a country is sufficiently large and well-endowed to limit these pressures, the need for participation in international markets remains, and this may pose severe constraints on governments' internal freedom of manoeuvre. Edward Friedman, for example, argues (in the way of Wallerstein) that the nature of the international political economy makes 'true' socialism impossible, since the imperatives of the world market 'force state power-holders to act in a capitalist manner, i.e. to organise their society for competition in world exchange'.[6]

The international scene also offers opportunities, as we shall see later. Dependence and vulnerability can be reduced to some degree by exploiting competition between industrial powers, both capitalist and socialist; certain countries can realise advantages deriving from natural resources or strategic location. Inimical political and economic pressures from the capitalist world can to some extent be counter-balanced by aid from and trade with developed socialist countries, notably the Soviet Union – and, in certain circumstances, vice versa.

Internal constraints are no less formidable, as Fred Halliday argues in his analysis of South Yemen which dramatically demonstrates, in his words, that 'if socialist revolution is an attempt to expand and consolidate the realm of freedom, ... such revolutions take place overwhelmingly in the realm of necessity'. Material scarcity exerts a stifling grip – the parameters of innovation are narrow. 'True' socialism, it appears, must await the economic millennium. The problems are familiar to students of the Third World: narrow and poorly-integrated economic bases, low levels of technology, widespread illiteracy and lack of trained personnel for development programmes. In the socio-political realm, nascent régimes in countries where national traditions were weak, such as South Yemen and Mozambique, must deal with social conflict based on religious, cultural, tribal or ethnic schisms; where national traditions were strong, as in China, Vietnam and Korea, the dead hand of a bureaucratic and authoritarian past claws at those who would seek a revolutionary break. More immediately, fledgling socialist governments face opposition and subversion from defeated political forces and those social strata threatened by revolutionary redistribution.

The crushing weights imposed by 'the realm of necessity', domestic and international, have raised serious questions about the viability of socialism in Third World conditions. Opinions among western socialists analysing the Third World are diverse, with two influential positions at each pole. On the one side, there is the idea of '*premature socialism*' of which Warren was the primary exponent. This argument draws on classical Marxian analysis of the progressive historical function of capitalism and its role as creator of the true social base of socialist revolution, the industrial proletariat.

As Third World capitalism grows, imperialism as a system of domination. . . declines, as Third World capitalism develops, the working class is destined to play the classic revolutionary role.[7]

Separated from its economic matrix and class base, Third

World 'socialism' is thus by definition either an historical mistake, an 'ultra-leftist' perversion, or a political fraud, a prettified populism fronting for petty bourgeois nationalism, statism or militarism.

On the other side of the debate are people working within various neo-Marxist or 'dependencia' frameworks, who see revolutionary socialism as saviour of the Third World. In this paradigm, capitalist development at the periphery tends to be seen as a subordinate expression of world capitalism which operates as a rapacious and destructive form of imperialism inimical to real national development, including capitalist. Revolutionary socialism thus provides the Marx-*ex-machina* which solves the problem of 'under-development', a combination of backwardness and dependence. In the words of Dieter Senghaas, 'it devolves upon socialism to save peripheralised societies from further peripheralisation ... socialism becomes a development policy without alternatives under conditions under which capitalism failed'.[8]

The first position is salutary, in that it highlights the dubious nature of various self-styled 'socialisms'. It is also a useful counter to the 'voluntaristic' currents common in newly-established socialist countries, which overestimate the extent to which 'objective' realities must yield to political mobilisation and institutional change. Christine White pinpoints this problem in her study of Vietnamese development policy, while Fred Halliday emphasises the obverse point when he cites South Yemen as a 'harsh reminder of the objective, material and cultural, preconditions for any full transition'. Yet the 'premature socialism' position is itself over-optimistic, nay starry-eyed, about the prospects for generalised indigenous capitalist development in the Third World, minimises its harmful social effects, and condemns political radicals to a passive waiting game. Moreover, the failure of revolutionary socialism to emerge from advanced capitalism in the West hardly augurs well for this historical scenario. Indeed, the particular form of social fragmentation and reintegration which capitalism introduces, both internally and externally, may make the construction of alternative co-operative forms more difficult – this is the nub of Mao's idea of a 'poor and blank' society on which new words can be inscribed, and it also lies behind the argument for national self-reliance and 'disengagement' as an essential precondition for socialist transformation.

On the other hand, any extreme view to the effect that revolutionary socialism is the *only* path to successful national development would have to be rejected, or at least heavily qualified, given the experience of the so-called 'newly industrialising countries' over the past two decades. While it is easy to puncture the superficial propaganda surrounding alleged South Korean, Taiwanese or Brazilian 'miracles', point to the inequalities, instabilities and dependencies embodied in such modes of development, and question their generalisability, development in material and cultural terms has still been impressive in some cases, not least in the eyes of their socialist competitors (for example, many contemporary Chinese economists regard Taiwanese economic progress as superior to the mainland's).

In my own view, 'proto-socialist' development in Third World countries is neither historically inappropriate, nor is it the only path to development. The experience of Third World socialist countries suggests, on the contrary, that they constitute a *distinctive* and *viable* mode of development, in terms of certain key social, economic and political indices, and – though this may be true to greater or lesser degrees – *preferable* to hypothetical capitalist alternatives in so far as the interests of the mass of the population are concerned. These judgements require more attention to the actual developmental performance of Third World socialism and we turn to this in the next section.

Revolutionary Socialist Developmental Performance

The basic argument of this section is that revolutionary socialism has many developmental achievements to its credit, but that it embodies many basic problems, more or less common to its various national expressions, which are 'internal' to this specific mode of development, and which cannot be attributed to objective constraints or external pressures. In making such judgements, however, it is important to avoid a static kind of cost-benefit analysis – the contradictory performance of revolutionary socialism is rooted in its historical origins, as we have seen, but also in the specific structure and dynamics characteristic of state socialist social formations, as we shall make clear in the last section.

Overall judgements on the developmental performance of 'socialist' Third World countries are hard to arrive at given the plethora of 'socialist' régimes, and the absence of precise criteria for differentiation. Jameson and Wilber, the editors of a recent compendium which included a wider range of 'socialist' countries than those covered in this volume (including Burma, Iraq, Syria and Tanzania) concluded that there has been a 'rough comparability in [per capita] growth rates' between 1960 and 1974, with thirteen 'Marxian socialist' countries (apparently including eastern Europe) growing at 3.68 percent p.a. and non-socialist Third World countries, including OPEC, growing at 3.06 percent.[9] They also tend to agree that socialist countries do better in terms of economic equality and provision for basic human needs, notably health and education. One could also add that socialist countries seem to have tackled the problems of unemployment and inflation more successfully than their capitalist counterparts. For Jameson and Wilber, the main black mark was the relative absence of 'human rights', especially but not exclusively when defined in conventional liberal terms.

It is, of course, hard to generalise from the small number of case-studies in this volume, but each provides evidence of solid achievement across a wide range of indices, as a perusal of the country profiles would reveal. Many of the most signal accomplishments, moreover, are hard to measure and do not show up in the statistics: enhanced national identity and pride, greater cultural self-confidence, abolition or reduction of previously exploitative or oppressive social relationships, the spread of 'modern' or secular attitudes towards nature and society, and the political mobilisation of previously inert strata.

At the same time, however, benefits conceal, indeed often entail, serious costs – the trade-offs are a familiar theme of political and academic discourse: equality v. liberty, collectivism v. individual initiative, redistribution/incentives, planning/market, political centralisation/political repression, political unification/conformity, self-reliance/insularity, mass mobilisation/the role of experts, positive/negative freedom, and so on. Some of these costs appear particularly stark in certain cases, notably North Korea, where remarkable social and economic progress has gone side by side with political stultification. These trade-offs are a basic element of the development process, common to all types of strategy; some of them, however, are particularly salient in socialist contexts.

Some of these dilemmas, and their developmental consequences, have been the object of reassessment in relatively mature socialist countries over the past decade – our case-studies of China, Vietnam and Cuba focus on this process which seems characteristic of a certain stage of socialist development. The 'models' of the 1960s, notably Guevaraism and Maoism, have been adapted or rejected in Cuba and China; a critical review of Kim Il Song's *juche* is long overdue in Korea.

Let us briefly review the main areas of debate and reassessment within socialist countries.

(i) *Development Strategy*

All state socialist societies are bent on eventual, and hopefully rapid, industrialisation for a mixture of economic, social and political reasons. Industrialisation is seen not merely as the establishment of conventionally defined industries, but a comprehensive process of both social and technical change throughout the whole economy. Industrialisation is seen as providing the only effective means of dissolving the ties of dependence and defending against hostile international pressures – military, political and economic. Domestically, it is seen as the essential basis for increased material and cultural standards, for transforming the realm of necessity into one of freedom. Politically, as Carciofi argues in the Cuban case, it is seen as laying the foundation for 'true' socialism resting on an industrial working class.

The Soviet precedent of crash industrialisation, with priority to producer-good sectors, has exerted a beguiling influence. For a considerable period, this strategy was virtually equated with 'socialist development' imposing a framework of priorities for state action – heavy over light industry, industry over agriculture, import substitution over international integration, investment (both productive and social) over consumption, speed over proportionality – which was, to varying degrees, incompatible with domestic factor endowments and social needs. Much of the policy dynamics of Third World socialist régimes revolves around the need to devise new strategic conceptions of 'socialist development' harmonious with national ecological potential and socio-political needs/demands. For relatively small, malproportioned and dependent economies such as Cuba, Mozambique and South Yemen, this pattern is clearly inappropriate, yet the Cuban leadership did make an abortive lunge towards crash industrialisation in the early 1960s before reverting to a strategy resting on comparative advantage in agriculture (predominantly sugar). Development strategy in Mozambique is still in an embryonic stage, resting on the principle (akin to the Maoist slogan) of 'Agriculture as base, industry as leading factor and motive force'. Though it embodies some of the ambiguity of its Maoist predecessor and is the subject of heated debate, it lays heavy stress on agriculture, and attempts to orient industry towards infrastructure and those industries 'that provide the people's basic needs'. Even in a large country with a relatively comprehensive resource base such as China, where the Soviet precedent seems to have more *prima facie* relevance, different factor endowments and a more rural-oriented political leadership have brought pressures for reorientation towards agriculture and light industry, beginning with Mao Tse Tung's re-evaluation, in the mid-1950s, in his speech 'On the Ten Great Relationships', through the stress on 'agriculture as the foundation' of national development from 1960 onwards, to the strategic 'readjustment' in favour of agriculture and light industry introduced by the Dengist leadership of the late 1970s. In the Vietnam case, the dynamic of development debates has been distorted by the exigencies of war, but Christine White's analysis of the late 1970s points to comparable rethinking and strategic readjustment prompted by changes in the international environment and stubbornly sluggish performance in agriculture. On the other hand, the North Korea case is a very distinctive one where a Soviet-style strategy was applied with apparently considerable success on *both* industrial and agricultural fronts and maintained, with relatively marginal adjustments, until the present. To the extent that one assesses this experience positively, North Korea can be cited to support an argument that, at least for medium-sized Third World countries with a relatively favourable resource base and geo-political position, a determined leadership and a relatively homogeneous population, the Soviet model cannot be discounted as a strategic option. The number of hypothetical conditions is large, however, and the range of application will be correspondingly narrow.

The Chinese and perhaps the Cuban cases demonstrate another dimension of changing development strategies which can also be seen in the evolution of eastern European economies. Strategic reorientation should not merely be analysed in static terms as a matching of strategic priorities to given economic conditions and socio-political demands. There is a *dynamic* element which reflects the basic movement of state socialist societies under endogenous and exogenous pressures. Focusing for the moment on internal pressures, there is only a limited amount of historical space in which a 'big push/high-accumulation' strategy can be pushed without unacceptably high economic cost, social tension and political conflict. Jam tomorrow must sooner or later be followed by jam today, and strategy must be oriented towards current consumption – social and individual – for the mass of the population. I shall expand my analysis of these dynamic processes in the conclusion.

(ii) *The International Dimension*

The case-studies in this book deal with the pressures exerted, and opportunities offered, by the international political economy, both socialist and capitalist. At the economic level, a basic decision must be taken on what kind of relationship a socialist country can and should adopt, at any given time, towards the international economy, especially the industrialised capitalist countries. The last decade has seen a trend towards growing interdependence between socialist countries in eastern Europe and the Third World on the one hand and capitalist countries and international markets on the other.

The pressure of 'the international law of value', of economic and technological advance among the industrialised capitalist countries, has been inexorable. To catch up with, or even to survive as, a socialist country in this changing environment, particularly in the absence of a comparable dynamic in industrialised socialist countries, requires that an industrialising socialist country must participate in international markets. The opportunities offered by the international political economy have changed over time. One can discern three broad stages: the first 'cold war' stage was eroding in the 1960s, and had evaporated to a considerable extent by the early 1970s with the end of the Vietnam War, the Shanghai communiqué, and the weakening of the US embargo against Cuba; the second stage, the early 1970s, seemed to offer an environment favourable to socialist leaderships who wished to participate more extensively in international financial and commodity markets; the third stage, from the mid-1970s on, was one of accelerating inflation and recession in most of the industrialised capitalist countries, instability and growing crisis in international trade and finance which, for those socialist countries already heavily committed outside, were disruptive and in some cases (e.g. Poland) traumatic, and which offered a far more treacherous environment for any socialist country newly seeking to reap the benefits of comparative advantage.

For all Third World socialist countries – and particularly for smaller countries for whom the prospect of self-reliance is chimerical, or for a larger country such as Vietnam, whose economy is prostrate after decades of devastation – international relationships are a crucial component of national development. If we focus on the smaller and/or weaker countries covered in this volume, each faces politico-economic threats from countries wishing to limit their developmental prospects and undermine their social system where possible: South Yemen from conservative Middle Eastern states, Mozambique from South Africa, Cuba from the United States and Vietnam from China and the United States. Each country has tried in distinctive ways to expand the positive developmental impact of external liaisons without a corresponding loss of sovereignty. This involves certain choices, between the industrialised capitalist and socialist economies and within each group. Each case provides a different pattern: Cuba, though heavily dependent on Soviet military and economic aid and political support, and a full member of CMEA with a high level of trade with the Soviet Union and eastern Europe, has been able to diversify its trading ties with capitalist countries during the 1970s. Though the latter trade was in deficit in the late 1970s, overall balance was rectified to some extent by an improvement of terms of trade with the Soviet Union, notably through agreements on the prices of sugar exports and oil imports. Vietnam, after heavy dependence on Soviet and Chinese aid during the war, made a serious effort to diversify foreign economic ties with capitalist countries in the late 1970s, but was unsuccessful, partly because of the lamentable state of the economy and conflict with China and Kampuchea, but partly because the United States exerted pressure to discourage foreign investment and political accommodation. In the Vietnam case, the eventual decision to join CMEA seems to have been taken as the only available option in a situation of economic crisis, military threat and virtual political blockade. Mozambique, on the other hand, though inheriting a colonial economy damaged by flight of capital and personnel after Independence, has enjoyed significantly more freedom of action, South Africa notwithstanding. Aid and investment have been forthcoming not only from socialist countries, but also from Europe and Japan and the degree of western political hostility to the Mozambiquan revolution has been relatively restrained given ambivalence about South Africa and the need to combat increased Soviet influence in the area. South Yemen has also been successful in attracting aid, trade and investment from both socialist and non-socialist countries and has benefitted from tensions between competing Arab powers. Most distinctively, it has received a major financial fillip from large numbers of emigrant workers to the tune of about £60 million per year.

Without pursuing details any further, certain general conclusions can be drawn on the basis of these cases. Third World socialist countries face many of the same external constraints as their non-socialist counterparts: distorted post-colonial economies, a weak base of available resources, dependence on a few commodities, chronic balance of payments deficits, etc. On the other hand, their capacity for internal socio-political mobilisation and their ability to establish strong states aid them in their attempt to make the best of the options available. And options there are, notably in the sphere of economic diversification and political non-alignment: the strategy of securing the developmental advantages offered by both capitalist and socialist industrialised powers by utilising the economic and political competition within and between each of these two groups. It is now not unusual to see countries such as Vietnam, South Yemen, Mozambique, which are full, associate or aspirant members of international institutions such as the IMF and the World Bank on the one hand, and the CMEA on the other – North Korean isolation is now the exception. There is now virtual consensus among the leadership of socialist countries – even including the North Koreans, who opened the door to joint ventures in 1981 – that there are considerable economic advantages to be gained from expanding the range of ties with the capitalist world and its international institutions, particularly in securing scarce developmental capital and much needed technology. Former radical versions of 'self-reliance' are no longer in vogue, particularly after the demise of the Maoist variant and the embarrassment of the Kim Il Songist variant.

The Soviet bloc also provides certain advantages: as a political and military counterweight to western pressures and as an economic partner, inside or outside CMEA, with certain inherent advantages: the opportunity for more stable and predictable trade relationships; for barter agreements and trading in 'soft' goods; for certain types of advanced technology and limited capital inflows. The Soviet connection is also crucial as a haven for countries under severe international pressure, the best examples being Cuba and Vietnam. It is worth remembering, moreover, that two cases of successful and relatively self-reliant industrialisation – China and North Korea – were heavily dependent on the Soviet Union in their early years.

Yet the availability of international opportunities positive to socialist development should not blind us to the fact that – with significant exceptions, notably China in recent years – the international environment for socialist Third

World countries has in general been less benevolent than for their non-socialist counterparts. Finance is less forthcoming and terms often tougher, private capital is more cautious about investment, hostile political pressures are stronger, and the technical and economic capacities of the industrialised socialist countries (not to mention their political will) are insufficient for the developmental needs of their poorer counterparts.

Analytically speaking, however, it is inadequate to deal with international alignments in terms of options to be chosen by national leaderships. The developmental implications of alternative choices are more fundamental than the policy choice paradigm can comprehend. To probe these deeper processes, we need a longer historical perspective. To this end, it is important to look at the two cases in this volume – China and North Korea – which are relatively long-established, and in which an initial stage of import-substitution industrialisation was successful, in both cases with Soviet help. The long-term impact of a period of Soviet tutelage has not as yet received a great deal of analytical attention. An initial judgement suggests the following hypothesis: that the major long-term impact of the Soviet Union on Third World socialist countries is not so much through economic relationships (which can be controlled or abrogated), or direct political intervention (which can be countered internally and internationally), but through a process of institutional *Gleichschaltung*, the imprinting of Soviet-type patterns of behaviour and attitude in the crucial genetic years of new socialist régimes. For all their Maoist and Kim Il Songist bluster, China and North Korea are still 'Sovietised' in their basic structures. As the case-studies by Carciofi and Wield suggest, moreover, Soviet institutional practices are contesting with indigenous patterns of democratisation in Cuba and Mozambique. The nature of Sovietisation and effective countermeasures need more systematic study.

In assessing the impact of growing ties with capitalist economies, we are on firmer empirical ground. In the Chinese and Korean cases – as in the case of small eastern European socialist countries such as Hungary and Rumania – their increasingly sophisticated economic structures have demanded greater participation in the international capitalist economy:

the need for raw materials, wider markets for finished products, or imports of advanced technology. One can detect two broad patterns of increased participation here: an '*introverted*' one in which foreign financial or trade ties are sought to improve domestic economic performance within a still largely 'self-reliant' import-substituting framework (for example, North Korea in the early 1970s and China from 1977–9), or even to solve fundamental politico-economic contradictions (for example, Poland's spending spree in the early-mid 1970s), and an '*extraverted*' pattern whereby international market participation, financial and commercial, is seen in more classical Ricardian terms as a stimulus to the domestic economy through competitive pressures and international specialisation (this resembles the Hungarian experience more closely and, to a more limited degree, Chinese policy since 1979).

In expanding relations with the international capitalist economy, a socialist country faces a Scylla and Charybdis. On the one hand, as its economy grows more complex, its requirements more differentiated and its productive capacity overspills the boundaries of national markets, and if its leadership wishes to absorb the technology necessary to increase labour productivity decisively and compete in sophisticated international markets, the need to expand international economic ties becomes economically (and politically) inexorable. As the North Korean and Chinese cases demonstrate, however, 're-linking' of a previously self-reliant economy may prove difficult, with many unforeseen costs: the North Koreans' optimism about markets for their exports proved faulty, and they were forced to default on foreign commercial debts; the Chinese avoided large-scale debt, but made poor import decisions, leading to wastefully inadequate absorption of expensive technology, and, perhaps of greater concern to the leadership, suffered substantial social and political 'contamination' from an irrationally precipitous expansion of foreign contacts. More fundamentally, one could argue that the greater the extent that a socialist country participates in the international capitalist division of labour, and endeavours to remain competitive therein, not only is its economy more vulnerable to uncertainty, instability and inflation, posing threats to socialist goals such as full employment and price stability, but it may also be forced to reorganise production relations in ways incompatible with a socialist transition. To beat capitalism, it seems, one must join it; if one joins it, there is the danger of internal restructuring and eventual absorption.

(iii) *Economic Management*

All the countries covered here have established some version of a central planning system to define developmental priorities and manage the economy. In Mozambique, this system is still in a relatively embryonic stage, state interventions in the economy still appear, from Wield's account, to have an *ad hoc*, incremental character and socialisation of the economy is still far from complete. In South Yemen, the planning system is more firmly established and the level of socialisation more advanced, but achievement of planning targets has been frustrated by uncertainty about external finance and imported inflation. In both cases, the planning process is highly vulnerable to external fluctuations; internally, they are both mixed economies, and thus face the familiar problems of securing plan discipline across socialised and private sectors. The other four countries surveyed have far higher levels of socialisation, thus alleviating problems of coordination and control between public and private, but moving to a new plane of problems characteristic of 'developed' systems of central planning, already familiar from eastern European experience in the 1960s and 1970s. These problems have been discussed widely elsewhere and do not need elaboration here:[10] the basic point is that, though a highly centralised system of directive planning may be effective in the initial stages of socialist transformation, as the economic structure stabilises and becomes more complex, traditional methods of planning become increasingly ineffective in managing the economy in an efficient, flexible and dynamic way. At a certain point in the evolution of most of the mature socialist economies, therefore, 'reform' projects have arisen with a critical diagnosis of traditional planning and a programme proposing a switch towards parametric planning, administrative decentralisation, and expansion of market mechanisms. Of the four relatively well-established countries covered, three – Vietnam, Cuba and China – have followed this pattern to varying degrees. The lack of reform in the North Korea case perhaps owes more to a sclerotic political system than to an economy without problems.

Though reform programmes are a response to systemic defects, however, they have themselves proven problematic in both conception and realisation – the Chinese case illustrates this well. The reform project is rooted in the idea of complementarity between plan and market: planning will still be the dominant principle of economic action but can be combined with market processes in mutually beneficial ways. But the relationship between them is also contradictory and, without a well-conceived programme of policy reform, the results may be the worst rather than the best of both worlds – an unproductive co-existence of inaccurate planning with 'anarchic' markets. If we focus on non-economic factors, moreover, reform programmes appear even more problematic. From a *political* point of view, 'planning' and 'markets' are systems of social power, each with its own structure of interests and ideological predispositions. 'Marketisation' opens up new opportunities for those in charge of and/or working in basic level production units, and diminishes the power of the former agencies of administrative control – the relationship between 'plan' and 'market' thus becomes a political battleground. Marketisation can, in theory, be defended on various social grounds (weakening of bureaucratic privilege, expanding the range of individual choice, linking material rewards more closely with effort, etc.) but in practice – particularly in situations of excess demand and financial disequilibrium – expansion of markets can bring price instability, inflation, profiteering and speculation, over-production, unemployment and increasing wage differentiation which release new wells of social discontent.[11] After two years of attempted economic reform in China, the new General Secretary of the Chinese Communist Party, Hu Yaobang, remarked that 'our present domestic problems are like a pile of dry kindling. A single match could start a blaze'.[12] This is one of the major reasons why the reform experiment was brought to a screeching halt in China in early 1981.

(iv) *Relations of production*

Several of our contributors deal with debates over the organisation of production relations in both industry and agriculture. Debates both inside and outside state socialist countries revolve around the question of how to establish a system of production relations which combine socialist goals of co-operation, self-management and collective commitment on the one hand with micro-economic efficiency on the other. This general question has led to specific policy debates about worker participation, management methods and incentive systems. The classic Soviet model of organisation in state industrial enterprises – in fact, if not always in theory – has tended to be authoritarian, with clear authority designated to managers and a limited role for worker participation or trade union power. The use of hierarchical chains of command and differentiated division of labour in complex organisations has led to comparisons with capitalist production processes and allegations of class exploitation and subordination.[13] In the Marxian tradition since social relations within basic production units are the source of class relations in society as a whole, they are the crucial context for evaluating progress towards the 'classlessness' of full socialism.

Of the countries covered in this book, some accepted Soviet institutional forms, sometimes wholesale, in their initial stage of socialist transformation, later attempting to adapt them in line with specific national conditions and political traditions: Maoism is the best example of (ultimately unsuccessful) adaptation. In other countries, such as Cuba, there was an attempt to create new forms in the initial period (notably the Cuban stress on *conciencia* in the 1960s).

In general, there have been two main concerns: democratisation and micro-economic efficiency. Experience of attempts to democratise industrial enterprises in state socialist countries suggests that, if the initial pattern of production relations adopted was in the authoritarian Soviet tradition, it hardens into habits of command and subordination and is perpetuated by the material and political differentials inherent in unequal authority. This pattern is reinforced by a legitimating logic which emphasises (i) the need for control of the workforce to promote accumulation in a context of scarcity; (ii) the need for a precise division of labour and a corresponding system of coordination to meet the growing complexity of technical conditions of production; (iii) the need for labour regulations and hierarchical controls to discipline an immature workforce still unequal to the challenge of self-management. This situation effectively resists later attempts to democratise, such as the Maoist.

These considerations add weight to Wield's stress on analysing debates about and changes in relations of production in state-owned enterprises in Mozambique's crucial genetic phase of institution-building. He focuses on the crucial role of the *grupos dinamizadores* (GDs) or 'dynamising groups', organised in both residential and work units, during the difficult period of transition after the departure of the Portuguese, and the later establishment of workers' councils in basic level units of production and service. The latter organisations are designed as weapons of worker power against any resurrection of pre-revolutionary relations of production and the encroachment of bureaucracy. But Wield points to the constraints on their influence: from workers' lack of technical knowledge and generally low level of education, and from growing managerial power and prerogatives apparently supported by President Machel on grounds of efficiency and class conciliation. The progress of these nascent mass organisations has been uneven and their future is uncertain; given the expansion and consolidation of the Party apparatus, government bureaucracy and managerial authority, it would not be surprising if they were reduced to a relatively marginal role characteristic of Soviet-style trade unions. As Wield's account suggests, however, the issue is still undecided, and the struggle for democratic control of the workplace continues.

Similar processes of workplace democratisation have also occurred in Cuba, though the historical rhythm is different. During the 1960s, massive mass mobilisation was not accompanied by a development of effective institutions for democratic participation and control among the workers — it was participation without power, involvement without real responsibility. Partly because of the adverse socio-economic consequences of this strategy, and partly as a result of the Cuban leadership commitment to mass participation, in principle, and as a counterweight to burgeoning bureaucracy. the 1970s brought certain institutional changes favourable to workplace democratisation, notably a significant increase in the role of trade unions as a check and balance within the planning system.

As Carciofi argues, however, the mere shift towards formally more democratic institutions in Cuba does not mean that they have a firm political foundation. In fact, the political logic of such 'sponsored' democratisation – as in Cuba or post-Mao attempts to establish 'workers' congresses' in Chinese enterprises – is decidedly problematic. Common sense would suggest that effective mass institutions are created by a strong impetus from below – otherwise, as Carciofi argues in the Cuban case, formally new institutions may be subordinated to the structural logic of the old system.

In dealing with changes in relations of production, we have so far emphasised the issue of democratisation. Efficiency questions, variously defined, have also been of paramount concern to socialist leaderships bent, in the official terminology, on 'harmonising the relations of production with the development of the productive forces'. Given the cardinal role of agriculture in most Third World countries, and its consequently vital role as the basis for eventual socialist industrialisation, there has been considerable concern about agricultural performance and increasing emphasis on readjusting rural production units in ways calculated to boost output and productivity. This has involved broad-ranging debates about the advisability of agricultural collectivisation (*vis à vis* state farms or peasant holdings), the precise pacing of collectivisation, different forms of co-operative/collective units and relations between collective units and the residual private sector. Since two of the editors have addressed this question in detail elsewhere,[14] I shall only refer here to the specific issues raised by the cases in this volume. First, the difficulties involved in mapping out a clear and consistent strategy of socialist agricultural development are highlighted by the case of Mozambique: policies have been ambiguous on the relative importance of socialised v. peasant agriculture and state farms and co-operatives. The resultant uncertainly has been unfavourable for *all* sectors. Second, turning to forms of socialised agriculture, Mozambique also illustrates the difficulties involved in setting up and running efficiently a system of state farms, owing to managerial, financial and technical inadequacies. The Cuban case, on the other hand, presents a more positive picture of the capacity of state farms, in the crucial sugar sector, to raise average yields and promote technical transformation, a case argued in more detail elsewhere by Pollit.[15]

Third, the cases throw light on the evolution and performance of collective agriculture. In the established socialist countries of East Asia, where most agriculture is collectivised, the collectivisation process was aided considerably by previous patterns of communal ownership (in Vietnam) and nucleated village settlement. In the East African context, however, progress towards co-operatives or collectives is impeded by scattered settlement patterns. Thus concentration of population is an essential precondition for communal production, and this is a socio-economically disruptive and politically divisive process. Where collective agriculture is well-established, there are continuing problems of sluggish growth in output, and productivity which impose constraints on national aspirations for industrialisation. The North Korean case seems a counter-example, but apparent progress may conceal serious and intensifying problems. In other countries – notably China and Vietnam – these problems have led governments to a wideranging reassessment of institutional forms in agriculture and to certain basic policy changes: a rethinking of the traditional Marxist-Leninist emphasis on the ultimate aim of introducing large-scale, industrialised production units in agriculture, caution about pushing the transition from small to larger-scale collectives, and emphasis on various ways of decentralising the production process within existing collective units. Particularly important in the Vietnamese and Chinese cases has been the recently increased recognition of the economic importance of the household economy – both as a separate sector producing and exchanging certain key foodstuffs and generating a considerable proportion of rural cash incomes, and as a specific form of production organisation which can be incorporated, on a contractual basis, into the framework of collective production. The recent moves towards subcontracting to households in Vietnam and household-based responsibility systems in China are important examples of this reorientation.[16] While the economic results of the reforms seem initially encouraging in terms of raising productivity and incomes, these policy changes also have economic drawbacks (for example, weakening rural infrastructural construction and local accumulation generally) and socio-political costs (increasing inter-household inequalities, weakening collective welfare services and collective political institutions) which make further re-evaluation and policy readjustment necessary in future. Though socialist agriculture remains a problematic area, however, such examples of ideological creativity and organisational flexibility give scope for optimism. Certainly, one should be sceptical about sweeping claims about the superiority of agriculture in non-socialist contexts, rooted in simple notions of allegedly 'individualistic' peasants, or superficial contrasts between collective and private, socialist and capitalist production. The depressing realities of rural life in many non-socialist Third World countries should also give pause to such judgements.

(v) *Social issues*

While the countries under scrutiny appear to have performed well in terms of basic social indices – notably economic redistribution and provision of education and basic welfare services – the areas of gender relations and female liberation remain problematic, a point to which several of our contributors refer. In most of the state socialist countries of which this author has some knowledge, considerable headway has been made in improving the social status of women, as compared both with their pre-revolutionary position, and their situation in non-socialist countries with similar cultural backgrounds and/or economic levels. Fred Halliday argues, for example, that 'the PDRY has gone further than any other Peninsula society towards ensuring the equality of men and women'. Though Jon Halliday paints a less favourable picture of North Korea, it may appear better when compared with certain aspects of the position of women in South Korean

˙society, such as exploitation of cheap female labour, widespread prostitution and 'sexual tourism'.

This progress has certain basic dimensions: significant improvements in the legal position of women, through laws on family, marriage, divorce and economic status; greater female participation in political activities and organisations, and access to positions of political and administrative authority; improvement in the social freedom of women (for example, erosion of the *sheidor* in South Yemen) and the social resources to which they have access, notably education, health and childcare facilities; greater opportunities for remunerated employment outside the home and some limited headway in breaking down male occupational preserves, including skilled manual industrial and technical-professional labour.

These gains seem particularly dramatic in the immediate post-revolutionary period when the memory of the 'old society' is still fresh. If one analyses the experiences of longer-established socialist régimes, one is struck by a certain slowing down of female emancipation – there is a tendency for established socialist régimes to claim that the 'women question' is basically solved, and then shunt it into a political siding. This is not merely a feature of Third World socialism; in their comparative study of the Soviet Union and China, Salaff and Merkle argue that

[the] oppression of women [has] remained culturally, politically and economically institutionalised: the traditional image of women, the subordination of women in the family, and the economic and political inequality of women were not eliminated by the revolution.[17]

How valid is this kind of judgement for Third World socialism in general?. I do not have the information necessary to make sweeping comparative judgements – the following remarks are based on a detailed examination of the Chinese case, and would also seem to have some application to the other Asian socialist societies (Korea and Vietnam), but should not be extended to other contexts without further research.

The general picture in the Chinese case is that, in spite of significant progress towards gender equality, women still lag behind in many areas of life, and in some – notably the political – lag far behind. First, in terms of strategic policy priorities, the separate question of women's emancipation is low. Women have in effect been asked to subordinate their sectional interests to the exigencies of industrialisation and/or the higher imperatives of 'class struggle'. Second, in the economy, the sexual division of labour remains pronounced – women's role in production has been far greater in light industry and agriculture than in heavy industry, in the collective rather than the state sectors, household rather than socialised sectors. Since these distinctions correspond to differences in income, prestige and, ultimately, political influence, they serve to perpetuate female inferiority in society at large. Third, serious attempts to change the distribution of work *within* the household are rare (Cuba may be an exception here). Since low levels of development limit the extent to which household tasks can be socialised, the vast bulk of domestic labour still rests on women's shoulders, creating a double burden if women also work outside the home. Fourth, there has been scant scope for independent women's organisations – official women's associations, like other 'mass organisations', are usually tame toe-ers of the official line and, while helping to improve the everyday life of women in various ways, do not raise the 'big issues'. This political weakness is reinforced by gross under-representation of women in the major state institutions – Party, government and army.

How do we account for these persistent inequalities? Though the influence of pre-revolutionary 'hangovers' and continued resistance from less progressive sectors of society are crucial factors, they do not constitute a full explanation. There is a strong argument to suggest that the post-revolutionary society itself still embodies a distinct realm of dominance and inequality rooted in gender relations, ultimately founded on power relations within the family. To the extent that socialist institutions reflect this pattern of male dominance, the logic of dissimilar interest will blunt the redistributive impact of policies designed to improve women's lot, declaratory good intentions and good faith notwithstanding. This kind of analysis would seem to lead inexorably to the conclusion that the pace of female emancipation and gender equalisation can only be accelerated by the formation of relatively autonomous women's organisations, to exert greater political pressure on gender issues, and provide a more critical perspective on official definitions of socialist development, sexual equality and women's liberation.

(vi) *The problem of the state*

The question of the state – its economic, political and social role – is perhaps the central question of socialist development. 'Actually existing socialism', in its eastern European and Third World forms (with the partial exception of Yugoslavia), has taken a strongly 'statist' form. To be specific, the state apparatus has played a dominant role in steering the development process in all its aspects; the Party, as the nucleus of the state, makes all major decisions, imposes ideological orthodoxy, monopolises channels of political influence and communication, and penetrates all major socio-economic institutions.

In analysing the role of the state, it is important to avoid slipping into *easy* positions: kneejerk liberalism, ahistorical anarchism, or simple notions of the allegedly Machiavellian machinations of evil 'statists' or totalitarians'. It is also important to discount for negative propaganda, a distressingly common feature of western media, which sometimes rival their eastern counterparts in one-dimensionality. Serious criticism can and must be sustained, but it should be situated in a careful historical analysis of Third World realities. Particularly in their crucial 'bootstrap' stages, revolutionary socialist societies require strong states. Internally, enemies of the revolution often retain their influence; the centrifugal force of tribal, regional, ethnic or cultural fragmentation may threaten national unity; there is need for a strong hand to mobilise and coordinate resources, material and human, in the struggle for development. Externally, powerful international hostility to nascent socialist societies includes economic blockade and sabotage, political subversion, military threat and terrorist violence. As I am writing this introduction in August 1982, Ruth First, a revolutionary socialist scholar and activist and a long-time opponent of apartheid, has just been murdered at her research institute in the Mozambiquan capital Maputo, by a letter-bomb – presumably sent by South African agents. In such conditions, the case for a strong and vigilant state is compelling. This said, however, to endorse the actions of socialist states uncritically would be to give succour to the forces of authoritarianism embedded therein. Even given the pressures listed above, there is significant scope for experimentation and change. But progressive change is impeded by the very nature of the revolutionary socialist state itself. It is an ambiguous entity best described by a series of oppositions: transformative/conservative, participatory/authoritarian, organisational/bureaucratic, liberationist/oppressive, mass-oriented/sectionally-oriented, mobilisational/militaristic, vigilant/paranoid, and so on. Historical experience suggests that, while the first (positive) terms are dominant during the early years of socialist transformation, as régimes become established the second (negative) terms gradually gain strength, for reasons to be explored in the last section.

To move towards the goals of 'full' socialism requires several basic processes: 'de-bureaucratising' social and economic life; questioning the vaunted infallibility of 'scientific socialism', and encouraging a more diverse intellectual and cultural life. The key to these and other necessary changes is thorough-going democratisation in at least three senses: (i) the democratic rights of *individuals vis à vis* the group, organisation, collective or state, to be strengthened and protected by an effective and autonomous legal system and by institutionalised channels of defence against bureaucratic or political injustice. The language here is liberal, but individual rights are surely human rights which cannot be dismissed as 'bourgeois', but must be incorporated into a truly humane socialism. (ii) the democratic rights of individuals or collectives as *producers* or members of the workplace. We have discussed this earlier, and the principle of self-management, already realised to some extent in Yugoslav institutions, is crucially important here. (iii) the democratic rights of individuals or groups as *citizens*, able to influence the direction of society as a whole through electoral processes, representative institutions and sectional associations.

A sceptic might retort that such talk of democratisation is utopian, adding that the room for political manoeuvre is small, that democratisation is incompatible with the basic assumptions and institutions of revolutionary socialism, and that recent experiences of democratisation, such as the Cultural Revolution and the Democracy Movement in China, were notably unsuccessful. The weight of vested interest within the state apparatus is enormous. To echo Stalin's words 'cadres [still] decide everything'; whether they be politocratic, bureaucratic or technocratic, they still have much to lose from genuine democratisation in terms of concrete interests and are ideologically armed to resist it, whether in terms of 'Party leadership', the supremacy of the state or the 'neutral' requirements of rapid modernisation.

However, a strong counter-argument can be made to the effect that democratisation in its various forms is not merely desirable but also inexorable. By its very success in the initial phase of development, state socialism creates the preconditions for its own dissolution and supercession. Whether one uses the analytical language of structural-functionalism or Marxism, the same case recommends itself. The main question is whether democratisation will make or break revolutionary socialism. Two broad scenarios are possible: in the first, established régimes try to ignore or suppress intensifying contradictions; this exacerbates the situation, either making progressive change conflictual or violent, or driving an aroused population to espouse anti-socialist causes. The Polish case is instructive here. In the second, more optimistic scenario, a coalition is forged between a progressive sector of the Party-state élite and democratic forces in society to sustain the momentum of change and push through an ultimately radical series of reforms.

The Dynamics of Socialist Transition

Though the experience of revolutionary socialist countries in the Third World is very diverse, there are strikingly common elements on which we can base some tentative judgements about their dynamics as a specific developmental genus. This task requires some historical depth, so I shall focus on longer-established cases, such as Cuba, China, Korea and Vietnam, with comparative reference to the state socialist nations of eastern Europe. The basic thesis is that state socialist countries undergo certain characteristic transitions and stages of development which reflect the influence of structural changes in society and state, historical conditions and ecological constraints (both internal and external) and certain basic problematic features of 'planned' economies and 'Partycratic' polities.

Each major transition manifests itself in specific policy changes but these are the tip of the iceberg. The key determining factors in each phase are first, the strategic context – domestic and international, economic and political, technical and social; second, the evolving nature of the social structure, notably the emergence and consolidation of new class forces; third, the nature of the state both as an agent of class formation and a matrix of political relations. At each stage, these conditions and pressures shape, and are shaped by the specific mix of institutional alternatives characteristic of socialism – state intervention, markets and mass participation – and the specific policy agenda of the period.

Using this broad analytical framework, one can distinguish three key phases and transitions in revolutionary socialist development: (i) *revolutionary voluntarism and its limits*: this involves the classic problem of transition from a revolutionary era of fierce politico-military struggle to the post-revolutionary stage of socialist construction. In the initial post-revolutionary period, the nascent state is dominated by radical elements representing the political aspirations of the revolutionary mass coalition; the social structure is in turmoil and transformation; and internal and external politico-economic conditions are threatening. Institutionally, state-building combines with mass mobilisation; markets are seen as matrices of antagonistic class power and subjected to increasing controls. The policy agenda calls for rapid social and institutional transformation. In this context, the methodological heritage of the revolutionary period is appropriate; as conditions change, however, its applicability is brought into question.

(ii) *Bureaucratic voluntarism and its limits*: To the extent that the strategic tasks of the immediate post-revolutionary period are achieved, the revolutionary model of social mobilisation is undermined. The burgeoning state apparatus is increasingly manned by people without revolutionary experience, a reorganised social structure is taking shape with institutionalised patterns of social mobility and a strategic role for educated, primarily urban, strata; as the state is consolidated, it manages to marginalise domestic counter-revolutionary opposition and establish a *modus vivendi* with the external world. The strategic task of the era becomes rapid economic development and the state takes on the key role in steering the social economy in the prescribed direction through a network of increasingly complex bureaucratic organisations. This is the era of bureaucratic voluntarism. In Weberian terminology, the revolution is being institutionalised; from the perspective of many former revolutionaries, 'revisionism' and 'degeneration' are setting in. Thus the transition between stages is usually marked by political conflict and ideological disagreement among the Party leadership. The 'revolutionaries' may maintain their influence for some considerable time (in Vietnam revolutionary methods were prolonged by the war; Chinese Maoists of different varieties lasted till 1978; and in Korea former guerrilla leader Kim Il Song still clings to power aided by the military confrontation with South Korea). However, the new phase of bureaucratic voluntarism also digs its own historical grave (but is remarkably resistant to being lowered into it).

(iii) *Reformism and market socialism*: In a transitional process much analysed in socialist countries and abroad, bureaucratic voluntarism becomes increasingly irrational economically and increasingly unacceptable politically. The new state apparatus has bred 'new men', reared in a post-revolutionary environment, who develop interests which are increasingly incompatible with those of the politico-administrative élite and press them by technocratic means. The population wearies of postponed consumption, and increased social differentiation leads to proliferating sectional interests and demands which beat on the doors of Party hegemony. The traditional methods of directive planning become more and more ineffective as the economic structure becomes more complex and social demands diversify. There are thus moves to change the institutional mix, with more scope for markets, greater political pluralism and cultural diversity.

The policy agenda focuses on economic efficiency and productivity, intensive rather than extensive development.

This three-stage transition is, of course, an ideal type, and sits uneasily with some cases. The uniformity of Kim Il Songist rule in North Korea is an apparent counter-example but, I would argue, one which has postponed rather than avoided these critical contradictions – when the dam breaks, the flood may be devastating. Looking to the future, moreover, the newer socialist countries, such as Mozambique and South Yemen, may not approximate this path, due to different historical contexts and political traditions. For the longer-established régimes, moreover, the transition between stages is not clear-cut, each new stage maintaining essential elements of the one preceding. The fit between 'objective' socio-economic requirements and the pattern of political demands on the one hand, and embedded socio-political structures on the other, is not a neat one; institutions stay up way past their historical bedtime.

It is important for socialists to confront these contradictory realities and not smother them in propaganda, antagonistic or approving. However, one should bear in mind that the revolutionary socialist mode of development has succeeded in establishing itself as an alternative to global capitalism, and has made enormous strides over the past three decades. Admirers of capitalist alternatives hardly have grounds for complacency at a time when the international system is moving into deepening crisis and clear cases of developmental success are few. Revolutionary socialism may have its problems, but it also has its own characteristic promise. There is a future to be won, but the struggle will be a hard and long one.

Notes

1 For an attempt to define the nature of a 'socialist economy', see W. Brus, *The Market in a Socialist Economy*, London, Routledge & Kegan Paul, 1972, p. 3.
2 Rudolf Bahro, 'The alternative in Eastern Europe', *New Left Review*, 106, November–December 1977, pp. 3–38.
3 For an interesting, though not wholly convincing critique of 'state capitalist' analysis of the Soviet Union, see David Laibman, 'The "State Capita-

list" and "Bureaucratic-Exploitative" interpretations of the Soviet social formation: a critique', *Review of Radical Political Economics*, vol. 10, no. 4, pp. 24–34.

4   Dieter Senghaas, 'Socialism in historical and developmental perspective', *Economics*, Tübingen, vol. 23, 1981, p. 95.

5   Michael Ellman views Marxist-Leninism as 'ideologies of state-directed industrialisation in backward countries', in his *Socialist Planning*, Cambridge University Press, 1979, p. 274.

6   Edward Friedman, 'On Maoist conceptualizations of the capitalist world system', *China Quarterly* 80, December 1979, p. 806.

7   John Sender, in his introduction to Bill Warren, *Imperialism: Pioneer of Capitalism*, London, NLB, 1980, p. xiii.

8   Senghaas, *op. cit.* p. 99. For other examples of this type of approach, see Samir Amin, 'Accumulation and development: a theoretical model', *Review of African Political Economy*, 1, August–November 1974, pp. 9–26; and Clive Thomas, *Dependence and Transformation. The Economics of Transition to Socialism*, New York: MR Press, 1974.

9   Kenneth P. Jameson and Charles K. Wilber, 'Socialism and development: editors' introduction', *World Development* vol. 9, nos. 9/10, September–October 1981, p. 804.

10   For interesting discussions of this process, see W. Brus, *The Market in a Socialist Economy*, London, Routledge & Kegan Paul, 1972; D. M. Nuti, 'The contradictions of socialist economies: a Marxist interpretation', in R. Miliband and J. Saville (eds), *The Socialist Register*, 1979; Ota Sik, 'The economic costs of Stalinism', *Problems of Communism* XX, 3, May–June 1971.

11   Compare W. Brus's analysis of the fate of eastern European reforms, in 'The East European reforms: what happened to them?', *Soviet Studies*, XXXI, 2, April 1979, 257–67.

12   Cited in Lowell Dittmer, 'China in 1981: reform, readjustment, rectification', *Asian Survey*, XXII, I, January 1982, p. 33.

13   For example, see Bob Arnot, 'Soviet labour productivity and the failure of the Shchekino experiment', *Critique* 15, 1981, pp. 31–56.

14   Christine White and Gordon White (eds), 'Agriculture, the peasantry and socialist development', issue of *IDS Bulletin* vol. 13, no. 4, 1982.

15   Brian H. Pollit, 'The transition to socialist agriculture in Cuba: some salient features', in White and White (eds), *op. cit.*

16   See the articles by Christine White, Barbara Hazard and Jack Gray in this same issue.

17   Janet W. Salaff and J. Merkle, 'Women and revolution: the lessons of the Soviet Union and China', in M. B. Young (ed.), *Women in China: Studies in Social Change and Feminism*, University of Michigan, 1973, pp. 145–77.

THE PEOPLE'S DEMOCRATIC REPUBLIC OF YEMEN: THE 'CUBAN PATH' IN ARABIA

Fred Halliday

The experience of the PDRY, independent since the British departure in 1967, is of interest for the study of the transition to socialism in a number of respects.[1] First, it represents by far the most radical experience of social and political transformation yet seen in the Arab world and, with the exception of the Islamic republics of Soviet Central Asia, the most far reaching yet seen in the Muslim world. The South Yemen revolution has therefore taken place in a context noted for particularly strong hostility to socialism at the mass level because of Islam, and in a part of the world where regional powers hostile to socialism, the oil states, exert considerable influence. Nevertheless, the record of the PDRY, despite the immense difficulties it has faced, stands in clear contrast to that of other Arab states which profess adherence to socialism: (a) it is the only such state where the transformation process has led to the outright expropriation of the indigenous landowners and bourgeoisie, i.e. has gone beyond nationalist revolution and social reforms to an attempt at socialist revolution; (b) as opposed to transferring ownership from an old to a new possessing class it has gone much further than any of these other states in socialising the means of production and installing a centrally-planned economic system; (c) whilst seeing itself as part of the Arab revolution, it has rejected any ideological compromise with the theories of a special Arab or Islamic socialism of the kind espoused by Nasserites, Qaddafi, the Ba'ath or the Algerian NLF; (d) unlike all these other régimes, the top state officials are not drawn from the army, and the Party is an independent force that itself controls the state apparatus; (e) it has militantly rejected compromise with the reactionary forces in the Arab world, and has taken up firm and (to it) costly internationalist positions in contrast to the equivocations of the other supposedly 'socialist' Arab countries.

Yet the revolution in South Yemen was not made by a communist or Marxist Party, and herein lies the second reason for interest in the PDRY : as an instance of the 'Cuban model', i.e. of radical nationalist experiences which, for a combination of internal and external factors, have gone beyond their initial political confines to attempt a full transition to socialism. Hence, while the South Yemeni process was not begun by a communist or even clearly socialist organisation, it illustrates the possibility of beginning a socialist transition, of vaulting from one path of development to another. This is the path already taken by Cuba, and one that may also be taken by certain Third World states in which a socially *radical* nationalism has triumphed – Angola, Mozambique and Nicaragua being cases in point. However, the conditions for such a successful transition are demanding and are not as yet fully satisfied in the South Yemeni case. Herein lies the third reason for studying the example of the PDRY in some detail; while the poverty of the mass of the population and the relatively weak implantation of a capitalist ruling class made the revolution of 1967 all the more possible, this restricted availability of material and human resources, and the relative superficiality of the revolutionary process itself, have acted as objective impediments to a transition to socialism. While much analysis of Third World revolutions has stressed the element of will, the South Yemeni case is a harsh reminder of the *objective*, material and cultural, preconditions for any full transition and of the difficulties involved in a voluntaristic approach to revolutionary transformation. Its economic base is too weak to allow for rapid and substantial growth. It is unable to conceive of an autarkic or 'de-coupled' economic growth. At the beginning, the revolutionary movement itself was lacking in trained personnel, riven by factional disputes, deluded by apparent developmental short-cuts, and ideologically isolated from the mass of the population. The political preconditions for a fully democratic system have *not* been present, any more than have the conditions for rapid economic growth. Moreover, the international context in which the South Yemeni revolution found itself has been distinctly unfavourable: in its first years it was surrounded by hostile states, deprived of its traditional sources of foreign income, at the moment of revolutionary triumph, and subjected to the consumerist attractions of the oil states. While certain external conditions have allowed the South Yemeni state to survive and in some degree consolidate, others have harassed and undermined it at both the economic and political levels. Hence if socialist revolution is an attempt to expand and consolidate the realm of freedom, the case of the PDRY has underlined that such revolutions take place overwhelmingly in the realm of necessity.

The discussion that follows is an attempt to outline the main characteristics of the South Yemeni experience. It begins by describing the colonial society, the course of the revolution, and the factors behind its particular outcome. It then goes on to analyse changes in the economic, social and political spheres. There follows a description of the international context of the post-revolutionary régime, while the final section suggests certain conclusions of more general relevance which may be drawn from the South Yemeni case.

The Revolutionary Experience

The revolutionary movement in South Yemen owes its radical outcome to the fact that it was directed simultaneously against three separate opponents: British colonialism, the indigenous ruling classes allied to British colonialism, and the state which sought to control the resistance movement in South Yemen, Nasserite Egypt. The radical nature of the movement, its break both with the local ruling classes and with hitherto dominant forms of Arab nationalism, has to be seen in the context of both the social and political conjunctures of South Yemen in the immediate pre-independence period.

Under colonialism the area now comprising South Yemen was composed of two politically distinct kinds of entity. The port of Aden was ruled as a Colony by Britain from the time of its occupation in 1839. It was not just the political, but also the economic focus of colonial rule. With the opening of the Suez Canal in 1869 it became an important link on the route to India and developed as an entrepôt and garrison city. In 1954 it acquired an oil refinery, and in the 1960s became the headquarters of British forces in the Middle East. Its population rose from 80,000 in 1945 to around 250,000 in 1967. In 1965 80,000 people were registered as being in employment.[2] Over a third of those who migrated to the growing town were from North Yemen, a separate state ruled by a conservative monarch, the Imam, and from the mid-1950s onwards, Aden became the centre of a strong trade union organisation, based in the port and service sectors. This Aden Trades Union Congress was Nasserist and so pro-Egyptian. Economic development in Aden was, however, limited to the international functions performed by the port: there was little industrialisation apart from the refinery, and artisanal activities, and the surplus generated by the port was either placed on deposit in the banks, or exported for investment elsewhere. The ruling class in Aden was dominated by merchant capital – Adeni, Indian and British – and supported by the upper ranks of the civil service.

The rest of the country was ruled under a quite different dispensation. Known as 'South Arabia', this covered nearly two dozen sultantes and other forms of local state over whom the British gradually extended the Protectorate system. In essence, this system meant that the rulers retained responsibility for running their internal affairs; they were guaranteed support by the colonial authorities in Aden, in return for their ensuring that no outside powers gained access in their domains. It was an arrangement comparable to the princely states of India. In social and economic terms, this meant that the hinterland states were not directly incorporated into the colonial-political or capitalist-economic systems of Aden. Muslim, not colonial, law applied here, and the colonial authorities did not seek to extend capitalist relations into the hinterland: the market was too small to merit serious attempts to promote access for goods, and virtually none of the port's surplus was transferred there; even the food imports for the expanding population of Aden were, in the main, drawn from other areas of British control – meat from Somalia, vegetables from Cyprus.[3] The British authorities preferred to draw the city's labour force from another state, *viz*. North Yemen, rather than from the Protectorates; such labour was easier to control politically, and this policy avoided any disruption of the social peace upon which the hinterland rested. For their part, the Sultans did not wish to see their local powers attenuated by greater political or economic integration with the port.

Information on the socio-economic system of the hinterland is scarce. It is not sufficient to establish either the full picture of pre-capitalist relations, or the degree to which these relations were being transformed by the introduction of capitalist ones. The ruling class was composed of Sultans and sheikhs, whose power rested both on the ownership of land and on their hereditary positions in a tribal hierarchy. Such non-labourers were flanked by the *sada* (singular *sayyid*), notables who claimed descent from Mohammed, and who performed religious and juridicial functions, as well as often having access to part of the surplus from the land.[4] Except in a few cases, there was no large-scale landownership. The surplus was meagre, and only in two cases was there substantial economic development: these involved cotton projects initiated by the British government in collaboration with sultans who were given a stake in the enterprises. Of the total of around 300,000 acres cultivated in the best years (a mere 0.5 per cent of the land area) only 50,000 acres were cultivated for cotton on irrigated land employing local labour. Yet cotton made up 56 per cent of the Protectorate's exports. The rest of the cultivated area was farmed by peasants who paid a percentage of their crop to the sheikh, sultan or sayyid, or who were engaged in livestock rearing that was similarly taxed. Available evidence suggests that the rural labour force was poor and exploited, but that absolute landlessness was comparatively rare. Only a small percentage of the population – 15 per cent at most – were tribal nomads. But the settled rural population was also organised on tribal lines.

The divisions between town and country, Colony and Protectorate, capitalist and pre-capitalist sectors were substantial. It would seem that monetary relations had begun in some measure to permeate the countryside, as workers who had been in the city, or who had worked abroad, remitted part of their income. In the eastern part of South Yemen, known as the Hadramaut, large sectors of the economy rested upon remittances from exiles in south–east Asia. Yet the pre-existing system of social and political power remained apparently unchallenged until the 1960s, strengthened as it was by the guarantee of British power. There were tribal revolts in the hinterland during the 1950s, but these followed traditional forms of resistance, and involved neither new ideas nor new forms of social and political organisation. They were an extension of tribal warfare, and were often encouraged by the Imam of (North) Yemen, from across the border, for dynastic reasons.

The transformation of the situation in the western part of the hinterland came about by the effect of political developments upon the social changes that were already in train. The guerrillas were based here. One such development was the attempt by the British to forge a new state uniting the sultans of the hinterland with each other, and with the capitalist port. Initiated in 1959, this project led to the creation of a Federation of South Arabia in 1963. This was resented by the urban trades union movement, which did not want to be dominated by the hinterland tribal rulers, yet at the same time it created a more cohesive political context within which an opposition movement could develop. The other political event was the revolution in North Yemen: the Imam died on 18 September 1962, his son was overthrown by Nasserite army officers a week later, and a protracted civil war then began, pitting the nationalist republicans, aided by Egyptian forces, against the royalists, led by the ousted Imam and an array of tribal leaders. The civil war in the North had profound effects on the South and it pioneered two forms of nationalism: it aroused Arab nationalist sentiment in support of Egypt's role, and at the same time mobilised a particular sense of Yemeni nationalism, directed against British rule in the South and towards a new sense of a common Yemeni identity.[6] The political context was shaped by these two integrated processes: on the one hand, the British desire to forge a new state as a preliminary step towards decolonisation, which tied the opposition to colonial rule into a struggle against local ruling classes; on the other a mobilisation of patriotic sentiment in support of the republic in the North. Once the British and their sultan allies in the South were seen to be aiding the royalists against Egypt and the republic in the North, then the two struggles were presented as being to some degree unified. With ideological and material support from the Egyptians in North Yemen, guerrilla struggle against the British and their allies in South Yemen began in 1963. From 1965 onwards it spread to Aden itself.[7]

Yet the division of South Yemen that had been created by colonialism reproduced itself within the opposition movement. This was divided into two rival factions. The Front for the Liberation of Occupied South Yemen was based in Aden itself, and led by former leaders of the trades union movement, and its following was based on immigrants from North Yemen. The National Liberation Front was led by Nasserite militants who had been politicised in Aden, and were members of a Nasserite pan-Arab movement of Arab Nationalists (MAN); but they were based in the hinterland and mobilised support in their own tribal areas. These were hinterland migrants who had been educated in Aden or had worked there. By 1966, when it was obvious that the British would soon leave, the struggle was taking place on two fronts: first, against the colonial army and the ruling classes of Aden and the hinterland who were trying to consolidate their position for the independence period; second, between the two fronts, FLOSY and NLF, who were competing for mass support and for the monopoly of power in the new state. By mid-1967, the NLF had been able to previal over FLOSY, even in areas where the latter had previously been dominant. Several of the Aden trades unions swung behind the NLF, and the federal army, recruited from hinterland tribes, was successfully infiltrated by the NLF.

This conflict between FLOSY and NLF was compounded by an additional factor – the shift in Egypt's position. Although it had initially backed the NLF, this support was gradually withdrawn in 1965. The NLF came to see Egypt as a state that would not support its struggle to the end. It accused Nasser of making concessions to the British, the Saudis, and the sultans of the South. The NLF leaders were therefore able to pose as more militant Yemeni nationalists than FLOSY. This particularly Yemeni conflict took place against a wider context in which significant sections of the Arab Nationalist Movement were becoming critical of Nasserism.[8] This radicalisation of the MAN occasioned a

critique of Egypt as a petty bourgeois state, one that was
prevented by its class character from giving full support to the
revolutionary movement in the Arab world. Egypt's equivocations in Yemen were one cause of this crisis. Its inability to
confront Israel, epitomised in the defeat of June 1967, was the
other. The result was that the NLF, which emerged victorious
in the conflict with FLOSY and which defeated the plan for a
Federation of South Arabia based on merchants and sultans,
saw itself as part of a new self-proclaimed Marxist-Leninist
vanguard in the Arab world.

The NLF's radicalisation reflected its formation at three
separate levels: the *class* base of the guerrilla movement,
i.e. the small peasants who fought the landowners and tribal
authorities in the hinterland, in a struggle that was both
anti-colonial and socially revolutionary; the *organisational*
trajectory of a grouping that had to turn to new models of
political and social organisation because of its conflict with
what had, till then, been seen as the leading state in the Arab
nationalist camp; and the *ideological* transformation of a
group that was, in both its Nasserite and Marxist-Leninist
phases, under the strong intellectual influence of the left-
wing Arab intelligentsia of Lebanon and the Palestinian
movement.

Post-revolutionary Transformation:

British rule in South Yemen ended on 30 November 1967,
and power was transferred to an NLF government. Although
the British authorities had, until the summer, hoped to hand
over either to the federal rulers, or to some coalition of
federal and FLOSY leaders, the strength of the NLF, in
both the hinterland and the city, made this impossible. The
NLF did not force the British to leave South Yemen: the
decision to withdraw from Aden had been taken by the
colonial authorities for other strategic and economic reasons.
The NLF did succeed in undermining Britain's plan for transferring power to a pro-western state that would be
accommodating to British and to western interests in the
Persian Gulf and Indian Ocean regions as a whole. Yet
despite their success in the guerrilla war, the NLF came to

power with many problems. Their own organisation was relatively small – at most a few thousand fighters – and lacked any experienced administrative personnel: as seen elsewhere, the qualities of leadership in guerrilla struggle are not necessarily those required for wielding state power. Not a single one of the NLF leaders had had higher education, or had spent a significant period abroad. The NLF was riven by factionalism – on ideological, political and, persistently, tribal bases; this was to continue long into the post-revolutionary period. The revolutionary period itself had been comparatively short – four years: it had not given the NLF experience in administering liberated areas, and its ties with the urban and rural population were often weak. Significant sections of the urban population sympathised with FLOSY. Above all, the NLF leaders had only a vague idea of what state power involved: beyond the struggle against foreign domination, they seemed to have little sense of what was involved in economic, social and political development. They placed rather too much trust in the Marxist-Leninist formulae which they had espoused in the last stages of the struggle when this meant no more than a radical critique of Nasserism.

Their objective economic context was hardly more favourable. The urban economy had had three main sources of income – the port, a British subsidy which made up 60 per cent of the state's budget, and the income from the British garrison. All three were discontinued in 1967, the latter two as a result of the British withdrawal, the first because of the closure of the Suez Canal in the Arab-Israeli war.

The closing of the Suez Canal cut the number of ships passing through yearly from 6000 to 1500; GNP fell by an estimatèd 15 per cent per annum in the first two post-independence years; the British subsidy was ended abruptly. This economic crisis, compounded by political resistance to the new régime, provoked a massive flight: up to 500,000 people, out of a total population of under 2 million, left the country. Even though many of these were migrants to South Yemen from other states (North Yemen and Somalia), the outflow disproprotionately lessened the number of skilled personnel available to the new government. Virtually all the Adeni merchants and upper civil servants departed, but the crisis removed many urban workers as well. As a result, although for the first few years after 1967 unemployment remained, the country later had a labour shortage for skilled labour.

The NLF faced multiple tasks: to create a new national economy out of the divided service and subsistence sectors; to overcome the division of the countryside into twenty-three separate sultanates; to develop meagre agricultural resources with the goal of self-sufficiency in food; to train administrative cadres and a new workforce to replace those who had left, and to perform tasks never attempted under the colonial régime; to raise the educational level of a country with adult literacy under 20 per cent; to finance a development budget when the coffers were empty, and when the country was required to spend considerable amounts on military defence.

It took time for a new economic machinery to come into operation. In 1968–9 all salaries, in public and private employment, were cut from a third to two-thirds; public sector salaries were cut again in 1972. At the end of 1969, all banks and insurance companies were nationalised. In 1970, an agricultural reform law limited irrigated holdings to 20 acres and unirrigated holdings to 40 acres. In 1971, the free port status of Aden was abolished, except for a small transit enclave. In 1972, a housing law ended all private renting, and allowed individuals to own only the house in which they lived. The expropriated housing units were then reallocated.

The key to the new economic system has been the gradual imposition of a centralised planning system. The first plan, from 1971 to 1974, was allotted only YD 40 million (about $96 million at 1971 rates). A quarter was to be spent on agriculture and another quarter on industry, but even this small target was not obtained. As a result of the failure of some of the foreign donors to honour their commitments, the plan was only 77 per cent fulfilled. The second plan covered the five years from 1974 to 1978, with an initial commitment of YD 80 million: of this 27.7 million was to go to agriculture, twice as much as to industry. The monetary figures rose considerably above the original targets reflecting both inflation in world prices and increased foreign aid commitments. By the end of 1977, YD 136 million had already been spent. Total investment at the end of the 1974–8 plan was nearly YD 200 millions.

State control now pervades all sectors of the economy, except the retail sector where private interests remain active. By mid-1975, land reform had distributed land to about 30,000 individual farmers, nearly all of these now grouped into co-operatives which rely on state funds and machinery with targets set by state officials. By 1980 there were forty-four such co-operatives covering a total area of 214,000 acres, or 70 per cent of the cultivated land, and with a total membership of 40,000 families. Most of these remain service co-operatives, but an increasing number have become production co-operatives, with no distinction of individual peasant plots. State farms, where the peasants receive a wage, were established on land reclaimed from the desert, and by 1978 there were thirty-five of these, covering a total area of around 30,000 acres. In both cases the produce is marketed through a state distribution system: together these account for 80 per cent of agricultural output.

An area of priority expansion has been fishing, controlled by the Ministry of Fish Wealth. Between 1969 and 1975 fish output rose by 38 per cent, and export earnings rose from $1.3 million in 1969 to $8.1 million in 1975, when fish had overtaken cotton as the main export. South Yemen borders some of the richest fishing waters in the world, and some officials believe that they can increase fish output by up to 300 per cent. This is important not only for future exports, but also as a source of protein for the Yemeni population. A system of cold stores is being built throughout the country to distribute fish inland where it previously never reached, and fish canning and fishmeal plants are being built for export. The main emphasis is on high value exports – cuttle-fish, squids, lobsters – to the Far East and the USA. Two foreign firms (one Japanese, one Russian) are operating under concessions in the fish industry.

The first five-year plan projected a substantial increase in industrial output. Production rose around 260 per cent between Independence and the end of 1975. Of the thirty-five factories in the country at the end of 1977, fourteen belonged entirely to the public sector, eight to the mixed sector (with the state having a 51 per cent share) and thirteen to the private

sector, with the state-owned units accounting for a dispro-
portionate share of workers and output. The state sector
alone accounted for about 60 per cent of industrial output by
1980. The Chinese-built textile factory in the Aden suburb of
Mansura is the largest: it employs 1400 workers, 60 per cent
of them women, and has an annual output of 7 million meters,
making the PDRY self-sufficient in some textiles. Other new
factories include a shoe factory, a cigarette and match
factory and other clothing and mechanical plants, all in the
small-scale import substitution area. Total employment in
industry in 1977 was over 16,000.[9] 1700 were in the refinery,
and about another 7600 people worked in units employing
ten persons or more. A substantial number – 6000 – still
worked in small non-factory units of four persons or less.

Until 1980, the refinery continued to run at a substantial
deficit. It was taken over by mutual agreement in May 1977
and BP runs it on a service contract. Capacity is 8.5 million
tons, and its breakeven is around 4 million tons, but through-
put was under 1.5 million tons and the deficit was over $10
million/year. Arab states were reluctant to provide oil: the
Saudis cut off their commitment in late 1977 to protest the
PDRY's foreign policy, and the Iraqi offer of considerable
quantities was on condition that they could station troops
at the refinery. The plant is also in great need of modernisation but the funds were not available. The international
bunkering traffic is no longer there, and new refineries
elsewhere in the Red Sea (particularly the *Petromin* plant at
Jeddah) offer cheaper prices. The refinery did, however,
get a temporary new lease of life in 1980 as a result of the
Iran–Iraq War. Ironically, the plant had been built in the
first place to replace BP's refinery in Iran, which Mosadeq
nationalised in 1951. In 1980 the destruction of refining
capacity at Abadan, and Iraq's problems in oil output, led
to greatly increased use of the refinery's capacity by these
states.

The port, once the centre of the South Yemeni economy,
was partially modernised under a $16.8 million loan from the
Arab Fund for Development in 1975, and its activities have
picked up somewhat since the post-1967 slump. The number
of ships calling went up from 110 a month to 150 a month
after the Suez Canal reopened in 1975, but this was still only

a third of the pre-1967 level; the lucrative passenger-ship market has, in any case, been replaced by air travel. A third of the goods landed are in transit to North Yemen: the brightly-painted trucks of the Taiz and Sanaa merchants can be seen clustered outside the dock gates every morning. This transit trade is conditional on political accord between the two countries, and since 1982 the North has been utilising new competitive facilities at Mocha and Hodeida. There have also been long delays in unloading goods at Aden port, reflecting a shortage of management personnel.

All banking is now controlled by the single National Bank of Yemen, and although individual traders still dominate retail trade, they are directed in a number of ways by state policy. First, 95 per cent of all imports are now brought in by the state; the private traders purchase from state trading bodies who set the retail price. Second, the state has intervened directly to set prices of basic foodstuffs, a move necessitated by world inflation and substantial shortages of some commodities in the mid-1970s. In 1977 in Aden market, fish cost 150 fils a kilo (about 44¢ a pound); bananas and melon cost 50 fils a kilo (about 15¢ a pound). This price system was also enforced at the national level – something quite new in South Yemen with its enormous regional variations in price. Third, a system of state retail shops has been established: at the end of 1977 there were thirty-six in Aden, many selling clothing. The availability of goods in these shops limited the ability of private traders to raise prices. In order to cushion the economy from the effects of inflation, the Ministry of Trade set up a special fund to bridge the gap between Yemeni and world prices and at the worst period, in 1975, a number of commodities was rationed. Although officials said at the end of 1977 only sugar was rationed, shortages of basic foodstuffs from one day to the other certainly occurred, at least in Aden.

The overall record of the South Yemeni economy has marked several substantial advances. The disastrous trends of the first years of independence have been overcome and the dependence on services and a fickle international trade have been broken. A national economy has been established – something 129 years of British occupation failed to do. A system of state control, through the planning and other economic ministries, has been created. Between 1970 and 1975,

GDP rose by about 25 per cent, and the World Bank estimates that in 1973–7 the South Yemeni GDP was growing at around 7 per cent per annum.[10]

At the same time, South Yemen faces enormous economic difficulties which over a decade and a half of transformation have only partly solved. First, it lacks any major source of foreign exchange. As a result, the country's balance of payments has remained in serious deficit. In 1975 exports, at around $15 million, equalled only 8 per cent of imports at $177 million. This deficit has been made up from two sources. First, emigrant workers remit over $200 million annually, and the state has encouraged this by giving them special rates of deposit three times higher than the domestic rate. Second, there has been an increase in international aid, which at the end of 1975 came to $314 million. China was the largest donor, followed by the USSR, Libya, Kuwait, the World Bank and Abu Dhabi. Saudi Arabia also provided up to $50 million in 1976, and the PDRY emphasises that it is willing to allow foreign investments by private firms under certain conditions. In 1976 foreign debt equalled $226 million, or 49 per cent of GNP. Foreign loans are scheduled to make up over half of the investment funds for the 1979–83 plan.

One possible solution would be the discovery of oil. As of 1980, no such breakthrough had occurred, and the PDRY imported 500,000 tons of oil a year: because of the Arab boycott against what was seen as too radical a régime, the PDRY acquired most of its oil from the USSR. In 1980, however, there were reports that the Italian firm Agip had discovered oil in commercial quantities off the eastern coast, and that there was a possibility that the PDRY could even begin exporting oil by 1983. If true, these would represent a significant breakthrough in the economic climate of the post-revolutionary period.[11]

There are, however, other major problems internal to the economy. There is a great shortage of skilled labour, and in order to prevent loss of skilled workers to the oil states, where wages are much higher, the government banned further emigration for some years after 1974. The agricultural base remains meagre: although output rose 25 per cent in the 1967–77 period, this barely kept pace with the increase in population: mid-1970s per capita food production was 80 per cent up on 1970. Only 2 per cent of the country is cultivable. The PDRY also pays substantial costs as a result of its international political options: western sources suggest that defence expenditure takes up around 20 per cent of total government outlays, and the armed forces draw off needed qualified personnel. Arab aid has been restricted, and subject to political conditions.

Given the political turmoil in the country and the lack of skilled personnel, it is hardly surprising that mistakes have been made. Many of these are now being blamed on the late President Salem Robea Ali, but the problem goes deeper than that. The 1969 bank nationalisation measure was in some ways disastrously executed – most of the accounts nationalised were overdrafts which had been granted by the international banks against deposits held in their other overseas branches. The 1972 housing nationalisation law had the immediate effect of cutting back the flow of workers' remittances. They sent money home to build houses and sustain their families, and since they technically qualified as 'absentee' they lost ownership of these houses until the law was appropriately amended. In addition, some of the projects involving foreign aid donors have been unsuccessful. A Bulgarian agricultural team, using a faulty survey prepared by a Lebanese firm, abandoned a major farming project in the Third Governorate after three years of operations. Many of the state farms were too hastily set up and made big losses. Yet the evidence available suggests that after a decade of extremely difficult economic problems, a small force of skilled and experienced personnel are now in place to make much better use of the PDRY's limited development possibilities. The administrative apparatus has grown with each of the central plans, and it is a reasonable expectation that the third plan, that of 1979–83, will have greater success than the two earlier ones.

Social Reforms

Among the most striking post-revolutionary social processes is the attempt to abolish the influence of tribalism in South Yemeni life, in marked contrast to North Yemen, Oman and the other Peninsula states, where tribalism is being built into the new state structures. This involves tackling institutional *and* ideological structures. Many of the tribal sheikhs have fled, and have had their lands confiscated. The main means of undermining the tribal system is not by banning its outward manifestations, but by creating a unified Yemeni nation. This involves in the first instance creating the material infrastructure of a nation: a unified economy, a road system, a national military structure. Less tangibly, it involves promoting a Yemeni culture through literature, dance, music and archaeology. This sense of a common Yemeni identity has an inward-looking aspect, uniting the fragments of South Yemen into a single country, but it also looks outwards toward North Yemen and the long-standing aim of reuniting all Yemenis within a single state. Yet the South Yemeni experience also points up the difficulties of altering attitudes and loyalties based on the tribe, even if the material bases and outward manifestations of tribal society have been altered. Indeed, it points to the need for a greater recognition that in post-revolutionary societies the transformation of political values, what can, in a revised materialist sense, be called 'political culture', is far more difficult and requires far more time than the transformation of political and social institutions.[12] All the major leadership disputes of the post-revolutionary period have involved, among other things, issues of nepotism and tribal loyalty, and there is no reason to suppose that this matter is simply a matter of the past. Indeed, it was in recognition of this fact, and of the need to be more open about the persistence of such loyalties, that in 1980 the People's Assembly re-introduced the tribal names for the local administrative units which had been replaced by numbered designations at the time of Independence.

A noticeable consequence of the revolution and, unwittingly, of the post-1967 economic crisis, has been greater income equality. After the salary and wage reductions of the 1968–72 period, fixed scales of remuneration have been introduced, with a ratio of around 1:3 for most payments. In 1977 the lowest wage for a worker in a factory was around YD 25 a month (exclusive of overtime), the highest YD 75. This applies in ministries too, although the ministers themselves get higher salaries, plus non-monetary privileges. Rent controls also contribute to income equality. Allowing for variations in practice, official rents for flats in Aden range from YD 1.5 ($4.35) to YD 5 ($14.50) a *month*, the latter being for a three-room flat with bathroom. Although the price level in Aden rose by 77 per cent in the period 1970–5, rents fell by 25 per cent, despite enormous shortages of living space.

There has also been an almost total stamping out of corruption. In every economic enterprise and ministry there are special supervisory committees (*lejan al-reqaba*) whose job involves overseeing the finances and ensuring that no irregularities occur.[13] The contrast with the other countries of the Arabian Peninsula is striking. No one claims that individual corruption has ceased absolutely, but the greatest danger now lies not in one person taking money surreptitiously so much as in the emergence of a new privileged élite in the Party and state.

Great emphasis is laid on the expansion and distribution of educational services. The number of teachers has risen from 2485 in 1969 to 9277 in 1976; in the same period the number of pupils in primary and secondary education has risen from 60,000 to 288,000. Officially, 26 per cent of secondary-age children are in school and 77 per cent of primary, with a goal of 100 per cent in primary school by the mid-1980s. The present figures are respectively six and three times higher than in North Yemen,[14] and although possibly overstated they reflect a major advance. Aden has a small university with about 1300 students in 1975, and another 1230 studying abroad. The great failure of the educational programme is the adult literacy campaign. Despite official enthusiasm, government figures show that of the 736,000 people who enrolled in the 1973–6 period only 44,000 actually graduated. The campaign was modelled on the successful Cuban campaign of the early 1960s: but whereas in Cuba the literate *majority* could instruct the illiterate *minority*, the ratios were reversed in South Yemen. There were simply not enough teachers to go around, and Arabic script is much more difficult to learn than the Roman one used in Cuba. In addition, Cuba had a much higher population density, and over twice the level of urbanisation (60 per cent) found in South Yemen. The government is now rethinking the adult literacy campaign as a prelude to relaunching it.

Health has also been the target of a major effort. Life

expectancy at birth in 1970 was forty-two years. This was ten years lower than India; although comparable with that in North Yemen, the much higher level of urbanisation in the South should have somewhat improved health conditions. In 1967 the PDRY had twenty-nine doctors and nine hospitals, with only two of the latter functioning properly. In 1977, it had 250 doctors and twenty-six functioning hospitals. There are one health centre and ten medical units in each district (*mudiria*) of the country, for a total of twenty-two centres and 256 units. Since 1973, all medical services are free, and the target is one doctor per 2500 inhabitants by 1983. If this programme is completed it will distinguish the PDRY from most of the rest of the Middle East, where medical services are often costly and disproportionately concentrated in the urban centres. Already by 1977 the ratio of population to physician, although rather unfavourable (7510) was far better than that in the North (13,830).

Considerable efforts have been made to transform the position of women within the framework of the orthodox socialist programme for emancipating women.[15] This involves: (a) establishing legal equality between men and women; (b) strengthening the family and parenthood – the latter seen in economic as well as ideological terms, given the PDRY's shortage of labour; (c) encouraging women to participate in economic activity outside the home – again reflecting the need for more labour as well as a commitment to the equality of women and men. Under the 1974 Family Law, polygyny, child marriages and arranged marriages are prohibited. The conditions of divorce for men and women were made almost, but not completely, equal. A parallel erosion of traditional values can be seen in the town where the number of women wearing the *sheidor* has declined. The *sheidor* is, however, not in any way prohibited. The Ministry of Labour's campaign to increase the participation of women in the labour force through training and allocation policies yielded by the mid-1970s over 2000 women out of a total of 16,000 in industrial employment. During International Women's Year in 1975, special training institutes were established in each of the six Governorates and dozens of women were trained in jobs conventionally seen as exclusively men's, such as tractor driving, mechanics and accounting.

This process of emancipating women is only partially completed. Conservative opposition is strong: Saudi radio as assailed the 1974 Family Law as contrary to the true practices of Islam. At least two of the six women's training institutes were closed as a result of traditionalist and local hostility to women in these institutes living away from home for up to nine months. Participation rates in education also vary noticeably between boys and girls: by official accounts, 38 per cent for girls in the 7–12 age group in 1975, as compared with 94 per cent for boys. While these problems reflect the resilience of traditional values, other problems derive from limitations within the official policy. As in more advanced post-capitalist societies, there is almost no concern with restructuring relations within the home; the result is that working women still face the full burden of domestic labour on top of their new extra-domestic jobs: the double shift. Moreover, the women's organisation is totally controlled by the Party, which is dominated by men, so the place of women in political life remains a very restricted one. Against this it must be emphasised that the PDRY has gone further than any other Peninsula society towards ensuring the equality of men and women.

The transformation of Yemeni society has involved a careful relationship with Islamic beliefs. Virtually all South Yemenis are Sunni Muslims (of the Shafei variety), and Islam is the official religion in the constitution. The mosques are open and used, and Muslim holidays are officially observed. On the *Eid* the President leads the prayers in the main mosque and Imams officiate at certain state functions, such as honouring the dead of the revolutionary struggle on Independence Day. At least one prominent Imam is a member of the Supreme People's Council. Yet Islam is not central in South Yemeni political life in the way it is in many other Arab countries. Islamic concepts were not prominent in the ideology of the nationalist movement against the British, and little use is made of Islamic themes or invocations in official statements. The latter are based, unequivocally, on 'scientific socialism', in implicit contrast with what is seen as the diluted and unscientific content of the various brands of 'Arab Socialism'. The Koran is taught in the schools – but by lay-teachers and as part of the normal curriculum, on the

basis of textbooks that stress what are presented as the
egalitarian and anti-imperialist themes of Islamic doctrine.
The Imams still perform their functions in the mosque itself,
but they have lost their central forms of social power: education is secular; the *sharia* (the religious legal system) has
been replaced by a new state-run legal code; and the religious
endowment or *waqf* lands were confiscated in the 1970 land
reform. The Imams now derive a salary from the Ministry of
Justice and Waqfs to compensate for their loss of income
through land reform. While it would be rash to assert that no
opposition based on Islamic sentiment could emerge, it
does appear that the régime has been careful to avoid pro-
vocative anti-religious positions.

No account of Yemeni life would be complete without
mention of the narcotic *qat*, a leaf traditionally chewed by men
in afternoon social gatherings. After many false starts,
going back to the colonial times, a partial ban on *qat* consumption was finally imposed in 1975. Not only is it harmful
to health, but it has very negative social effects – encouraging
idleness and diverting family expenditure away from food. A
good afternoon's chewing of moderately-priced *qat* involves,
if you included the drinks normally taken with it, up to YD 2,
or a day's wages. Now *qat* chewing is restricted to the weekend
(Thursday afternoon and Friday) and casual observation in
Aden indicates that public *qat* consumption has ceased
completely on working days. The conviction of people
involved in illegal *qat* trading is given prominent coverage
in the press. But the ban on *qat* has had at least one unanti-
cipated negative result: a rise in the demand for alcohol.
Beer and whisky are available in Aden at least, and many who
earlier sought solace and social company in the mastication of
qat have simply transferred their dinars elsewhere.

Political Transformation

Since 1967, South Yemen has been dominated by one political
organisation, the National Liberation Front, with its two
small and dependent allies, the Ba'ath and communist
groupings. The construction of this new political system
has involved the reorganisation of the state apparatus, and

the transformation of the Party from a loosely structured and radicalised nationalist front into a more orthodox centralised communist party.

At Independence, the NLF inherited a civil service and an army whose structure and orientation were stamped by colonialism. The civil service in Aden was an urban adjunct of the port and the British base, and the army was a tribally-recruited force for rural law enforcement. Many of the top civilian and military officials fled the country at Independence or soon after, and today there is limited personnel continuity within any section of the state apparatus between the pre- and post-Independence periods. All ministers are veterans of the guerrilla struggle, or are Party militants subsequently trained abroad. The state apparatus is very much under the control of the political leadership. Party functionaries are located at each level and play an active role. Civil service employment in 1977 numbered about 31,000 (more than double that at Independence) and, given the state's role in the economy, a majority of those in other employment were also under some degree of state influence.

The 'Defence of the Yemeni Revolution' does not just involve a strong and well-armed army along the country's extensive borders. Western estimates give a total of 21,000 in the military in 1978–9, with 19,000 of these in the army. In addition to the regular army the NLF has, since June 1973, developed a people's militia force based on the place of residence. The NLF has apparently firm control of these military units, and the army plays a rather less prominent role in public life than in other Arab countries. Yet in both the 1969 and 1978 crises one of the explosive issues was that of officer promotion and demotion, indicating that the factional disputes within the civilian political apparatuses find a continuing reflection inside the armed forces themselves.

A pervasive security consciousness has certainly become a much more marked facet of Yemeni life. The Yemenis aroused hostile criticism even among friendly Arab parties when in their 1975 State Security Law they made it illegal for any Yemeni to talk to a foreigner except on official business. 'Foreigner' .means non-Yemeni, and the law was in fact especially aimed at other Arabs – Egyptians, Iraqis and Saudis – who were suspected of setting up, or attempting to set up, client political groupings in the PDRY. It was also aimed at foreign aid missions suspected of recruiting spies (as in the case of one foreign advisor in Mukalla) or of encouraging prostitution. South Yemen's security measures have also provoked considerable criticism abroad: Amnesty International has attacked the PDRY's human rights stand. Yemeni officials concede that in the early years of the revolutionary régime violations and repression occurred, and Salem Robea Ali has been publicly blamed for many of these in the period since his fall. Officials insist that the PDRY is a country at war, and that many of those reported as being in jail or as having disappeared were killed in clashes with security forces along the border. They are also indignant at what they see as foreign silence on human rights violations in North Yemen, Saudi Arabia and Oman. The officials emphasise too that outside money can be used to bribe individuals in their impoverished country. It is not by chance that the 1975 anti-fraternisation law was passed a few months prior to the announcement of diplomatic relations with Saudi Arabia in March 1976. While it may be impossible ever to establish the real record, it certainly seems to be the case both that major violations of socialist legality have occurred in the PDRY and that, at the same time, the extent of these violations has been greatly exaggerated by a 'black propaganda' campaign against that country. The number of political prisoners is, at most, a few hundred.

In October 1978, after a fifteen-year process, the NLF became the Yemeni Socialist Party. This process involved a 'double radicalisation'. In the first phase, from its establishment in October 1963 to June 1969, it was radicalised within the parameters of the Arab nationalist movement, from a loose Nasserite front to a more centralised organisation professing Marxism-Leninism, in part influenced by a similar and simultaneous ideological radicalisation within the Palestinian movement. Although Marxism-Leninism was prominent at the Third and Fourth NLF Congresses (October 1966 and March 1968), much of the Party apparatus remained in the hands of an opposing group led by Qahtan ash-Shaabi. The Marxist-Leninist faction came indisputably to power in June 1969. Yet this radicalisation left many questions unanswered: its Marxism-Leninism was rather inchoate, borrowing ideas from the more utopian parts of Lenin, from Mao, and from Guevara. It lacked three essentials for being the ideological basis for a ruling Party: it had no coherent theories of Party organisation, or of social and economic development of South Yemen, and it was unclear about South Yemen's international alignment in circumstances where the country desparately needed foreign support in order to survive. Over the next nine years this radicalised nationalism was itself transformed into the 'scientific socialism' of the Yemeni Socialist Party. This second radicalisation led to the fall of a Party leader, this time President Salem Robea Ali.

The beginnings of this second radicalisation were evident at the Fifth Congress of the NLF in March 1972 when the Arab nationalist organisational structure of the 'General Command' was replaced by a Central Committee and a Political Bureau. The same Congress decided on the establishment of the militia and of the popular defence committees which were designed to combine educational and social welfare activities at the neighbourhood and block level with security surveillance duties. This second radicalisation was marked by greater political restraint, and the conference tone was more composed than that of the heady post-Indepence Fourth Congress: there were fewer attacks on the petty bourgeoisie in the Arab world, less emphasis on the efficacy of armed struggle, and the phrase Marxism-Leninism was being gradually displaced by the less outspoken scientific socialism. At what was called the Unification Congress, in October 1975, the NLF went a stage further. It moved into a transitional phase, establishing the Unified Political Organisation of the NLF, incorporating the Vanguard Party, a Ba'ath grouping and the Popular Democratic Union, the Communist Party. Between October 1975 and October 1978 this Unified Political Organisation evolved into a new, formally constituted 'Vanguard Party', which became the Yemeni Socialist Party in October 1978.

The YSP now has a fully articulated organisational structure, very different from the nationalist NLF of the late 1960s. The controlling bodies are the Politburo with five full members, and the Central Committee of forty-seven full members.[16] Membership of the NLF stood in late 1977 at around 26,000 including 1000 women, and around 2000 workers. No later figures are available. The Party's ideological school in Aden has trained over 3000 members since it was set up in 1973, and many cadres have been abroad for political training courses. Beyond the Party itself are the mass organisations: the largest, the General Union of Yemeni Workers, has 84,000 members; the Democratic Yemeni Youth 31,000; the General Union of Yemeni Women 15,000; and there are other student and young pioneer groups. Significantly, in the light of their weight in the population and the rural origins of the NLF; the peasants did not have an organisation until the mid-1970s. In May 1973, Popular Defence Committees, modelled on the Cuban system, were set up in the urban areas, but this project is believed to have not been successful: popular enthusiasm was low, and the security functions of the committees came to predominate. The media are also firmly under Party control. The most important publication is the party weekly *ath-Thawri* (The Revolutionary) with a circulation of 26,000. Some left-wing papers from other Arab countries, such as *al-Horria* and *al-Hadaf*, are on sale, and despite the political control of the media inside the country, there is no apparent restriction on listening to foreign radios: government officials openly quote the BBC or the Voice of America, and the radios in cafés also tune in to these stations, among others.

The highest legislative body is the Supreme People's Council, originally set up in 1971 with a nominated membership. In 1978 it was filled by direct elections for 111 seats and it elected a presidium (eleven members) and a Council of Ministers (nineteen members). At the provincial level, in a development modelled on the Cuban system of Poder Popular, People's Councils with limited financial and administrative powers were elected in each of the six Governorates in 1976 and 1977. Screening of candidates certainly occurs, but there is a plurality of candidates and out of 111 members, forty of the Supreme People's Council's members are not in the YSP.

By the end of 1978, the process of constructing a new set of political institutions for Party and state had been completed with the founding of the Congress of the YSP and the first elections to the SPC. Casual observation of the 1977 local assembly elections in the First Governorate indicated that there was considerable enthusiasm – indeed pride – in the new electoral process. People pointed out that whereas under colonial rule there had been elections only in Aden, these elections were country-wide, that women voted for the first time, and that most of the candidates were of working-class background. Indeed, expectations may have gone beyond what the candidates can deliver: one member of the First Governorate Assembly remarked that his electors now regarded him 'like a British MP' and were 'besieging my home with requests for help with their problems, especially housing problems'.

Despite the democratic presentation of these new institutions, no one doubts that real power rests with the top leadership. The Party not only selects those candidates who stand in elections, but also controls the discussion in the various Councils. In the YSP itself there is limited room for debate; most discussions take place in private and informal circumstances.

The issue of what kind of Party to have – its internal structures, the relation between it and the people – lay at the centre of the dispute with President Salem Robea Ali. He was one of the leaders of the 1963–9 radicalisation, and President throughout the second phase. As early as 1972, divergent lines were clear. In July 1972, soon after the Fifth Congress, he launched his anti-bureaucratic campaign of urban 'uprisings', a form of mass mobilisation influenced by the Cultural Revolution in China, and designed to break the hold of the 'bureaucrats' in the Party and state. Later, he used his influence to restrict the unification of the NLF with what he regarded as the unrepresentative Vanguard and PDU groupings, and he criticised the new Party model for creating an élite structure. His opposition ranged across all three issues: Party structure, development programme, international alignment. Although hostile to the model of his opponents within the NLF leadership, he was unable to offer a coherent alternative.

The crisis between Salem Robea Ali and his opponents came to a head in June 1978. On 24 June the President of North Yemen was killed by a bomb sent to him disguised as a present from the South Yemeni government. The majority of the NLF Central Committee accused Salem Robea Ali of having organised this, in the hope of provoking a crisis in the North in which he could intervene, and so oust his rivals in the South. On 26 June fighting broke out in Aden between units loyal to the President and forces backed by the Central Committee majority. By the end of the day Salem Robea Ali and his two leading associates had been captured and executed. Many issues contributed to this dénouement, but central to the dispute was the question of what kind of political structure to have. Salem Robea Ali favoured mass mobilisation, the promotion of politically militant at the expense of technically competent cadres, and an egalitarian life-style for Party cadres. His opponents argued that this approach was simply unworkable in South Yemen, where the material problems facing the régime were too great, and where the administrative incompetence, combined with nepotism, of the 'spontaneist' approach would lead to further catastrophes. In a small scale, this conflict reproduced the 'red' versus 'expert' dispute of the Chinese Revolution, and the debates in Cuba over Guevarist versus Soviet-style planning. Salem Robea Ali was, like Mao and Guevara, groping for an alternative, but the evidence is that he did not have one.

The defeat of Salem Robea Ali might have been expected to open a new period of orthodox Party consolidation within the YSP, which was established four months later. In fact, factional disputes continued to rage for the next two years. In 1979 the powerful head of the Ministry of State Security, Mohammed Said Abdullah, was dismissed and sent into exile in Ethiopia. Accused of being responsible for violations of legality, he was also involved in a growing conflict between YSP members from North and South Yemen: as a Northerner, he was blamed for many of the troubles which the country faced. Then, in April 1980, the powerful Secretary General of the YSP and President of the PDRY, Abdul Fatah Ismail, was dismissed and his place taken by the Prime Minister Ali Nasser Mohammad. The issues behind his fall were a mirror of those leading to the fall of Salem Robea Ali: Abdul Fatah was criticised for having been too loyal to the Soviet development model, and for relying too much on Soviet economic aid that was often deficient. He was also regarded as being too far removed from the concerns of the masses to take appropriate initiatives. It would appear that although the USSR disapproved of the fall of Abdul Fatah they did respond to the April 1980 events by increasing their aid, and meeting some of the complaints which the Yemenis had voiced. Whether the disputes of 1978–80 will mark the end of this factionalism within the YSP or whether further conflicts will arise to weaken the Party and state leadership, remains to be seem. Based as they were on both personal issues, and substantial disagreements over policy, they showed that the transformation of the old nationalist grouping was still not complete.

International Dimensions

From its inception, the PDRY has been involved in conflict with the other Arab states of the region: it has been the subject of attack by these states, which seek to undermine its social system, and it has itself encouraged revolutionary forces in these other countries. The key to South Yemeni foreign policy is its position on North Yemen: that Yemen – North and South – is one country (as much so as Vietnam, Korea and Germany, states divided by the conflict between capitalism and socialism, and as much so as Somalia or the Camerouns, colonial areas divided by rival imperialisms and only reunited at Independence). The division of Yemen is seen as a compound of both of these processes: first, the partition between Ottoman and British imperialisms in the nineteenth centruy, and second, the division between the revolutionary régime in the South and the right-wing capitalist régime, supported by Saudi Arbia, in the North. The régime in the North is seen as having usurped the revolution of 1962, and the tasks of reunification, which would involve fulfilling the programme of the 1962 revolution in the North, remain the overriding concern of the Southern leadership. A united Yemen would be economically viable in a way that the South on its own is not, and would, with a population close to 9 million, be the most populous state in the Arabian Peninsula. On two occasions since 1967, in 1972 and again in 1979, the two Yemens have been at war. Yet on both occasions these conflicts have given way to agreements on step-by-step unification of the two countries. Full unity between the two is inconceivable before the two social systems are more comparable; but the dialectic of unity, oscillating between collaboration at the state level, and support for opposition forces in each other's domain, is the central concern of policy-maker in the PDRY.

Aden has supported the guerrillas in the neighbouring state of Oman, and has had only intermittently favourable relations with Saudi Arabia: successive Saudi attempts to wean the PDRY away from the USSR, and to force Aden to allow exiled merchants and landowners to return and repossess their property, have not succeeded. The PDRY's relations with the rest of the Arab world have been fraught – especially with Iraq, which has promoted its own Ba'athist followers in both Yemens against the NLF and its allies. The PDRY's major ally in the region has been Ethiopia: although favouring negotiation rather than a military solution in Eritrea, the South Yemenis have welcomed the advent of the Ethiopian revolution as a whole.

The international orientation of the PDRY has led it increasingly into a close alliance with the communist countries, and since the late 1960s it has enjoyed growing military, political and economic ties to the Soviet Union and its allies. Most military aid and equipment has come from the Soviet Union, and Soviet bloc countries participate in a wide range of development projects. The Cubans too play a significant role: they train the militia and the air force, and provide many doctors and educational experts. Thousands of Yemenis have been trained in eastern Europe and Cuba, and it is on the basis of this new generation of qualified personnel that the new structures of Party and state are being built up.

Despite a general alignment with the USSR, the PDRY has been careful to sustain its relations with China. The Chinese have built the largest factory in the PDRY (the textile plant at Mansura) and the 315-mile road linking Aden to Mukalla. There is a Chinese-staffed hospital in the Crater district of Aden, and at a day-to-day level Chinese technicians remain rather popular with the Yemeni population.

Faced with the threat of annihilation in the years since Independence, it is obvious enough why the PDRY has opted for a general alignment with the communist world. The more interesting question is why the PDRY opted for the USSR rather than China, especially given the fact that in the late 1960s the Marxism-Leninism of the radical Arab nationalists was anti-revisionist in tone (i.e. anti-Russian) and tended to look to China for political inspiration.

The first reason is that the overriding aim of the PDRY government is survival: only the Soviet Union has the military power to guarantee that, both in providing arms and training, and in giving a general guarantee of support via its air and naval power. Second, the rightwards turn in Chinese foreign policy has, since the early 1970s, disillusioned many Yemenis. The turning-point was probably China's support for Sudan's President Numeiry in his July 1971 execution of Communist Party leaders, but Chinese recognition of Haile Selassie in 1970, the Shah in 1971 and Sultan Qabus in 1978 confirmed the shift. A third factor has been the influence of the small communist group in South Yemen itself, the PDU, which has in common with most other Arab communist parties an alignment with Moscow rather than Peking. Its gradual incorporation into the NLF has strengthened the links with the USSR. A fourth factor, and one not to be underestimated, is the relative inapplicability of the Chinese model to the PDRY: 'self-reliance' is not a feasible economic strategy, and in the absence of a long pre-history of revolutionary organisation before the advent of the organisation to power, the NLF has had to build up its cadres after Independence in a way that precludes ventures of the Cultural Revolution type. The failure of Salem Robea Ali's 'Maoist' initiatives has confirmed this trend.

If there is a criticism of the Soviet role, it is that Soviet non-military aid is *too small*, and that the USSR has not made clear a commitment to help transform the country economically, as it did in Cuba. There are some indications that since the establishment of the YSP, South Yemen has been allocated a somewhat higher ranking in Soviet foreign relations, and that since 1980 more economic aid has come as a result. But on the evidence so far, this is a just criticism. The Russians do not consider South Yemen to be a socialist country, merely 'a society of socialist orientation'. They retain reservations about the political character of the YSP as well as doubting the feasibility of South Yemeni economic development.

Conclusions

Any attempt to define the nature of the South Yemeni social formation encounters the problem of definition, the absence within Marxism of an agreed specification of what constitutes socialism. This is not the place to enter into that debate: suffice it to say that socialism will be treated here as a transitional stage between capitalism and communism, and in which two basic criteria are met: (a) that the major part of the means of production have been socialised; (b) that there exists a system of democracy at the level of the state and of the workplace. In other words, a combination of socio-economic and political conditions. In this light, it is clear that South Yemen is not a socialist country. Nor, indeed, does the YSP claim this: rather it states in its official documents that the PDRY is going through a national democratic phase of the revolution 'for the purpose of paving the way for the transition to the construction of socialism'.[17]

Although it is not yet socialist, it would be mistaken to see the PDRY as a capitalist country: elements of capitalism survive, as do, to a lesser extent, elements of pre-capitalist society, above all in the ideological realm. But the basic features of capitalist society, private ownership of the means of production and the possibility of private accumulation, do not *dominate* the South Yemeni economy, in practice or in law. In fact, industry, agriculture and foreign trade are all dominated by the state: 60 per cent of industrial output is by the state sector alone; all land is owned by the state, and service co-operatives are gradually giving way to producer ones; nearly all foreign trade is state-controlled. The private sector survives in a part of industry and agriculture, and in domestic trade. Of equal importance, however, is the fact that, in contrast to other experiences of 'Arab socialism', there is very little room for private accumulation, even in law: Party cadres have certain privileges, but they do not use these privileges or monies obtained through their position to accumulate and acquire control of production. The new 1978 constitution specifies clearly that the state must play a leading role in the economy, dominating although not totally excluding private capital. Were the present process to lead to one in which private accumulation was taking place under the guise of state control, and this is a possibility in the future, then it would represent a definite reversal of the present trends, and an alteration of the real and legal conditions of ownership in South Yemeni society. One can, therefore, state that whilst South Yemen is not yet a socialist society, as far as the system of ownership is concerned, it has certainly ceased to be one in which the capitalist mode of production is dominant: it is a transitional formation, marked by features of both capitalism and socialism.

The second part of the definition of socialism concerns the exercise of deomocratic controls: this does not exist in South Yemen, nor, on the available evidence, would it be possible in a full sense. A greater degree of political democracy is certainly possible in the PDRY, but what the South Yemeni case underlines are the objective preconditions for such democracy to be implemented fully, where this is interpreted both in relation to the decisions of the workplace and in relation to the broader political concerns of the society. These would include a certain level of development of the productive forces, such that education and a degree of time for political activity were generalised;[18] the overcoming of pre-capitalist and capitalist ideological structures within the society; a degree of international security for the social formation in question; and a general commitment on the part of the mass of the population to the transition to socialism. For reasons both internal to South Yemeni society and related to the international and regional contexts in which it finds itself, none of these conditions is yet adequately satisfied. As in economics, so in politics: the transition to a higher form of organisation and society cannot be effected merely by an act of will, however great the degree of mobilisation. This transition involves objective preconditions, the realisation of which may lie outside the influence of the political forces involved. Yet such objective limits on democracy do not justify the denial of all democratic forms, they merely point to the difficulty of attaining socialism amidst such scarcity.

These objective constraints help to explain South Yemen's relationship to the Cuban model, why South Yemen both moved along that path, but has not proceeded anything like as far as Cuba. In both cases a radical nationalist tendency was converted into one that was socialist in intention as a result of the transformation of the revolution itself at home, and the conflict with counter-revolutionary forces outside. Both these cases involved the assimilation into the transformed Party of formerly separate, even hostile, urban-based communist groupings (the PDU, the PSP) and the establishment of closer relationships with the USSR. In both, an initial period of somewhat utopian experimentation in domestic and foreign policy led to serious reverses which had a jack-knife effect: having for some years scorned the policies advocated by Moscow, both régimes seemed to abandon their reserve and become almost too loyal imitators of the Soviet line. This reflected the longer–term failure of their radicalisms to produce an independent model. Such a process was associated with the departure from power of elements associated with the earlier, less orthodox, experimentations (Salem Robea Ali, Che Guevara). Both states suffered from the undermining of their social and economic development by the consumerist attractions of neighbouring countries – Miami in the case of Cuba, the oil states in the case of Yemen. Both had overgrown urban centres that went into severe decline when their international links were broken (Aden, Havana). Yet both managed to rally a measure of patriotic support, drawing on the long histories of struggle prior to the revolution in which the two régimes remained rooted. Above all, both demonstrated that possibility, under certain conditions, of making the transition from radical nationalism to a commitment to socialism, one quite distinct from the statist capitalism presented as a 'third way' or as 'socialism' in many other Third World countries. Yet the differences are also important: for all its problems Cuba is a far richer country than South Yemen – in 1978, per capita income at $810 was twice that in South Yemen; it has a far higher level of literacy, technical personnel and mass consciousness; pre-capitalist ideological factors have virtually no role in Cuba, as opposed to South Yemen. Whatever the regional problems of Cuba, these pale besides those to which South Yemen is exposed in the Arabian Peninsula.

What then are the conditions for South Yemen progressing further along the path towards a transition to socialism? Three at least can be specified: the first is the development of the national economy, with a corresponding increase in levels of health, education and political confidence. This depends partly on internal factors (such as the discovery of oil), and partly on the international aid which it receives. Secondly, it involves the growth of freer political norms inside South Yemen, both within the YSP and between the YSP and the population as a whole: this will not follow automatically from a development of the economy, since much higher levels of production are quite compatible with the absence of democratic norms, as is seen in eastern Europe. Indeed, the availability of Soviet economic aid, while favourable on one score, may well contribute to the reinforcement of centralised political control by the YSP leadership. Finally, progress towards socialism involves changes in the regional climate in which the PDRY finds itself, so that its general insecurity and the ideological pressure on its population are reduced and so that its ability to relate to other Third World states without relying so heavily on the USSR is expanded. The noteworthy achievements of the South Yemeni revolution should not obscure the great difficulties which it still confronts.

Notes

1   This article is based on research conducted during three visits to South Yemen in 1970, 1973 and 1977. An earlier version was published in *MERIP Reports*, no. 8. My thanks are due to all those who read earlier versions and commented upon them – Perry Anderson, Helen Lockner, Maxine Moluneux and Robin Murray. For further details of the historical background to the South Yemeni revolution, see my *Arabia without Sultans*, Penguin, 1974, part three.
2   Details as follows: port 7555; building and construction 12,789; industrial undertakings 13,301; retails and wholesale trade 10,714; government, police and army 18,231; domestic service 17,000; others 1385. *Source*: M. S. Hassan, *Report to the People's Republic of Southern Yemen on Guidelines for Industrial Planning and Policy*, Aden, 1970, p. 6.

3   So restricted was the development of the productive forces that at Independence production only made up 40 per cent of GNP, services and British finance making up the rest. A striking illustration of the enclave could be seen in the hills west of Aden bay. At Bureika was the modern oil refinery which employed some local labour. Within five miles lay the fishing village of Fukhum, where the population lived, as they had done for millenia, in wattle huts.

4   The best available study of one part of the South Yemeni hinterland is Abdalla S. Bujra, *The Politics of Stratification: A Study of Political Change in a South Arabian Town*, Oxford, 1971. Bujra's study is of a town in the eastern, Hadramaut, region: we have no comparable study of the more densely populated western part of South Yemen, where the guerrilla movement was strongest.

5   The reason for this promotion of cotton in the late 1940s was the loss of Indian supplies following Independence, and the desire to guarantee supplies of cotton to Britain. A similar motive lay behind the much larger Gezira scheme in the Sudan.

6   The Imams of Yemen had ruled what is now North Yemen and much of the western part of South Yemen in the early eighteenth century, and there are strong common features in Yemeni life – in dialect, dress, eating habits, consumption of the narcotic *qat*, etc. The first modern nationalist movement was the liberal opposition to the Imams who fled to Aden in 1948 after a failed uprising. These Free Yemenis are the forefathers of the radical movement in both North and South.

7   From early 1963 onwards, the British were supplying arms and financial aid to the royalists in the North, and this was an added reason for Egypt to support an underground in the South. The Southern Yemenis were Muslims of the Shafei branch of Sunni Islam as were the inhabitants of southern and central North Yemen. The royalists tended to Zeidis, followers of a branch of Shiite Islam.

8   On the history of the MAN, see Walid Kazziha, *Revolutionary Transformation in the Arab World*, London, 1975.

9   *Source*: Ministry of Industry and Planning, Aden. This figure is much lower than the World Bank figure of 27,000. The discrepancy may be accounted for by the inclusion in the latter of additional artisanal labourers not included in the other figure.

10 *World Bank Study*, p. 5.

11 *New York Times*, 7 July 1980.

12 The concept of 'political culture' was originally developed within orthodox political science, where it had an idealist – a historical and unmaterialist – connotation. It is possible however to revise the concept, taking into account those historical and social factors which shape existing political values, and ascribing a less determinant role to them. The persistence of ethnic, tribal and sexual prejudices in post-revolutionary societies can be ascribed to the endurance of political cultures, understood in this revised sense.

13 Penalties for financial misdemeanors are heavy. In November 1977, a man convicted of embezzling YD 642 (under $2000) from the Mukalla Hotel was sentenced for prison for $2\frac{1}{2}$ years, and banned from public employment for life (*Al-Sharara*, no. 267, 9 November 1977).

14 Comparable figures for North Yemen were 25 per cent and 3 per cent. *Source: World Development Report*, 1980, p. 154.
15 Maxine Molyneux, 'Women and Revolution in the PDRY', *Feminist Review*, no. 1. London, 1979; and *State Policies and the Position of Women Workers in the PDRY*, ILO, 1982.
16 *BBC Summary of World Broadcasts*, part 4, 16 October 1980.
17 *Constitution of the PDRY*, October 1978, Article 1.
18 As an antidote to the somewhat over-optimistic analysis of mass action prevalent on the Left, it is worth remembering Lenin's remark that 'an illiterate person is outside politics'. This may be too absolute a dismissal: illiterate people can certainly revolt, but the ability to construct a new society, let alone fulfil the economic and political preconditions for the transition to socialism, must be dependent on a generalised level of education.

South Yemen: Country Profile

Official name:	People's Democratic Republic of Yemen (named People's Republic of South Yemen from Independence on 30 November 1967 till 1969).
Population:	1.84 million (1979).
Capital:	Aden, 271,590 (1977).
Land area:	333,000 sq km, of which 0.7 per cent arable land, 27 per cent pastures and 7 per cent woodland and forest. Large areas are mountainous and desert terrain.
Official language:	Arabic.
Membership of international organisations:	UN, IMF, Arab League, Islamic League, CMEA (associate member).
Political structure	
Constitution:	Of October 1978 (supersedes that of 30 November 1970).
Highest legislative body:	People's Supreme Council (111 members).
Highest executive body:	Council of Ministers (nineteen members).
Head of state:	President Ali Nasser Muhammad, assumed office in April 1980.
Prime Minister:	Ali Nasser Muhammad, assumed office in August 1971.
Ruling Party:	The Yemen Socialist Party, constituted in October 1978.
Secretary General of the Party:	Ali Nasser Muhammad, assumed office in April 1980.
Party membership:	26,000 (c.3.5 per cent of the adult population, 1977).

Armed forces: 23, 800 (c.5 per cent of total labour force, 1980), based on draft, plus a people's militia of up to 100,000 or c.12 per cent of the adult population.

Population
  Population density: 5.6 per sq km.
  Population growth (%):   1.9 (1970–8).
  Population of working age
  (15–64, %):   51 (1978).
  Urban population (%):   37 (1980).
  Ethnic groups: Predominately Arab population, with small Indian and Somali minorities.

Education and health
  School system: Twelve years of primary and secondary education free, but not universally available. Six years of universal primary education target for 1985.
  Primary school enrolment[I]:   78 per cent of primary school-age children enrolled in 1976.
  Secondary school enrolment[II]:   19 per cent of secondary school-age children enrolled in 1976.
  Higher education enrolment: 0.1 per cent (1976).[c]
  Adult literacy (%):   27 (1978).
  Life expectancy: 44 (1978).
  Infant death rate (per 1000):   114 (1977).
  Child death rate (per 1000):   31 (1977).
  Population per hospital bed: 810 (1977).
  Population per physician: 7095 (1977).
  Access to safe water
  (% of population):   24 (1975).[18]
  Access to electricity
  (% of population):   22 total, 1.6 rural (1975).[c]

Economy
  GNP: US$ 770 million (1978).
  GNP per capita: US$ 420 (1978).
  Gross domestic investment
  as % of GDP: 41 (1977).[c]
  State budget (expenditure)
  as % of GNP: 50 (1977).[c]
  Defence expenditure –   (1977).[c]
    % of total state budget: 19.
    % of GNP   9.5.
  GDP by sector (%):   Agriculture 13, fisheries 9, industry 19, (manufacturing 8), services 59[III] (1976).
  Total labour force: 476,000 (1979). c.25 per cent were working abroad in 1976.[c]

by sector (%):	Agriculture and fishery 60, industry 21, services 19 (1978).
Structure of ownership:	*Industry*: partly nationalised with state-owned enterprises representing c.60 per cent of output value (1980); the remaining units are under either private or mixed (with 51 per cent of shares owned by the state) ownership. *Agriculture*: All land nationalised. Co-operatives[IV] cover 70 per cent of the cultivated area, state farms c.10 per cent (1980). Livestock, (the bulk of which is produced by Bedouins) is mainly privately owned. *Fishing*: (by gross value, 1976): co-operatives 26 per cent, joint ventures 9 per cent, state-owned enterprises 16 per cent, foreign ownership 49 per cent.[c]
Land tenure:	The 1970 Land Reform limited irrigated holdings to 20 acres (8.1 ha) and unirrigated holdings to 40 acres (16.3 ha).
Main crops:	Wheat, cotton.
Irrigated area:	56,000 ha or 25 per cent of arable land (75 per cent of land used for crops).
Food self-sufficiency:	60–5 per cent (1977).
Energy balance – commercial consumption	(1978).
per capita:	523 kg coal equivalent.
liquid fuels (%):	100.
net imports (%):	114.
Growth indicators (% p.a.)[c] –	
GDP:	c.7 (1973–7).
GDP per capita:	c.5 (1973–7).
manufacturing industry:	7 (1969–76).
refining:	− 13 (1969–76).
agriculture:	2 (1973–6).
fisheries:	6.5 (1973–6).
food production per capita:	0.6 (1969/71–9).[6]

Foreign trade and economic integration
  Main source of foreign
  exchange: (1978).[9]

	US$ m.	% of GNP
Workers' remittances	256	35
foreign aid (loans and grants):	123	17
exports (goods):	39	5
oil refining:	13[VI]	
Imports (goods):	367[9]	50

Main exports:	Fish 37 per cent, petroleum 37 per cent, cotton 8 per cent, coffee 8 per cent (1977).[c]
Main imports:	Machinery and transport equipment 35 per cent, food 23 per cent, petroleum 18 per cent (1977).[c]
Main trading partners:[VII]	Japan, the UK, the USSR, Italy (1975–7).[c]
Destination of exports (%):	Industrialised countries 35, developing countries 51, socialist countries 10, capital surplus oil exporters 4 (1978).
Foreign debt –	US$ 349 million (1978).[c]
as % of GNP:	47.5.
by creditors (%):[VIII]	Arab governments and funds 42, the USSR 23, China 14, IDA 9, other largely socialist 13 (1977).[c]
Debt services ratio (%):	1.7 (1978).[18]
Foreign aid:	43 per cent of total state budget in 1977. Total disbursed 1969–77: US$ 250 million in medium-and long-term loans ($\frac{2}{3}$ from socialist countries), US$ 113 million in grants (mostly from Arab countries).[c]
Foreign investment:	The 1978 constitution allows foreign investment under certain conditions. So far, some joint ventures have been initiated in fishing and oil exploration.

Sources

[a]Fred Halliday, *Arabia without Sultans*, part III, London, 1974.
[b]Richard Nyrop, *Area Handbook for the Yemens*, Washington DC, 1977.
[c]World Bank, *People's Democratic Republic of Yemen. A review of Economic and Social Development*, Washington DC, 1979.
[d]Robert Stookey, *South Yemen*, London 1982.
[e]Moshe Efrat, 'The People's Democratic Republic of Yemen: Scientific Socialism on Trial in an Arab Country', in Peter Wiles ed. *The New Communist Third World*, London 1982.

Notes

[I]See text. Gross ratios (1977, %): 77; males 100, females 54.
[II]See text. Gross ratios (1977, %): 26.
[III]Services include port activities.
[IV]With co-operative management of services or production.
[V]Calculated from data in source c.
[VI]1977.
[VII]Non-petroleum trade only.
[VIII]Disbursed and undisbursed.

South Yemen: Chronology

1839	Britain occupies the port of Aden.
1869	Opening of the Suez Canal.

First decades of the twentieth century: extension of the Protectorate system into the hinterland.

1948	Emergence of the first Yemeni nationalist movement in North Yemen.
1950–2	Adeni nationalists call for self-rule in Aden itself.
1956	Founding of the Aden Trades Union Congress; pro-Egyptian, it organises a series of strikes.
1959–63	Establishment of the Federation of South Arabia.
1962	Revolution and civil war in North Yemen; intervention of Egyptian troops; formation of people's Socialist Party by Aden trades unions.
1963	Establishment of the National Liberation Front (NLF) of South Yemen, and start of a guerrilla war in the South Yemeni hinterland.
1965	First Congress of the NLF in North Yemen; guerrilla war in Aden.
1966	PSP and other organisations form FLOSY, Front for the Liberation of Occupied South Yemen, with Egyptian backing.
1967	Withdrawal of British forces from the hinterland; civil war between NLF and FLOSY; British hand over power to the NLF on 30 November.
1968	March: Fourth Congress of NLF, followed by evictions of the Left; first land reform.
1969	June: Left returns to power; October: Aden breaks relations with the USA; November: nationalisation of all banks and insurance companies.
1970	Second land reform.
1971–4	First three-year plan; 1971 free port status of Aden abolished.
1972	All rented property nationalised; Fifth Congress of the NLF establishes militia and People's Defence Committees; September: first border war with North Yemen, followed by Tripoli agreement on unity.
1974	Family Law; First Congress of the General Union of Yemeni Women; emigration banned.
1975–8	Second five-year plan.
1975	October: Unification of NLF, People's Democratic Union and Vanguard Party into United Political Organisation of the National Front.
1976	Establishment of diplomatic relations with Saudi Arabia.
1977	May: government takeover of BP refinery, by agreement.
1978	June: government crisis, execution of President Salem Robea Ali; October: founding Congress of Yemeni Socialist Party.
1979–83	Second five-year plan.

1979	February: second war with North Yemen; Kuwait unity agreement.
20 November 1979	Year Treaty of Friendship and Co-operation with USSR.
1980	April: Abdul Fateh Ishmail replaced as President and Secretary-General by Ali Nasser Mohammad. Discovery of oil reported.
October 1980	Extraordinary Congress of YSP. New Politburo and CC.
February 1981	Execution of Saleh Mohammad Motieh, former Foreign Minister and Politburo member, charged with spying for Saudi Arabia.

MOZAMBIQUE—LATE COLONIALISM AND EARLY PROBLEMS OF TRANSITION

David Wield

Introduction

This chapter first describes the social and economic changes which occurred during the colonial period. Portuguese colonialism left Mozambique with a particularly backward and distorted economy; and Portuguese capital was one of the weakest in Europe and depended on coercion to a greater extent and for longer than other colonial powers. For example, a system of forced labour was widespread in Mozambique until the mid-1960s. In the second section, I discuss the process of anti-colonial struggle, notably the formation and development of the only serious Nationalist party, Frelimo, and its radicalisation during the 1960s. The next two sections discuss the crisis in the colonial political economy between 1974 and 1976, and between 1976 and 1981.[1] Since it is impossible to be comprehensive, some important theoretical and empirical themes have been omitted, or considered only briefly.[2] I have, however, tried to cover some important theoretical themes: people's power and post-Independence democratic institutions; the social relations in industry and agriculture; the question of planning and the balance industry-agriculture; the relationship between the Party and state; as well as to include considerable descriptive detail.

The Colonial Background

Historically, the colonial domination of Mozambique can be split into three periods: (a) until the second world war, (b) 1945 to the early 1960s, and (c) 1960 to 1974. During each of these periods the particularity of Mozambique (and of Angola) lies in the fact that the level of Portuguese capital accumulation was so low that it could never exploit the labour and natural resources of the colony unaided;[3] foreign capital investment always predominated.

(a) *The period before the second world war: foreign capital dominates Portugal and the colonies*

The 'Scramble for Africa' and the Berlin colonial conference of 1884 presented Portugal with a cruel choice – either to move from its small merchant activities to effective territorial colonisation, or to leave the field to make way for Britain, France and Germany. Though the former policy was adopted, Portuguese capital was so weak that effective colonisation had to proceed by leasing out Mozambique to foreign investors. The colonial authorities generated revenue by leasing out about two-thirds of Mozambique – most of the centre and north – to non-national chartered companies. These companies, usually controlled by British capital, had powers to tax, police, sub-let land, and force people to work.[4]

More important for Portugal's revenue was the sale of transport services to neighbouring colonies, mostly British. Lourenço Marques became the most important harbour for South Africa's gold industry, and Beira was Rhodesia's major port. The large port and railway system, built with finance from London, never carried more than 10 per cent Mozambican traffic until Independence. But the most important source of revenue was the institutionalised sale of labour for mine work, largely in South Africa.[5]

The Portuguese state also encouraged foreign investment in agricultural production, and several large plantations were set up in the centre of the country to produce sugar, copra and sisal.[6] The major Portuguese presence was administrative – for colonial control and revenue gathering. Portuguese settlers tried small agricultural, industrial and commercial ventures, but could not count on support from the Portuguese state in their unequal struggle against foreign capital.[7]

As in other parts of Africa, both taxation and administrative coercion were required to generate the quantities of labour required for all of these activities. In the Portuguese colonies the Labour Law of 1899 stated that all men had to work for six months of every year.

They have full liberty to choose the means through which to comply with this obligation but if they do not comply in some way, the public authorities will force them to comply.[8]

These forms of labour generation were not unusual in Africa in the early twentieth century; however the Portuguese colonies were unique on two counts: first, the labour generated worked directly or indirectly for foreign capital and not for capital of the colonial power. (The Portuguese gained by skimming revenue from its 'leased out' colonies.) Second, the forced labour system was retained, rationalised and extended until the early 1960s. Let us see why.

(b) *The strengthening of the Portuguese bourgeoisie: the second world war to the early 1960s*

During the Salazar period (1930s to 1960) the Portuguese bourgeoisie grew stronger, and this was reflected in Mozambique by an increase in labour control and forced cotton cultivation. Attempts were made to rationalise the colonial administration; and a uniform system was imposed all over the country, including the foreign-controlled chartered company territories. For the first time, an attempt was made to use Mozambican products directly for Portugal's own needs through cotton cultivation for Portugal's nascent textile industry. By 1944, 790,000 families – probably one-third of the population – were involved in forced cotton cultivation.

But it was only after the second world war that the Portuguese bourgeoisie began systematically to use Mozambique for its own accumulation needs. Settler-interests took over some of the 'big' concessions for cotton buying and ginning, and invested in tea plantations and production of food crops for the local urban market. Settler-investment in industrial and commercial activities also grew but was overshadowed by the rapid expansion into Mozambique of the Portuguese monopoly groups (Champalimaud, Espirito Santo, CUF, Banco Nacional Ultramarino, etc.). After their growth and consolidation in Portugal in the depression and war years they were at last able to mobilise the resources to develop both Portugal and the colonies simultaneously. *The labour needs of these new forms of production in addition to expansion of labour export, plantation production and transport and transport and tourist services required an intensification of labour coercion in the period 1945–60.* The forced labour system was continued, including much increased forced cropping and a *de facto* pass law system. Its effeçts have been described in detail elsewhere, for example, the Bishop of Beira described the impact of forced cotton production as follows:

I know a region which used to be a granary for lands afflicted with hunger. After the cotton campaign was begun there the fertile fields ceased to supply food for the neighbouring population and the people of the region itself also began to feel hunger.[9]

In the 1950s, almost no effort was made to improve productivity even as the labour shortage grew. In one district (Zambesia, with one-fifth of Mozambique's population) a surplus of 26,000 men over labour needs in 1947 had been almost completely taken up by 1957.[10] Oppression increased in Mozambique at a time when colonies to the north were moving towards political independence. Portuguese capital was not sufficient to change Mozambique's predominant role as a service economy for Southern Africa, but could only use ever more violent techniques to ensure labour supplies for internal production within Mozambique.

Strikes (particularly by dock-workers, the last in 1963) and unrest (including peasant demonstrations like that in Mueda in 1960) and their failure, with death and deportations, were the initial impetus for the development of armed liberation struggle.

(c) *The early 1960s until 1974*

This period was marked by Portugal's determination to maintain political domination over Mozambique and its other colonies which were economically crucial. This was achieved through a closer union between Portuguese and other capitals in investment in Portugal and its colonies.[11] It was a period of relative 'boom' in the sense that large increases in settler numbers occurred, tens of thousands of Portuguese troops were stationed in Mozambique, and Portuguese capital expanded rapidly in agriculture, industry, commerce, insurance and banking. Joint agreements were signed with non-Portuguese, increasingly South African groups, for the bigger projects, and foreign capital found it more easy to invest, though usually linked to Portuguese capital. Only in the biggest projects was Portuguese capital not represented (or represented very weakly), as for example in the Cabora Bassa scheme and in prospecting for minerals. Integration with Southern Africa grew as South African manufacturing industry increasingly supplied industrial inputs as well as consumer products to Mozambique. By 1973, South Africa had become Mozambique's biggest source of imports (over 20 per cent), exceeding even Portugal.

The absolute shortage of labour and Frelimo's increasing strength led to some reforms during this period. Forced labour was officially banned in 1962, although it continued well into the 1960s in some guises. Administrative intervention became more indirect and arbitrational. Employers had to improve housing, food and wages and, for the first time during the century, real wages began to increase. A few black and mixed-race children were given a secondary education. In industrial production there was an impetus to mechanise and to encourage permanent as opposed to migrant labour, but this was still not generalised even by 1974. The movement towards accumulation through production of relative surplus value had progressed but very unevenly. Of the million or so wage-earners out of a population of 9 million, only about a quarter had permanent jobs, and many of these were paid by the day.

This bare information underestimates the degree of proletarianisation, since almost all men had some experience of wage work. In southern Mozambique, for example, almost all African males had worked in the South African mines. In central Mozambique, wage work was widespread in the plantations, in Rhodesia, and at the port, railway and tourist terminus of Beira. Only in the north was peasant production undertaken by the whole family, but even that was distorted by much short-term male contract labour.

However, the extent of proletarianisation was reduced by two factors. First, there was no absolute land shortage in any part of Mozambique; every family had the right to some land; the shortage was a relative shortage of good

Table 1   *Estimated employment, 1974*

Total white wage employment	100,000
Black agricultural workers (90 per cent on contracts)	300,000
Black servants and hotel workers (temporary)	300,000
Black migrant workers abroad	200,000
Black industrial, construction and transport workers	250,000
Total	1,150,000

land and land for crops given the large-scale cashew and coconut tree planting along the richer coastal strip. Secondly, the stable, black working class was rather small, as can be seen from Table 1.

The development of other classes by 1974 can be summarised as follows: peasant production was very unstable; the end of forced labour brought a movement from peasant cotton production to cashew nuts; and Mozambique became the world's leading exporter by the early 1970s. But in most of the country, female labour on small peasant plots was combined with male labour outside the household. Household labour thus lowered the costs of reproduction of the wage labour force (average black wages in 1974 were lower than $20 a month), but was not sufficient to improve and stabilise a middle and rich peasantry. Most peasant households can in fact be characterised as worker–peasant households, and only in a few zones, for example in the rich Limpopo valley, had a rich peasantry begun to develop.

The big bourgeoisie was largely foreign. Non-Portuguese capital controlled significant parts of the plantation, industrial and transport sectors. The Portuguese monopoly groups controlled most banking, insurance and big commerce, industry, agricultural commercialisation of cash crops, and a part of plantation agriculture. A settler-based section of the Portuguese bourgeoisie controlled large quantities of rich agricultural land and smaller commerce and industry, as well as part of certain service industries like tourism.

The petty bourgeoisie was a largely Portuguese immigrant settler class with a growing local black group. The latter were concentrated in lower clerical posts in the civil service (only fifty had secondary school qualifications in 1970), or in primary school teaching and nursing. The number of black

Mozambicans who had reached ninth grade ('0' level equivalent) must have been only a few hundred by 1974.

Anti-colonial Struggle

It is against this background that the armed struggle and the development of Frelimo and the consolidation of the Marxist current within the nationalist movement took place. The consolidation of Frelimo as a movement with popular support was closely linked to the politics of the armed liberation struggle. The original decision to start an armed struggle for national independence was taken almost unanimously by the Frelimo leadership. This happened not because of an extreme radicalism within the whole movement, but because of the heavy repression against earlier movements and against the 1963 dock strikers, and the impossibility of forming a legal nationalist movement.

The earliest Mozambican nationalist associations had grown up in the 1920s during the liberal Republican period of Portuguese history. These early groups split up in the years following the dictator Salazar's accession to power. It was not until the late 1940s that more groups emerged. The secondary-school students' organisation was founded by a group who later joined Frelimo. Eduardo Mondlane, Frelimo's first President, was a founder member of this school group. (He later obtained a doctorate in sociology in the United States and was invited back to Dar Es Salaam by various nationalist groups in 1962 to head a new united nationalist front Frelimo in 1962.)

Founder members of Frelimo came from exile groups in Kenya, Malawi and Tanzania. Some were skilled and semi-skilled workers from the ports and railways of Beira and Maputo; others were secondary school students and young teachers and nurses. Samora Machel was a young nurse with six years of education when he left Mozambique to join Frelimo. What almost all had in common were parents with a small or middle peasant background and some education, usually of only a few years. Some were linked to religious groups, others to tribal groups, student associations, peasant co-operatives and workers' organisations involved in the strikes of 1960 and 1961. To join Frelimo all had to leave Mozambique to travel to Tanzania, knowing that it would be impossible to return legally given the level of Portuguese repression.[12]

By the end of 1968 Frelimo forces had increased from 250 to 7000 in four years, and an estimated 70,000 Portuguese troops had been drafted into Mozambique to hold them back. The rural zones of the northern provinces of Cabo Delgado, Niassa and parts of Tete were under Frelimo control. This was over one-quarter of Mozambique's land area with about 1 million people. It was in these liberated zones where the new Frelimo forces were found and where new political organisation was developed.

Sharp differences emerged over the conduct of the independence struggle; and it was the resolution of these differences which resulted in Frelimo's ability by 1974 to change its programme into an anti-capitalist one. Of course, it is important to realise that the armed struggle was only successful in so far as there was class support for it; Frelimo's development depended on the class forces within Mozambique. But the playing out of the class struggle in this period was concentrated particularly on the politics of the armed struggle.

Differences within the movement revolved around questions of political, social and economic organisation in the liberated areas, notably the following: (a) *How to replace the organs of colonial state power in the liberated zones.* Should the new institutions be staffed by chiefs and elders, or by democratically appointed representatives? (b) *The nature of the armed struggle*: whether political and military aspects should be integrated; whether Frelimo should attempt to take urban centres or consolidate the rural liberated zones; whether they should concentrate on a regional victory for Cabo Delgado and the Makonde peoples, or on an ongoing national struggle. (c) *Social relations of production*: whether there should be collective production, or private ownership of land, and exploitation of labour on the land; whether to encourage private or co-operative shops. (d) *Education and health*: whether training should be organised in brief courses for people who would then return to their villages, or through prolonged higher education overseas. (e) *Youth and women*: whether women should be allowed to join the armed struggle;

over policies towards polygamy, bride prices and child marriage; whether youth had equal rights with elders.[13]

These conflicts lasted from 1966 to 1970, and culminated in assassinations, including that of the Frelimo President, Eduardo Mondlane, and expulsion of members of the Central Committee, including the Vice-President, Uria Simango. Those in the leadership representing tribal chiefs and elders and those educated cadres refusing to return to the liberated zones were expelled from the movement. The movement was strengthened through the support of poor peasantry who had reacted against continued exploitation by Frelimo political leaders, through their corrupt co-operative ventures and shops and employment of labour for low and sometimes non-existent wages. The Marxist current was strengthened by growth in the numbers of military leaders who supported and applied a revolutionary class line. In Cabo Delgado, for example, where the struggle was most fully developed, the delegation for the Second Party Congress in 1978 was split between political and military wings. The political wing had unsuccessfully tried to exclude the military representatives of the People's Forces from the Congress. In the end, they themselves boycotted the Congress and the military remained taking up a strong pro-poor peasant position in favour of collective production and against private ownership of trade and wage labour in the liberated zones.

The liberated zones

The necessity of building an alternative to the colonial form of government in the liberated zones is considered by Frelimo to have been the most important focus of political struggle and change in the pre-Independence period. In the liberated zones policies gradually emerged on political structures, forms of production, distribution and trade, and on education and health. These had a crucial impact on post-Independence policy-making.[14]

Production forms were various, but the tendency was towards collectives. In some areas, however, such as Cabo Delgado, Frelimo leaders, including Nkavandame, used co-operative labour for their personal interests. In other areas, peasants produced on a family basis and villages produced an extra collective plot for army needs. Frelimo schools, army bases and hospitals had Frelimo farms cultivated by militants. With the breakdown of colonial production where men had to engage in wage work for six months usually away from home, agricultural production began to change. New techniques, and products such as salt and soap, were tried. By 1974 more land was under cultivation than before the war even though fields had to be camouflaged by day and cultivated by night with the constant threat of bombing and destruction of crops by the Portuguese troops. Annual exports grew to over 1000 tons of cashew, sesame and groundnuts by 1969, all carried by people over the border to Tanzania. In return, imports of salt, oils, textiles and agricultural implements were sold through the Frelimo People's Stores. These stores had to be defended not only militarily but also politically from those who wished to set up private commerce in the liberated zones.

In these zones Frelimo was able to work with the peasantry in organising a new way of life and making a qualitative break with the past. People who previously had been forced to work for others on their terms were now working for themselves on their own terms. In this way, Frelimo gained the support of the peasantry in the liberated zones. It was this support which enabled Frelimo to beat back a major Portuguese offensive in 1972, and then to advance very rapidly into central Mozambique. From 1973 there were almost daily reports that Frelimo were cutting railway communication on the important Rhodesia/Beira line. Portuguese troop morale dropped dramatically, a major factor in the 1974 Portuguese *coup d'état*.

By 1974 Frelimo defined the anti-colonial struggle more overtly in class terms. Its revolutionary policy and practice in the liberated zones had built class politics on its anti-colonial foundations. Thus victory in the anti-colonial war and the right to national political independence were not seen as bringing the end of exploitation. This important change in political outlook was to prove crucial in the period of transition which followed, years in which, it was argued, 'the enemy is using more subtle techniques regarding the continuation of exploitation'.[15]

The Crisis of the Colonial Political Economy, 1974–6

We shall tentatively divide the post-Independence transformations into two periods:[16] April 1974 to 1976–a period of crisis and disintegration of colonial society which includes the year before independence (this section); and 1976 to the present (1981)– a period of early restructuring of the state and the economy. This has been coupled with the beginnings of economic recovery and with a closer analysis of the realities facing Frelimo throughout the country and not only in the liberated zones (see the following section).

Even before the defeat of the Portuguese dictatorship in April 1974, the 250,000 settlers had begun to desert the colony – 40,000 had left between 1971 and 1973. Between the *coup* in Portugal in April 1974 and Independence in 1975[17] at least another 100,000 left. The balance at Independence was thus about 100,000, and the bulk of those left within one year of Independence.

Three months elapsed after the 25 April *coup* before the Portuguese authorities recognised the right of the colonies to independence. Frelimo's military advance in this period was dramatic. In addition, on the Portuguese side, left-wing documents supporting Frelimo circulated amongst the troops and were signed by them. Strikes took place in many sectors in Mozambique. The colonial bourgeoisie and petty bourgeoisie began to organise politically in a more open fashion in this period. Forlorn attempts were made to organise and support anti-Frelimo movements, the most sophisticated involving sections of the African petty bourgeoisie. However, Frelimo's mass support in Maputo was already sufficient for these movements to be defeated after their attempted *coup* in September 1974. The killing of Frelimo soldiers in the city by settlers led to a massive reaction from the African population. The Lusaka Accord, which gave the right to Independence with Frelimo as sole representative party of the Mozambican people, and the unsuccessful settler reaction to it, were followed by two years of disintegration of settler society through emigration, and the destruction of much of what could not be taken out.

This flight affected every sector in some way: in the cities construction almost came to a complete halt, leaving unfinished high-rise blocks; owners of small and medium industrial enterprises – from brick-producers to garage repairers – left the country; larger industries kept going with a steadily decreasing number of managerial and skilled workers; as settlers left, the market for locally-produced consumer goods, particularly luxury goods, severely diminished; and most domestic servants lost their jobs as settlers left.

In the rural areas, settler farms were almost all abandoned by their owners. The complex commercial network which bought peasant crops such as cotton, and transported them for export or processing, was controlled by the settler bourgeoisie and petty bourgeoisie and collapsed almost completely around Independence. In the south of the country, the resulting unemployment was partially offset by increased migration to South Africa, numbers increasing by over 40 per cent in 1975. In other parts of the country this was not possible.

Early government policy and actions

Government actions in this period were two-fold: first, to press ahead with policies with historical links to pre-Independence struggles in the liberated areas, like nationalisation of the social services; second, to hold out against international calls for 'moderation' and 'realism' caused by the crisis of settler withdrawal, and to move forward with new methods of control and restructuring of production, relying on mass mobilisation. The period is thus characterised by relatively clear policies in some sectors where Frelimo had long experience and by a 'learning' situation in others. Machel has said about the period as a whole that the leadership were like firemen moving rapidly from one crisis to another. Top- and medium-level political cadres were spread molecule-thick throughout the state apparatus, usually with several jobs at the same time.

Nevertheless, the first months after Independence brought nationalisation of land, medicine and social services, education, legal services and rented property. Nationalisation of land eliminated speculation on building land and helped to restructure property relations in the countryside with the beginnings of state farms and co-operative production.

Nationalisation of private medicine and schools, including the mission system, allowed the beginning of mass-based services. Educational enrolment increased almost three-fold in two years. In the cities the secondary schools began operating a three-shift system (morning, afternoon and evening) to accommodate the expanded intake, which included large numbers of adults who were working full-time. In the rural areas new schools sprang up without any facilities at all, with older students teaching younger ones. The minority of students in higher education who stayed in Mozambique found themselves involved in part-time teaching as well as in their own studies. 'All must teach and all must learn' was an early slogan.

Medical services, concentrated as they were in the urban areas, at first almost collapsed. The number of doctors dropped from 550 in 1974 to eighty by the end of 1975. But those health workers who remained, supported by crash training programmes and foreign health workers,[18] made it possible to cope with the massive increase in the numbers of those appearing in health units as a result of nationalisation.

Nationalisation of rented property included not only the huge flat-blocks which had been erected speculatively in the last decade of colonial rule, and which dominate the skyline of Maputo, Beira and Nampula, but also large numbers of rented, galvanised tin and reed huts which were rapidly increasing to accomodate newcomers to the cities.

The nationalisations hit settler interests. They could no longer buy their social services, and many had put their savings into real estate. This greatly contributed to the early post-Independence settler withdrawal. This has been designated as a 'problem' for Mozambique. It is common for foreign observers to argue that the nationalisations were senseless acts which strangled the prospects for future development. From another perspective, however, they can be seen as victories for the Mozambican people. They were, in fact, the first post-Independence concrete expressions of the revolutionary line which had emerged within Frelimo in the post-1970 period. Moreover, the early nationalisations contained both defensive and offensive elements. In health, the defensive element involved resuscitating a defunct colonial medical system; nationalisation of land was one way of coping with the land abandoned by settlers. Offensive elements were crucial in restructuring services to meet popular needs. In education, the three-fold increase in intake required radical restructuring of the colonial educational system, dominated by the missions for Africans, and with a small state sector serving only the settlers and *assimilados*.

Political organisation and the Grupos Dinamizadores

In this crucial period of transferring power, Frelimo was faced with the lack of a mass political organisation in two-thirds of the country containing 80 per cent of the population. It responded by moving to extend its political structures throughout the country. Of critical importance was the forma-tion of the *Grupos Dinamizadores* (GDs) – literally translated as 'dynamising groups'. These were popularly elected groups of 8–10 people set up according to both residence and work-place. In rural communities they reached down to villages, to every suburb in the urban areas, and to factories, commer-cial and banking institutions, schools and hospitals. They became the focus of mass political activities as the colonial state dissolved, the principal vehicles through which class forces expressed themselves in this period.[19] Their functions were variable and often extremely complex arising from the crisis situation. Their initial role was to consolidate the politics and practice of Frelimo in the whole country; their slogan was 'unity, vigilance, work'. They were the 'school of democracy' which sought to unite the population in discussion and po-pularisation of the Frelimo line of *unity* of all democratic elements, *vigilance* against all attempts by the colonial bourgeoisie and petty bourgeoisie[20] to sabotage Mozambican independence and the economy, and *work* in a collective way to continue production as settlers left. Mass assemblies were held weekly, with large attendances. They discussed a wide range of issues: problems of production; the nature of their collective activities; more general political questions like racism, tribalism and the sabotage which accompanied settler withdrawal; and the personal behaviour of GD representa-tives. According to one Frelimo spokesman, these meetings 'created a new sense of confidence in the oppressed masses and helped convince them that they had the capacity to transform Mozambique. The GDs are the very essence of People's Power.'[21]

There is considerable evidence of the ability of the Party and the GDs to mobilise large numbers of the population. For example, the national vaccination campaign in 1976 involved a turnout of 30 per cent more people than had been counted in the last colonial census six years previously. The mobilisations for national elections and Party selection in 1977 and 1978 again demonstrated the effectiveness of these basic-level political organisations.

The economic role of the Grupos Dinamizadores

Even before Independence, but especially after it, the GDs were an important means by which Frelimo defended its economic line against the colonial bourgeoisie. Detection of sabotage and subversion could best be done at the grass-roots level and with mass participation.

The settler withdrawal from the end of 1975 was such that many small and medium enterprises were abandoned. In January 1976, in one day alone, twenty firms in the capital were abandoned. The government responded through its 'state intervention' law of early 1975 which allowed the take-over of such companies. But the role of the GDs in controlling the worse aspects of sabotage was much more important. The state called on the 'creative energies of the workers led by the GDs' to keep enterprises running. The best GDs were able to stop breakage and robbery of equipment, to discover whether top and middle management were failing to renew stocks and spare parts, and to maintain equipment and keep accounts. In consequence, very few enterprises were closed down. Production was kept going, though usually at a much reduced rate, by attempting to draw in the talents of all sections of workers in the enterprises through the GDs.

A government publication of early 1977 shows that of the 319 commercial and industrial enterprises under state control, 141 had fewer than twenty workers, and 131 had only between 20–100 workers. Only forty-seven had more than 100 workers.[22] Production control in such a wide spread of enterprises could only have been achieved with the kind of mobilisation effected by the GDs. Even so, considerable energy was expended at ministerial and high and middle cadre level in coordinating and combating the worst effects of abandonment of so many small enterprises. In fact, the government in this period did not move to nationalise bigger enterprises except after abandonment or particularly bad sabotage. Eighty per cent of tea plantations, which were principally Portuguese investments, were taken over, and some of the larger cashew factories. CIFEL, the large steel-rolling mill, was another enterprise where administrators were appointed by the state. These large, often very crucial, enterprises did not receive the attention they deserved because of the emphasis put on keeping the small and medium enterprises going under state control. Some, like CIFEL, were, in consequence, *de facto* under workers' control.

In agriculture, the GDs played a large role in avoiding large-scale land seizure by private interests as settlers left. The land went mostly to state farms set up rapidly to keep production and employment going. Some went to co-operatives, and a little was distributed in some areas to peasants with poor land.

The commercial sector, particularly in the rural areas, broke down dramatically. GDs tried to control this, but less successfully and with disastrous results for peasant sales. Abandonment of settler farms led to a drastic (55 per cent) fall in production between 1973 and 1975; the fall in peasant marketed production at 60 per cent was even greater.[23] The inability of the commercial sector to buy peasant crops led to a longer-term problem, since peasants did not produce so much for the market in future years. It was 1978 before peasant sales began to increase once more. The plantation sector, largely non-Portuguese foreign capital, held its production more steadily with only a 16 per cent decrease in production during this period.

The ability of the GDs to mobilise politically was important in those social services which were nationalised after Independence. It became increasingly important after 1976 with the campaign to restructure the state apparatus and defend the state services against bureaucratisation, corruption and uneven use of facilities.

In many of their tasks the GDs played contradictory roles, related to the breakdown of the colonial state and the need to build Frelimo's political structures from scratch. In the factories, for example, the GDs often acted both as agents of mass mobilisation and representation on the one hand, and as *de facto* management on the other. In the rural areas, the GDs gradually built up their capacity for mass mobilisation, while at the same time substituting for the colonial state apparatus at the level of the district and below. At provincial level (ten provinces presently exist) the major state officials came from Frelimo. All the provincial governors, for example, came from the Frelimo Central Committee. At district level (a little over 100 districts exist) this was not the case. The district administrator and his staff were the senior Mozambican staff left at Independence. Below district level, the colonial chiefs *regulos* were disestablished, and the GDs at locality level took over their functions. These varied from making decisions on land use, solving intra- and inter-family disputes, and controlling movements in the rural areas.

These contradictory roles, and the fact that the GDs were amalgams of all classes, led to political struggles;[24] It was even reported that early GDs were sometimes dominated by PIDE (Portuguese security) agents. Sometimes their members came from the foreman and manager level at the factory and not from the shopfloor. As a result, the GDs were continuously shaken up and reconstituted.

To summarise, the period 1974–6 began in chaos with continuous settler withdrawal. It was a time of crude sabotage, abandoned small enterprises in all sectors, and increasing unemployment of wage labour. It was also a time of military victory over the colonial forces, of the political consolidation of Frelimo throughout the whole country, and of class struggle within and outside the GDs at local and higher levels.

Restructuring of State and Party, and the Struggle to Re-establish Production (1976–81)

Analysis of this period is difficult in view of the short period since Independence, the dramatic breakdown of colonial society and economy, and the lack of quantitative information.[25] We shall only discuss some tendencies and emerging problems, concentrating on questions of production and the relationship between agriculture and industry. I shall first consider Frelimo's view of Mozambique's social structure, then discuss Mozambique's relationship with Southern Africa and finally problems of agricultural and industrial production.

Frelimo's analysis of social structure at Independence

Between 1976 and the Third Congress in February 1977, Frelimo responded to the challenges of Independence by producing a series of policies on the political situation, the Party, the state apparatus, health and education, and agricultural and industrial production.[26] Their official analysis of social structure in early 1976 was based on the assumption of sharpened class struggle in a phase of open struggle against capitalism. The analysis suggested that the colonial bourgeoisie had weakened the economy by leaving the country, and had also attempted to infiltrate the new political organisations such as the *Grupos Dinamizadores*. Though the small and medium national bourgeoisie had applauded the fall of colonialism and supported Frelimo, their position was ambiguous. They had always taken the colonial bourgeoisie as their model, and their support for Frelimo was weakened by the nationalisation measures. Thus this was a potentially dangerous social category, given its economically exploitative character and its important position in the state apparatus and the economy.

Strengthening of the 'popular masses', the 'workers' and 'peasants', was seen as essential to prevent the growth of a national bourgeoisie.[27] The number of workers had increased rapidly since 1960, but colonial coercion 'had impeded political work within the working class',[28] and workers tended to have an 'economistic' outlook, even after Independence, thus a greater effort was needed to improve political organisation among workers. The large domestic servant group, in spite of a low level of political consciousness, had supported Frelimo's policies and the new *Grupos Dinamizadores*.

A seminar on the state apparatus emphasised the need to change the mentality of state employees, altering their class composition through the influx of workers and peasants, and controlling bureaucracy, arrogance and abuse of power.

In the rural areas a complex situation existed, but there was 'a strong nationalist sentiment, a weak implantation of colonial values and a consciousness of the misery imposed by the colonial system with a consequent willingness to struggle against exploitation'.[29] Rural living conditions could be improved through the organisation of state farms and co-operatives. The communal village was seen as the 'spinal column' of this development strategy.[30]

In two speeches in late 1976, the President concentrated on the need to set up new organisational forms. In health, ward councils were proposed in the Central Hospital in Maputo in order to 'mobilise, organise and politically unify the different categories of workers in the hospital'. The President stressed the need for democratic control in the workplace to avoid increasing bureaucratisation. A call was made for a new organisation in the factory, the production council, elected by the workers, which would plan and control production and thus allow workers to participate in factory mangement.

The Southern African connection

In 1976 international constraints grew, and Mozambique's extreme dependence on non-Portuguese external forces became clearer, especially its economic relations with Southern Africa. Overshadowing everything was the international recession which brought a stop to the high economic growth rates of the 1950s and 1960s. For Mozambique itself, the problem was exacerbated by the crisis of the colonial economy. 1976 brought the closure of the Mozambican border with Rhodesia. Rhodesia had supplied over half of the railway and port receipts, and gave work to Mozambican migrants. The direct costs of closure were estimated at £90 million, but these were compounded by the costs of war damage by Rhodesian army incursions into Mozambique. The port of Beira was the worst affected, since it lost the bulk of its freight charges and tourist receipts. Experienced political cadres have remained 'tied-up' first with the Rhodesian war, and more recently with the South African backed armed terrorist groups, called the Mozambique National Resistance, operating inside Mozambique. In 1981 South African troops attacked the suburbs of Maputo.

Southern Mozambique was badly affected by the decreased numbers of migrant labourers allowed into the South African gold mines. Increased South African unemployment, coupled with increased mine wages after the strikes of 1973 and 1974, enabled South Africa to increase its local component of mine labour from 20 per cent in 1973 to 43 per cent in 1976. This particularly affected Mozambique with a fall in recruitment from 115,000 in 1975 to 45,000 in 1976. This also meant a huge fall in foreign exchange from a situation where gold payments for migrant labour had reached an estimated 35 per cent of total foreign exchange earnings in 1975. A study in 1977 in southern Mozambique showed that 84 per cent of men interviewed were third generation gold miner migrants; well over 90 per cent of men in the rural areas had worked in the mines. The average period of adult life spent in the mines was 40 per cent.[31] In 1975 the response to the collapse of the colonial economy in the south had been increased migration to the mines, but by 1976 the Southern African recruitment authorities were refusing work except to the most experienced and skilled miners. The employment situation has worsened and the financial squeeze has continued to tighten up to the present.

Agricultural policy and relations of production in agriculture

The Third Congress of Frelimo in February 1977 gave considerable emphasis to development strategy and to the predominant role of the state in executing it. The basic formulation at Independence was 'agriculture as base, industry as leading factor and motive force'.[32] This approach is often assumed to embody a programme for balanced development, and to emphasise the role of the peasantry for capital accumulation. It is deficient, however, in that it does not explicitly discuss class structure and social relations of production in agriculture and industry.

Mozambique's agricultural policy has shifted several times since Independence as the government grappled with specific problems requiring a more sophisticated analysis than that at Independence.[33] In early 1976, co-operative production was emphasised rather than state farms or family production. Co-operatives were to be linked to the development of communal villages which would 'involve poor peasants, workers and exploited labour'.[34] The Third Congress appeared to change policy in favour of state farms. Co-operatives were to receive only 'supporting infrastructures', whilst state farms were to be 'dominant and decisive'.[35] The co-operatives were to be based on political, economic and social aims, whilst the state farms were to be developed predominantly within a technical framework.

But uncertainty and conflict over agricultural strategy continued. In the middle of 1978, the Agriculture Minister was dismissed because 'he refused to implement the priority defined by the leading bodies in relation to communal villages . . . giving priority to technique, he does not place trust in the people'.[36] Since that time family plots and production have received more emphasis. In June 1979 other problems were publicised. In communal villages, 'choosing of sites has not always been correct, and there have been problems of seed delivery, insufficient collective production and weak participation of the villagers in preparation of production plants'.[37] More recently, in August 1980, strong criticisms were made of the co-operative development section of the Agriculture Ministry (GODCA) that 'there is an absolute incompetence in the direction of GODCA made worse by a lack of conviction of the importance of co-operatives . . . and isolation from the peasantry'.[38]

These variations in policy point to an increased awareness inside Frelimo of the complexity of class relationships in the rural areas and the difficulties of applying generalisations about social structures. Recent studies have indeed shown the vast regional variations in colonial agricultural production and related class developments; the south served principally as a migrant labour reserve, the centre as a plantation agricultural producer and the north as a peasant cash-crop producer (see Table 2). What seems clear is that early drops in production were of marketed crops (see Table 3). The worst affected were peasant commercialised crops and Portuguese settler production. The state moved to nationalise abandoned settler land, and turn it into state farms with large technical inputs. The state also encouraged collective peasant

Table 2   *Colonial agricultural production, 1970*

	South[a] (*labour reserve*)	Centre[b] (*plantations predominate*)	North[c] (*peasants predominate*)
Population (%)	28	41	31
Total agricultural output (%)	17	43	40
Subsistence production (%)	49	52	60
Marketed production (%) of which:	51	48	40
Peasants produced (%)	20	19	65
Plantation produced (%)	4	57	5
Settlers produced (%)	76	24	30

[a]Maputo, Inhambane, Gaza provinces.
[b]Zambesia, Manica, Sofala and Tete.
[c]Cabo Delgado, Niassa, Nampula.
Source: See Note 15.

Table 3   *Agricultural production changes from 1973 to 1975*

Subsistence production of peasants	+ 12%
Marketed production of which:	− 43%
peasants	− 60%
plantations	− 16%
settlers	− 54%

Source: See Note 15.

production, but did not immediately assist the crucially important peasant household producer by providing credit or transport. These difficulties have not been made any easier by a continuous succession of natural disasters since 1976; first floods and then drought.

The post-Independence record of agricultural policy is thus marked by a continuous attempt to respond to short-term problems, but to improve the possibilities for longer-term planning by moving closer to an understanding of rural social structure and economy. The southern provinces provide the following strands for an analysis of agricultural policy issues.[39] The long-term distortion of agriculture by male labour migration was exacerbated by the collapse of settler agricultural production at Independence; family household production was not firm enough for easy recruitment of labour for co-operative experiments; the state farms which have taken over abandoned land are not strong enough to absorb migrant labour, or to act as advice and support nuclei for co-operative experiments; state farms which engage in mono-culture (like rice in the Limpopo Valley) make it difficult to change seasonal and migrant labour forms to more permanent ones; the lack of land shortage means that a policy of land restriction on bigger peasant holdings will not increase production. A more important problem in household production is equal access to agricultural implements, ploughs, oxen, irrigation, tractors and storage. Some co-operatives were formed by stable peasant producers in order to obtain rights over state inputs like tractors. Thus ex-migrant labour and their families, with a generally lower production base, have been reluctant to join co-operatives managed by peasants of higher strata than themselves.

The state farms do not have sufficient machinery to utilise all the land they have, and their policies to improve land use involve rapid mechanisation, irrigation, fertilisers and electrification, rather than intensive labour utilisation; while the preoccupation of the state farms to increase food production for the cities leaves less manpower and technical services to develop the household agricultural sector. The production of surpluses from this sector is made correspondingly difficult.

Marc Wuyts has recently pointed out that concentrated mechanisation of state farms implicitly assumes that peasants don't need help.[40] But it is clear from recent studies of southern Mozambique that the heavily proletarianised peasants are in crisis. He suggests that planned industrialisation and proletarianisation involves a stabilisation of worker–peasants on the land, and a steady, planned absorption into industry. The alternative, he believes, may well be an unplanned absorption, leading to urban unemployment. The signs are that these problems, the interdependence of each sector, and the importance of complex social relations, are becoming more apparent to the Party. Production has slowly increased since 1977, but it does not yet seem to have reached the highest levels of the colonial period.

Industrial strategy and relations of production in industry

Unlike agriculture, policy-making in industry seems more integrated and less subject to rapid changes. Industrial strategy must take account of the inherited colonial industrial structure, and the nature of the crisis of the colonial society. Industrial development before Independence was substantial compared with most other African countries. For example, intermediate producer-good industries, such as petroleum refining, machinery repairs, fertiliser, cement and iron and steel rolling existed along with agro-industries and simple consumer-goods industries.[41] Much industry was owned by Portuguese capital, but industries producing for export had the highest proportion of non-Portuguese capital, mostly a mixture of South African, British, German and French. Production for local consumption– both mass and settler– was controlled predominantly by big Portuguese groups or Portuguese settlers. Even goods for local consumption depended principally on imported raw and semi-finished materials– from plastic pellets through to steel bars. The industrial centre was Maputo, with 56 per cent of total industrial production in 1973. Maputo gained from its proximity to Johannesburg not only for industrial inputs, but also for technical know-how.

Settler withdrawal and sabotage led to a rapid collapse of production in many of the companies they controlled, and declines began in the bigger concerns controlled from Portugal. For example, the nationalisation of Champalimaud in Portugal had indirect repercussions, since Champalimaud owned all three cement factories, the only iron and steel factory, and the only fertiliser factory in Mozambique. State intervention in this period was essentially defensive. Nationalisations took place only when enterprises were abandoned, where production was threatened, or where major irregularities of foreign exchange were unearthed.

The general policy for industry at the Third Congress was: 'Industry is the dynamising factor for economic development.' More specifically, it was seen as important in the short term to increase production from those factories 'that provide the people's basic needs' and to convert luxury product factories as quickly as possible. New investments were to stress industries producing machines and materials for other industrial branches.

The Third Congress had not considered the differing organisational forms of industry in the same way as in agriculture. State farms, communal villages, co-operatives and households were considered as sectors with separate problems. Industrial policy did not consider small or large factories, private, state or co-operative enterprises as separate. The emphasis was on production rather than on differing production relations and methods. The approach was essentially economic, considering the sectoral balance and the overall place of industry in the economy, rather than enterprise management of the labour process. But some months previously, in October 1976, a new organisation for workers had been proposed – the production council. In a major speech, the President emphasised the low level of workers' consciousness and organisation, and admitted that 'authoritarian labour relations remain intact within firms and hinder the creative initiative of the working class'. The new councils to be set up at factory level, were to be

a weapon which will lead to the destruction of the old capitalist relations of production and to the establishment of new social relations of production. ... The workers will participate in an active, collective and conscious manner in the discussion and solution of problems, and will plan and control production.[42]

Within a few months of this speech workers in every section of most of the big factories were meeting regularly to discuss production relations in their sections. Production councils, with workers elected from each section, discussed and proposed ways to organise workers, increase production and productivity, and to develop new forms of discipline and promotion. In 1978 they were given the further task of drawing up a perspective plan for the year.

Thus the production councils appear to have had a dual role in this period: to control production, and to represent workers in the enterprise. They seem to have been proposed in the belief that increasing workers' knowledge and control of the production process in a political way would lead to productivity increases.

There are now three important institutional organisms

in the factory. The management, the *Grupo Dinamizador* (now usually a Party cell) and the production council, an embryo trade union. During a visit in September 1979 all of these, together with the representative of the women's movement, were present when I visited factories.

How much has changed? The social relations of production in the colonial period revolved around owners (foreign), management (non-Mozambican, usually Portuguese), technicians and foremen (almost all Portuguese, some mixed-race and South Asian), skilled workers (usually Portuguese) and unskilled workers (Mozambican). Within a year of Independence almost all of the Portuguese had left. Many enterprises, whether private or under state control, continued with a division of labour from the colonial period. It could not work if only because of the sheer lack of supervisory manpower. Take the steel rolling mill, CIFEL, for example:

In July 1977 an Administrator was appointed by the Ministry of Industry ... he had been a member of the City Council ... and still owned a couple of factories .... He consolidated a pyramidal structure with him at the apex and the six Portuguese technicians as departmental heads ... the Production Council was constantly being reminded it was first things first and they should be playing a policing role against indiscipline, lateness and absenteeism.[43]

Thus the old division of labour could not easily be reinstated through Mozambicanisation because of the lack of trained Mozambicans, and because of new structures (like GDs and production councils which, however fragile, had some impact on management decision-making). But the CIFEL example illustrates that the new structures were not working well in many factories. In CIFEL the workers were in danger of losing even the small knowledge they had gained over the production process, and there was a total differentiation of mental and manual labour. Peter Sketchley working in the factory, reports

I telephoned the clerk in the mechanics workshop to go and read a serial number from the plate of the truck. His reply was 'you must wait for Senhor Martinez [the Portuguese head of the department]. He is the one who understands these things.'[44]

But the CIFEL case also illustrates how controls over

management are possible in Mozambique. Changes began in 1978 during a mass examination of Party candidates as ordered by the Party. At the end of the meetings with the Party brigade, its leader

asked for any other contributions, nothing is too big or too small. Finally an elderly worker whose job was sorting out the scrap in the scrap yard came forward and stood at the front of the workers in his bare feet and endlessly patched work clothes. He stood there for a moment with his eyes to the floor. Suddenly he cleared his throat and in a loud voice cracking with emotion he said 'Imperialism is still here in CIFEL.' He went on to denounce the Administrator for having nothing but contempt for the workers and behaving just as the others had done before. He sat down to a roar from every throat in the room. Now everyone wanted to say his piece. . . .It was as if this ordinary barefoot worker had pulled the cork out of the bottle and all of the frustration and anger was pouring out. . .within a few weeks the Administrator was removed and replaced with two young black Mozambiquans. The GD secretary was also replaced. The Administrator joined in the weekly production meetings in each section, often sitting on the floor in the circle of workers.

During this one year, production at CIFEL doubled.

This case and others provide some early evidence that Mozambican industrialisation policy does not concentrate exclusively on economic questions, but has attempted to change relations of production inherited from the colonial period. Changes have affected ownership relations, the division of labour, forms of management and workers' control. These efforts have been held back at many levels, not least by the lack of simple technical knowledge and the low educational level of most of the workers.

Recent works on socialist industrialisation have concentrated heavily on overall economic strategies and the need to increase the means and forces of production.[46] But a successful analysis of what is happening in Mozambique depends on understanding of the relationship between three levels: overall management of the economy; management of the enterprise; and organisation of the labour process. In the case of Mozambican industry, all three have progressed, but each constrains the advance of the others.

Although data on industrial production are as yet unavailable, indications are that it has recovered from the throughs of 1977–8, but is still not up to colonial levels. Thus the continuing crisis of transport and commerce, and a huge increase in consumption of foodstuffs, has led to the shortages and queues which are an inevitable part of any press report from Mozambique.

Economic constraints and the reforms of the 'Presidential Offensive'

The Third Party Congress in 1977 suggested that the economy would take until 1980 to recover to the late colonial level. This is one illustration that this chapter has looked at at a very preliminary period of revolutionary development in Mozambique. We have seen that the colonial economy was based on providing services to Southern Africa. Imports cost twice the receipts from exports. The balance was met by 'invisibles', coming mostly from South Africa and Rhodesia. Receipts from South Africa have dropped and from Rhodesia fell to zero until 1980. Colonial production, particularly large-scale agriculture and industry, required big imports. Mozambique needs to restructure production, but this restructuring cannot take place overnight, nor can it rely totally on internally-generated capital. The supply crisis in late 1979 threw these problems into relief and a series of economic reforms in a 'Presidential Offensive' led by Machel in late 1979 and 1980.

The reforms covered a wide area. Let us consider the international aspect first. Mozambique has few foreign debts but, contrary to popular belief, does not receive aid from socialist countries on particularly easy terms, or in particularly large quantities. Recently, some major contracts have been signed which signal capital inflows. Contracts in industry include two textile factories (with China and the GDR), a lorry assembly plant (GDR), some light industries (North Korea), and a large agricultural implements factory (USSR). Investments in the fishing industry have been made by Japan, Spain and the USSR. These helped to increase prawn exports to $25 million in 1979, and trebled local urban fish consumption.

Assistance from socialist countries is considered insufficient for all of Mozambique's needs, and it is emphasised that certain industries must have capitalist technology. Sweden has given aid for feasibility studies for iron and steel and paper industries. The Scandinavian countries have an agricultural mechanisation programme. In mid-1980 a $110 million contract was signed with French and Italian companies to instal power lines and sub-stations from Cabora Bassa dam to the two most populated provinces of Nampula and Zambesia. Cabora Bassa is the fourth biggest hydro-electric scheme in the world, and was designed in the colonial period to send power to South Africa.

Mozambique is thus intensifying its campaign to attract foreign capital. 'Can we wait ten years for our own cadres to be trained before beginning to use our natural resources?' one minister asked. The agreements signed all involve state investment, include training courses, and rules to buy and sell only through the state. The dangers are obvious: the desire to move fast may lead to a neglect of local initiatives; control of big projects is notoriously difficult.

To consolidate these moves Mozambique has been considering whether to join international financing bodies. Mozambique is already a member of the African Development Bank, had observer status in the recent Lomé Convention talks, and is considering participation in the IMF, World Bank and Comecon. President Machel said recently that the government had been observing the behaviour of these bodies in differing countries, and assessing the ways in which they affect a country's ability to defend its national interest.

The move to increase foreign capital investment in new development projects coincided with encouragement for local small capitalists. The crisis of production and supply has been linked in official statements to the failure to control the bureaucratisation, corruption and inefficiency of the state-run enterprises.[47] Machel has said that the state should never have taken over small farms and shops in the early crisis period. He called on Mozambicans wishing to invest in small business to come forward so that the state could help them take over badly-run state enterprises. He also suggested that co-operatives should expand to take over some of these concerns.

At the same time greater powers and privileges have been given to managers of state enterprises and to senior civil servants. 'The manager must manage ... the manager must organise, lead and control production. The manager must decide. This power must be concentrated,' the President said in 1980.[48] These new policies are in part a response to earlier attempts to appoint managers solely for their political abilities rather than managerial competence. The policy of strengthening management powers has taken place simultaneously with the provision of certain privileges. The skills of the bureaucrats and the petty bourgeoisie are seen as crucial at this time and the encouragement of these strata involves giving concessions to some of their class practices. For example, in a hospital in late 1979 the President argued that 'we must make wards for those with responsible posts'.[49]

It is important to realise, however, that all these recent decisions coincide with moves to strengthen Party organisation. The Frelimo Central Committee, meeting in July 1980, criticised itself for neglecting Party organisation.

The leading structures of the Party, both at central and local levels were not filled. Party work was carried out as a secondary task and not as principal ... the work of the Party cells was weakened, and militants frequently remained without tasks.'

The meeting analysed the 'Presidential Offensive' against bureaucratisation in the state apparatus, which began in December 1979, as 'the offensive which forced a break with the spirit of routine. We were stuck in a rut. ... Routine thinking led us to let problems accumulate.'[50] The decision to move leading militants, like Marcelino dos Santos, to the Party from government is a result of this policy.

Conclusions

The top leadership of the Party remains those who fought for a popular line during the guerrilla war; those who developed policies in a close symbiosis with the peasants of the liberated zones in northern Mozambique.

The taking of state power brought a series of new problems: lack of seasoned cadres; a population with low literacy and technical skills; a very low level of worker organisation; and weakened household agricultural production. Early social policies involved government intervention wherever production was in serious trouble. The new political organisations and real enthusiasm for state policies allowed production to continue. Continued progressive social and economic policies have maintained mass support for Frelimo.

The new policies to make the state apparatus more efficient and less bureaucratic, and simultaneously to encourage foreign capital and local private entrepreneurs pose a set of questions with which we conclude. Will Frelimo be able to control local private investment in small commerce, industry and agriculture with its consequent class developments? Can the Party and its various linked organisations impose effective controls on the impact of foreign capital investments in Mozambique? Can the Party control the rapid growth of technical strata within the state apparatus? Will the increasing destabilisation tactics of the South African government allow any priority to be given to internal social and economic development? Though the recent history of Mozambique shows a leadership which has learned from experience and responded to changing realities, the challenges which lie ahead will test its political skill and revolutionary will.

Notes

1   This chapter is based on a talk given to the IDS Study Seminar in Social-ist Development in 1979. The initiative for my attendance at this Seminar came from the *Centro de Estudos Africanos* in Maputo, where I was attached between 1976 and 1978. Much of the information was gathered by the *Centro*. I am particularly grateful to Aquino de Braganca, Ruth First, Marc Wuyts and Martha Madoren for their inputs into the chapter. Important comments on an earlier draft were given by Martha Madoren, Laurence Harris, Martin Hobdell, Naomi Richman, Malcolm Segall, Pam Smith, Gill Walt, Richard Williams, Judy Bloomfield, Robin Murray and Gordon White. Responsibility for the finished product is mine.

2   For example, there is very little on social questions such as education or health. Published information does exist, for example, on health, see 'Revolutionary Practice in Health', *Peoples' Power*, no. 13, Mozambique, Angola and Guinea Information Centre, London, 1979; on education, see Frelimo, 'Educational Policy in the People's Republic of Mozambique', *Journal of Modern African Studies* 14, 2, 1976, pp. 331–9.

3   Sources on Portuguese economic and social history are few. The following are important: Armando Castro, *A Economia Portuguesa do Seculo*, xx,

Edicoes 70, Lisbon, 1973. ABC, *Portugal: Capitalismo and Estado Novo*, Edicoes Afrontamentos, Porto, 1976. In English we have Perry Anderson, 'Portugal and the end of ultra colonialism', *New Left Review*, nos. 15–17, 1962. Works relating to colonisation and particularly to Mozambique include: Eduardo Mondlane, *The Struggle for Mozambique*, Penguin, Harmondsworth, 1969; Armondo Castro, *O sistema colonial Portugues em Africa*, Editorial Caminho, Lisbon, 1978; A. de Braganca and I. Wallerstein, *Que e o inimigo*, 3 vols., Iniciativas Editoriais, Coleccao XX–XXI, Lisbon, 1978.

4   On chartered companies, see Leroy Vail, 'Mozambique's Chartered Companies: the Rule of the Feeble', *Journal of African History*, XVII, 1976, pp. 389–419. B. Neil-Thomlinson, 'The Niassa Chartered Company, 1891–1929', *Journal of African History*, XVIII, 1977, p. 1.

5   Luis de Brito, 'Dependencia colonial e integracao regional', *Estudos Mozambicanos*, no. 1, Maputo, 1980, pp. 23–32.

6   On the plantations, see Judith Head, 'Sena sugar estates and migrant labour', in *Mozambique*, Centre of African Studies, University of Edinburgh, 1979; S. Ishemo, 'Some aspects of the economy and society of the Zambesia basin in the nineteenth and early twentieth centuries', ibid.; Carlos Serra, 'O Capitalismo Colonial na Zambezia', *Estudos Mozambicanos*, no. 1, pp. 33–52.

7   'The Province of Mozambique is little nationalised [by Portugal]. The commerce of imports and exports is almost exclusively done by foreigners. The principal firms of the Province are all foreign, down to the commercial retailers of the interior which are in the hands of Indians of British nationality ... with Portuguese character there is only the feeble farmer, the poor grocer and wine salesman and a plethoric bureaucracy, excessively paid, it is said, with [South African] gold.' M. Guedes, quoted in E. de Saldanha, *Perante o Pais*, Lisbon, 1928, p. xv.

8   Native Labour Regulations, section 1, 1899, Lisbon.

9   Cited in Perry Anderson, *op. cit.*, p. 14.

10   Judith Head, *op. cit.*, p. 66.

11   This crucial period is very poorly researched. Some works concentrating on the post-colonial period have devoted space to an analysis of the late-colonial period. Ruth First, *Black Gold*, Harvester, 1982, gives some indication of the changes taking place in southern Mozambique; Marc Wuyts, *Peasants and Rural Development in Mozambique*, Centro de Estudos Africanos, Maputo, 1978, gives a summary of rural development; and J.E. Torp, *Industrial Planning and Development in Mozambique*, Scandinavian Institute of African Studies, Uppsala, 1979, describes the developments in colonial industry.

12   Eduardo Mondlane, *op. cit.*, gives more details of the social origins of the early leadership.

13   For a prolonged discussion of these issues see pp. 4–17 of The Central Committee Report to the Third Congress, 1977. An English translation entitled *Central Committee Report to the Third Congress of FRELIMO* was produced by the Mozambique, Angola and Guinea Information Centre, London, 1978. References are to this translation. John S. Saul, 'Frelimo and the Mozambique Revolution', in G. Arrighi and J.S. Saul,

Essays on the Political Economy of Africa, Monthly Review, 1973; S. Machel, 'Our health service's role in the Revolution', in *Mozambique: Sowing the Seeds of Revolution*, TCLSAC, Toronto, 1974.

14 *Central Committee Report*, p. 17.

15 J. Chissano, *Datas e Documentos de Historia de Frelimo*, Maputo, 1975.

16 The division into two periods derives from the work of the Centro de Estudos Africanos, Maputo. See, for example, Marc Wuyts, *Peasants and Rural Economy in Mozambique*, p. 29.

17 This includes the period April–September 1974 when warfare continued as negotiation between Frelimo and the new Portuguese government took place, and the period after the agreement (in the Lusaka Accord) to decolonise through a joint Frelimo–Portuguese transition period, followed by a Frelimo government at Independence.

18 'Militants who share a common cause and have put personal considerations in second place in order to help with national reconstruction.' S. Machel, in *Tempo*, Maputo, no. 315, 17 October 1976, p. 23.

19 For descriptions of the GDs, see *Central Committee Report*, pp. 20–5; John Saul, 'Free Mozambique', *Monthly Review*, December 1975, p. 8; and 'Mozambique: the new phase', *Monthly Review*, March 1979, p. 1; Allen Isaacman, *A Luta Continua*, Binghamton, 1978, chapter 2.

20 The local petty and medium bourgeoisie was seen as comprising local owners of means of production that exploited labour and the local faction of the colonial state apparatus. Thus, for example, 'The medium and small national bourgeoisie, composed of Mozambicans, is the fruit of the measures of "social promotion" taken by colonialism ... with the objective of stopping Frelimo's progress ... it is a social sector extremely avid for power and riches, prepared by colonialism in its image.... Although it is weak economically, its tastes, preoccupations ... reflect the ideas of the Portuguese colonial bourgeoisie which is its model and font of inspiration.' *Documentos de 8ª sessao do Comite Central*, Frelimo, Maputo, February 1976, p. 38.

21 Marcelino dos Santos, interview with Alan Isaacman, 1979.

22 *Empresas sob controlo*, Facim, Maputo, 1977.

23 Marc Wuyts, *Peasants and Rural Economy ...*, p. 30.

24 In 1976 and 1977 many issues of Maputo's weekly magazine, *Tempo*, carried stories on the *Dynamising Groups* and the struggles surrounding them.

25 For more details of these statistical problems, see Ruth First, *Black Gold*, Harvester, Brighton, 1982. Colonial statistical data were almost always incorrect. The 1970 population census showed 30 per cent fewer people than those treated in mass vaccination campaigns of 1976 to 1978. The colony never had a calculated GDP, and the various calculations have been shown to be gross overestimates. To make matters worse, the Government Statistical Service collapsed at Independence. At provincial level the situation is even worse. Evaluation of social and economic policies by Party and state organisations is thus debilitated, as are we!

26 These documents and speeches include, *Central Committee Report* 1977; Frelimo, *Directivos Sociais e Economicas, Third Congress 1977; Documentos da 8ª Sessao da Comite Central*, Frelimo, 1976, contains the

important Eighth Central Committee resolutions of politics, the Party, the state apparatus, communal villages, education and health. Machel's speech on health is in *Tempo*, no. 315, 17 October 1976; and on production councils in *Tempo*, no. 316, 24 October 1976.

27 *Documentos de 8ª Sessao da Comite Central*, p. 40.
28 ibid., p. 40.
29 ibid., p. 42.
30 ibid., p. 85.
31 *Black Gold*.
32 *Central Committee Report*, 1976, p. 43.
33 The early part of this section rests on the analysis in Laurence Harris, 'Agricultural co-operatives and development policy in Mozambique', *Journal of Peasant Studies*, July 1980.
34 *Documentos*; in English in *People's Power*, no. 5, p. 30.
35 'Economic and social directives', *People's Power*, nos. 7 and 8, p. 21.
36 *Tempo*, no. 412, 27 August 1978.
37 Report of the National Assembly meeting of June 1979, in *Mozambique Information Agency* (AIM), *Bulletin*, no. 36.
38 *Tempo*, no. 515, 24 August 1980.
39 This analysis is based on the work of the Centro de Estudos Africanos.
40 Marc Wuyts, *On the Question of Agricultural Mechanisation of Mozambican Agriculture Today*, Centro de Estudos Africanos, Universidade Eduardo Mondlane, 1979.
41 Jens Erik Torp, *op. cit.*, is the most comprehensive published analysis of colonial industry.
42 *Tempo*, no. 316, 24 October 1976, pp. 16–28. Reported in English in *People's Power*, no. 10, pp. 21–9.
43 Peter Sketchley, 'Problems of the transformation of social relations of production in post-independent Mozambique', *People's Power*, no. 15, p. 35. The use of CIFEL for this case-study relies on the excellent work of Sketchley in analysing his own work in that factory.
44 P. Sketchley, *op. cit.*, pp. 31–2.
45 ibid., pp. 37–8.
46 For example, see Clive Thomas, *Dependence and Transformation*, Monthly Review, New York, 1974.
47 S. Machel, 'Vamos declarar guerra no Inimigo Interno', *Tempo*, no. 493, 23 March 1980.
48 ibid., p. 53.
49 S. Machel, 'Organisar a Batalha na Frente da Saude', *Tempo*, no. 479, p. 38.
50 *AIM Bulletin*, no. 49, July 1980.

Mozambique: Country Profile

Name of the country:	People's Republic of Mozambique, established on 25 June 1975.
Population:	12.1 million (1980 census).

Capital:	Maputo, 750,000 (1980 census).
Total land area:	76,550 sq km, of which 4 per cent arable land (1978), 58 per cent pastures, 25 per cent woodland and forest.
Official language:	Portuguese.
Membership of international organisations:	UN since 1975, OAU, African Development Bank. (Membership of the IMF, the World Bank and CMEA is being considered.)

Political structure

Constitution:	Of 14 August 1978, superseding that of 1975.
Highest legislative body:	Popular Assembly, of 226 members.
Highest executive body:	Cabinet of ministers.
Head of State:	President Samora Machel, assumed office on 25 June 1975.
Ruling party:	Frelimo (Mozambique Liberation Front), formed in 1962, established as a party in 1977.
Party President:	Samora Machel, elected May 1970.
Party membership:	Not available.
Armed forces:	24,000 (0.5–0.7 per cent of total labour force, 1980).

Population

Population density:	16 per sq km.
Population growth (% pa):	2.5 (1970–9).
Population of working age (15–64, %):	53 (1978).
Urban population (%):	9 (1980 census).
Ethnic and linguistic groups:	European and Asian minorities less than 1 per cent (of the 250,000 Portuguese settlers 100,000 had left by Independence, and most of the remainder within a year). About twenty African languages; Portuguese is taught in the literacy campaign.

Education and health

School system:	Primary schools have 1st–4th years; secondary schools, 5th–11th. Technical schools exist for agriculture, commerce and industry.
Primary school enrolment:	700,000 in 1975, c. 1.4 million in 1978[b] and 1980[e].
Secondary school enrolment:	33,000 (1974), 91,000 (1980)[e].
Literacy (%):	15 (1975)[b].

Life expectancy:	46 (1978).
Child death rate:	27 per 1000 (1978).
Population per hospital bed:	772 (1972).
Population per physician:	16,300 in 1974, 115,000 by the end of 1975; 40,300 in 1981.

Economy

GNP:	US$ 1390 million (1978).[II]
GNP per capita:	US$ 140 (1978).[II]
Gross domestic investment % of GNP:	10 (1978).
State budget (expenditure):	41,900 million escudos (1981 plan)[5].
Defence expenditure % of state budget:	13 (1981 plan)[5].
GDP by sector (%):	Agriculture 45, industry 16, services 39[II] (1978).
Economically active population:	3.9 million (1979).
by sector (%):	Agriculture 67, industry 18, services 25 (1978).
Structure of ownership:	*Industry*: partly nationalised, with three forms of ownership – state-owned enterprises; enterprises run provisionally by Administrative Commissions; and private companies (the latter estimated to represent less than 50 per cent of all enterprises).[c] *Agriculture*: The land nationalised and in process of organisation into communal villages with co-operative production (embracing c. 10 per cent of rural population in 1979) and state farms. Most land still farmed individually,[a] but few large private investments remain.
Land tenure:	2–4 ha maximum for private holdings in irrigated zones only (i.e. no limit on 98 per cent of land).
Main crops:	Sugar, cotton, cashew, tea, maize.
Irrigated area:	68,000 ha, or 2 per cent of arable land (1978).
Energy balance – commercial consumption per capita:	(1978). 151 kg coal equivalent
liquid fuels (%):	48.
net imports (%):	15.
primary production by kind of energy (%):	Hydroelectric 62, solid fuels 38.
Growth indicators (%, pa) –	(1976–9).

GDP:	$-0.2.$[14].
GDP per capita:	$-2.7.$[14]
Agricultural production:	$-0.5.$[6]
food production per capita:	$-3.0.$[6]
Food self-sufficiency (in 1000 contos: NS$1 = 30 escudos; 1000 escudos = 1 contos):	1973: food imports 1353, exports 3254, 1979 food imports 2977, exports 524.[e]
Principal food exports:	Prawns, fruit, tea, oil and oil-nuts, sugar, cashew.
Principal food imports:	Fish, milk products, cereals.

Foreign trade and economic integration

Trade balance –	(1979).
exports:	US$ 270 million.
imports:	US$ 620 million. (Remittances from migrant workers in South Africa and income from transit trade contribute to foreign exchange earnings.)
Main exports:	Agricultural and fishery products.
Main imports (%):	Food products 14, crude oil and products 17, machinery, vehicles and spare parts 38, industrial raw materials 24 (1978).[d]
Destination of exports (%):	Industrialised countries 71, developing countries 29 (trade with socialist countries insignificant) (1978).
Main trading partners:	*Exports*: US, Portugal, UK, South Africa. *Imports*: South Africa, West Germany, Portugal, Iraq (1977).[3] 1973–9 trend away from Portugal and S. Africa, towards USA, eastern Europe and China.
External debt:	US$ 111 million (1978).[IV]
Foreign aid:	Not available.
Foreign investment:	A new policy encouraging greater foreign investment being developed in 1981. There have been joint ventures with foreign firms (including Portugal and US) and some previous Portuguese, French, British, German and South African investments have not been nationalised.

Sources

[a]Ian Christie and Allen Isaacman, 'Interview with Samora Machel', *Southern Africa*, July–August 1979.

[b]Frances Moore Lappé and Adele Beccar-Varela, *Mozambique and Tanzania: asking the big questions*, Institute for Food and Development Policy, San Francisco, 1980.
[c]Jens Torp, *Industrial Planning and Development in Mozambique*, Scandinavian Institute of African Studies, Research report no. 50, Uppsala, 1979.
[d]UNDP, 'Country Programme for Mozambique', *UNDP Assistance Requested by the Government of Mozambique 1979–81*, New York, 5 April 1979.
[e]*Informação Estatística*, no. 1, Comissão Nacional do Plano, Maputo, May 1980.

Notes

[I]Includes foreign advisers.
[II]Estimates in international sources vary a great deal, this one, World Bank,[18] is on the low side. UNDP[d] gives 170 per capita for 1976; UNCTAD[14] 205 for 1977.
[III]About half of agricultural production is for own consumption only. A large part of services is made up of earnings from railway and port charges.
[IV]Excluding debt of parastatals and other enterprises.

Mozambique: Chronology

1498	Portuguese navigator, Vasco da Gama, reaches Mozambique.
1500s and 1600s	Trading controlled by Portuguese (ivory, gold).
1700s	Arab trading control.
1800s	Portuguese regain trading control.
1890s	Forced labour laws instituted. Non-Portuguese plantations (sugar, copra, sisal) begun. Portugal signs agreement with South Africa to send gold mine-workers in return for use of Maputo as Johannesburg's seaport.
1920s	East African resistance to Portugal crushed.
1930s	Portuguese dictatorship of Salazar imposed. Forced cotton cultivation begun for Portuguese textile industry.
1940s to 1960s	Portuguese investment begins in industries, tea and cashew nuts.
1962	Foundation of Frelimo nationalist movement.
1964	End of forced labour.
1964–70	Beginning of liberation war.
1970	Assassination of Eduardo Mondlane, first President of Frelimo. Recognition of two opposing factions in Frelimo. Election of Samora Machel as President consolidates socialist leadership.
1974	*Coup d'état* in Portugal destroys the dictatorship. Transference of power to Frelimo begun.
1975	Independence. Nationalisation of health, education and justice.

1976	Rhodesian incursions begun. Border between Mozambique and Rhodesia closed.
1977	Third Congress. Proclamation of Frelimo as a Marxist party. Election of First People's Assembly.
1979	Rhodesian ceasefire.
1980	Zimbabwean Independence. Offensive against internal corruption and inefficiency. Launching of Southern African Development Co-ordinating Group aimed at reducing dependence on South Africa.
1981	South African attack inside Mozambique.

THE NORTH KOREAN ENIGMA[1]

Jon Halliday

North Korea, or the Democratic People's Republic of Korea (DPRK), is an isolated enigma in north-east Asia. No state in the world lives with such a wide gap between its own self-image as a socialist 'paradise on earth' and the view of much of the outside world that it is a bleak workhouse ruled by a megalomaniac, Kim Il Sung.

This gap demands explanation – and needs to be bridged. The DPRK has largely been excluded from general discussions of Third World development and socialist transformation; yet its experience is important. It has achieved remarkable economic growth and advances in social services. It raises important issues concerning the possibility of agricultural self-sufficiency and rapid, self-reliant industrialisation for a medium-sized Third World country. At the same time, most observers agree that its political system is one of the most dreadful ever constructed in the name of socialism. This too raises major issues, especially concerning the cult of personality. This text is an attempt to look at both parts of the equation, and at the relationship between the régime's political practice and its economic success, within the terms of socialism.

A Devastating Modern History

Korea is a single nation, with a rich culture and a deep sense of identity stretching back thousands of years. It is one of the most homogeneous countries in the world, 99 per cent of the population being ethnic Koreans. Yet the country was divided by the United States across the middle, along the 38th Parallel, at the end of the second world war. South of the parallel the US set up a separate régime, the Republic of Korea (ROK), based on Seoul, the traditional capital.

114

This régime, headed by Syngman Rhee, was formally installed on 15 August 1948, and exercised sway over two-thirds of the population (approximately 17 million out of some 26 million).[2] The DPRK was officially inaugurated on 9 September 1948. Both régimes claimed jurisdiction over the entire nation, and both recognised Seoul as the nation's capital.

It is impossible to understand the DPRK without a brief look at its immediate past and the particular factors which made it what it is today. In the space of one decade it went from extremely harsh Japanese colonialism (which had lasted an entire generation), through Soviet liberation and occupation for three years (1945–8), two years of difficult independence (in a divided nation), and three years of devastating war (1950–3), during which 90 per cent of its territory was occupied and almost the entire territory laid waste. This concentration of external pressures and tragedy has few parallels, if any, in world history.

Japanese colonialism

Japan formally occupied Korea as a colony from 1910 (*de facto* from some years earlier) to 1945, and integrated it as a subordinate component of a highly militarised empire. By 1938, 99.3 per cent of Korea's foreign trade was within the yen bloc (80.8 per cent with Japan proper, and 13.9 per cent with Manchuria).[3] There was 'spectacular industrial- isation',[4] combined with large-scale extraction of mineral resources, construction of large dams, an extensive metro- polis-oriented communications system, Japanese takeover of large amounts of land, a big increase in agricultural output combined with a sharp decline in Korean consumption, the expulsion of millions of Koreans from their homes, and severe political and cultural oppression. In brief, distorted growth with maximum extraction, plus harsh repression and cruel dislocation on a large scale.

By 1939 industry and mining together (39 per cent and 6 per cent, respectively) had overtaken agriculture (42 per cent) as a proportion of total output by value. Within industry, heavy industry in the same year accounted for 47 per cent of produc- tion (28 per cent in 1936) and the chemical industry ranked first, having ousted food-processing (first in 1936).[5] The chemical industry (including the second largest petrochemical plant in the world) was made possible by the development of hydroelectric power, with large dams in the area of the River Amnok (Yalu) on the border with China. Most of the heavy industry was in the north of the country (see Table 2). The communications system was far more extensive than in either colonial Vietnam or pre-1949 China.[6] By 1945 Korea had roughly the same length of railway track as the whole of China except for Manchuria and half the number of passengers carried by the entire Chinese system. The road network in 1945 covered just over 50,000 km, compared with 100,000 km in China in 1950. With the exceptions of the middle part of the east coast and the mountainous regions, the railway system penetrated the whole of Korea by 1945.

Japan's agricultural policy was to increase rice production in Korea for export to the metropolis. Between 1912 and 1933 rice output rose by about 50 per cent, exports rose over seventeen times, and per capita consumption in Korea fell by almost half.[7] Most of this increased rice production was in the south, while wheat production was promoted in the north.

The Japanese also took over large tracts of farmland.[8] By 1939 the tenancy figure (full-time and part-time) had reached 77.2 per cent for the whole country; almost 2 million people were living off fire-field agriculture. There was mass starvation. In 1934 the Japanese Governor-General 'spoke of the fearful misery of the Korean peasantry. He stated that every spring the number of wretched farmers lacking food and searching for bark and grass to eat, approached 50 per cent of the total peasant population.'[9]

In spite of the increase in industrial and mining output, Korea remained a predominantly rural society. At the end of the 1930s, only 11.5 per cent of Koreans were living in urban areas (in contrast with 71 per cent of the Japanese population in Korea, who made up 3.2 per cent of the total population). In 1938, 73.6 per cent of the total population made their living in agriculture, 7 per cent in commerce, 3.9 in the professions, and 3.1 in industry.[10] These figures obscure the difference between the Japanese and Korean workforces, as can be seen in Table 1.

By the end of 1944 there were an estimated 421,229

Table 1. *Japanese and Koreans by occupation
(per cent of each population, 1938)*[11]

	Japanese	Koreans
Industry	16.6	2.6
Commerce	23.4	6.5
Public officials and professions	38.1	2.9
Agriculture	5.3	75.1

workers in industry. The increase in the mining labour force was steep: it rose from about 36,000 in 1931 to about 220,000 in 1938. From the point of view of technical skills, there was a marked imbalance: of the 8476 engineers and technicians in the country at the end of 1944, only 1632 were Koreans.

Political repression and police surveillance were harsh and efficient; torture was standard police practice.[12] Cultural oppression was also bitter. In the late 1930s, as Japan expanded further into China from its base in Manchuria, policy in Korea hardened even further. From 1938 on, the use of Korean was banned completely in schools, and newspapers in Korean were abolished.[13] Koreans were obliged to give up their family names and take Japanese names – a particularly tragic imposition for a people with a strong attachment to family nomenclature and lineage. By September 1940, 80 per cent of the population had complied.

By 1945 Korea was a battered but seething land. Vast numbers had been dispossessed. Some 2 million Koreans had been dragooned into working in Japan, usually in the worst and most dangerous jobs;[14] there were 1½ million Korean emigrants in Manchuria by 1944, and about 200,000 in the Soviet Union; there was also a system of forced labour within Korea which conscripted over 2½ million people; and in 1942 a military draft was introduced for Koreans. By the end of the war, millions of families had been broken up. The culture and language of Korea, far older than that of Japan, had been suppressed. Women had suffered especially; many were forced or tricked into prostitution; some were taken to the front lines where 'apparently many were killed in the fighting'.[15]

The early communist movement

Given the ferocity and efficiency of Japanese police repression in Korea, organised resistance was extremely difficult. The history of the early communist movement is one of heroic resistance to the Japanese everywhere, in Korea, China and Japan, with the communist forces rapidly overhauling the Nationalist movement.[16] But it is also a history of enforced fragmentation; communication between the different communist groups was virtually impossible.

Korean communists played a big role in the early history of the Comintern:[17] they took part in the Canton Commune of 1927; they formed the only foreign contingent on the Long March; they accounted for perhaps as much as half the entire Japanese Communist Party during the toughest years; and they played a major part in fighting the Japanese and the Kuomintang in north-east China.

The official DPRK history of Korean communism focuses overwhelmingly on the role of Kim Il Sung. It excludes both the heroic internationalism of Korean radicals and virtually all individuals except Kim Il Sung.[18] It also massively falsifies the history of Kim, who, it is claimed, founded the movement in 1926 (at the age of fourteen!), unified it under independent Korean leadership, and led it to victory over Japanese colonialism and imperialism. In fact, Kim was an important guerrilla leader in north-east China in the 1930s, commanding perhaps about 400 people under extremely difficult conditions. He was not the leader of a unified movement, nor, for much of the time, of a wholly independent movement, but part of the North-east Anti-Japanese United Army (NEAJUA). His greatest achievement was a major raid on the border town of Pochon (Pochonbo) in 1937. But by the end of the 1930s Japanese repression had become so efficient in north-east China that Kim and his group were obliged to take refuge in the Soviet Union. There is no sign of activity by Kim and his group in the years 1941–5.

The specificity of the liberation of North Korea, 1945

The northern part of Korea was liberated from the Japanese in August 1945 by the Soviet Red Army. Soviet occupation continued until late 1948, when the DPRK was formally established. The DPRK is the only Third World country which has ever travelled the particular route of Soviet liberation and occupation plus revolution. It is also the only Third World country in which the Soviet Union has *directly* displaced colonialism, and the only one liberated and occupied by the USSR while Stalin was alive.

Indigenous political organisation was weak inside Korea itself. A few Korean guerrillas assisted the Soviet Red Army, and liberation involved mass participation, but the current official DPRK account – *viz*. that northern Korea was liberated by Korean forces headed by Kim Il Sung – is false. [19] It is not clear that Kim was even in Korea in the period immediately after the Soviet Army moved in. Thus, although there had been an active Korean communist movement and mass resistance to the Japanese, the liberation was more akin to that of, say, Romania than that of Yugoslavia or Albania. The combination was: liberation by Soviet Army + popular resistance to Japanese + small Korean guerrilla movement *outside* Korea.

A second distinctive feature concerns the collapse of colonialism. In August 1945 Japan was defeated not just in Korea, but on a world scale – and by a world coalition of powers. This, in combination with the Soviet presence, meant that the usual problems of neo-colonialism did not exist at the *political* level. There was an economy distorted by Japanese intervention; but the exclusion of Japan from the world capitalist coalition prevented it from sustaining neo-colonial interests in North Korea. In contrast to more recent times, Japanese interests could be seized and nationalised without a word of protest from world capitalism, the IMF or the World Bank; there were no foreign tourists; no foreign airlines or communications links with the West; there was no 'brain drain' to the colonial metropolis; Japanese colonial personnel in Korea were either imprisoned, expelled or, if technically useful, put to work.

The third distinctive feature of liberation was that it coincided with the *de facto* division of the nation. From the economic point of view, the division brought fresh difficulties. The North was left with a battered heavy industrial and mining base, a severe lack of skilled personnel, and a very

Table 2   *Distribution of resources at partition, 1945 (%)*

Sector	North Korea	South Korea
Heavy industry	65	35
Light industry	31	69
Agriculture	37	63
Commerce	18	82

Source: US Central Intelligence Agency, National Foreign Assessment Center, *Korea: The Economic Race Between the North and the South*, January 1978, p.1.

weak light industrial and agricultural base. An estimate for the distribution of resources in 1945 is given in Table 2. The North had the overwhelming proportion of the chemical industry (88 per cent), metal production (85 per cent) and electricity generating capacity (92 per cent).

Early reforms

By the time of the Moscow Conference in December 1945, it was widely assumed that Korea was not about to be reunified, nor left to determine its own fate. In the North, the Russians appear to have adopted a generally 'hands off' approach. They provided a military guarantee for the external security of the régime, and a context for measures of expropriation and reform. They also provided extensive aid.[20]

At the time of liberation a nationwide network of People's Committees was set up, grouping a broad spectrum of radical and nationalist opinions; the Russians recognised them as the base of the new administration. The returning Koreans grafted themselves onto this internal base. The new system was not a takeover nor an adaptation of the colonial state apparatus; it was something completely new. Nor was the régime purely communist at first. The Communist Party was fairly weak in this early phase; Kim Il Sung claimed a membership of only 4350 in December 1945.[21] In the immediate post-liberation period, Kim Il Sung was not the all-dominant figure which subsequent propaganda has claimed: he did not become head of the Party until December 1945, and of the state administration until February 1946.

Between March and August 1946 a series of radical reforms

was introduced covering every major field of policy: Agrarian Reform (5 March), a Labour Law (24 June), the Law on Equality of the Sexes (30 July) and the Law on the National-isation of Industry, Transport, Communications, Banks, etc. (10 August).[22]

After an initial reduction in tenant rents in October 1945 (which fixed the percentage of harvest yields to be given to landlords at 30 per cent), a 'land to the tiller' reform was carried out in March 1946. This was the most peaceful and the fastest land reform in Asia (or, to my knowledge, anywhere in the world); it is also the least studied.[23] In the pre-Liberation period, landholdings in Northern Korea were generally very small (in 1940 72 per cent of all farms were less than 1 *chongbo* (one chongbo = 2.45 acres or 0.992 ha) and only 4 per cent were more than 5 *chongbo*); 58 per cent of the arable land was owned by landlords, accounting for 4 per cent of all farm households. Land confiscated in the reform accounted for 54 per cent of all cultivated land, or 95 per cent of the land rented out before Liberation; about 76 per cent of peasant households received land. The state confiscated all land of the Japanese state and nationals, Korean 'traitors and deserters', and holdings over 5 *chongbo*, as well as some $3\frac{1}{2}$ million *chongbo* of forests, 1165 irrigation facilities, buildings, animals, farm implements and 2692 *chongbo* of orchards.

The reform was reportedly carried through in three weeks. It gave a fairly small plot of land to each peasant family. Most landlords had already fled to the South; those that remained were given the same holding as others provided they moved to another province. The reform appears to have had mass support, and to have exercised a big effect on the population in the South. By liquidating the remaining landlord class through relocation (after 90 per cent defection), the régime minimised the level of violence around the reform.

The Labour Law laid down an eight-hour day, banned child labour, instituted equal pay for equal work, 77 days' pregnancy leave, fixed vacations, overtime pay and social insurance, as well as protection and special conditions for dangerous work. The Law on Equality of the Sexes formally enacted full equality in all fields, including property in-heritance, divorce and child maintenance. It also banned prostitution, polygamy and concubinage, which had been widespread under Japanese rule (and before). The Nationalisation Law of 10 August confiscated all industrial, financial and other assets held by Japanese or Korean collaborators. Prior to Liberation, according to DPRK sources, Koreans held only 5 per cent of total industrial capital. The 1946 Law thus established a large state sector in industry which in 1947 accounted for 80.2 per cent of gross industrial output value.[24]

These reforms were accompanied by a big drive in education, and a blitz on illiteracy. The régime claims that illiteracy, which afflicted 50 per cent of the adult population in 1947, was completely wiped out by the end of 1948.[25] This claim is hard to verify and, if true, would make it one of the most successful campaigns ever. But the restoration of the national culture and language after the ravages of Japanese colonialism did have tremendous impetus, and this could well have made the Korean case exceptional, even if the 100 per cent claim is exaggerated.

On the basis of these reforms, the régime claimed major advances in all fields by 1949. Most of these claims are impossible to verify and the base year, 1946, is statistically unsatisfactory. On the other hand, it is the point from which the régime had to start. Composite estimates are given in Table 3.[26]

The Korean War

The war which started on 25 June 1950 was, in essence, a qualitative escalation of an ongoing struggle for unification. Whatever the causes of this escalation, the DPRK took a decision to cross the 38th Parallel in force and try to topple the US-backed Rhee régime in the South. There were mass

Table 3   *North Korea: indexes of key economic variables, 1946–53*
(*1946 = 100*)

	1946	1949	1953
National income	100	209	145
Gross value of industrial production	100	337	216
Production of the means of production	100	375	158
Production of consumer goods	100	288	285
Gross value of agricultural production	100	151	115

popular uprisings throughout the South, and the ROK army disintegrated. Ninety per cent of the South was liberated by September 1950. The People's Committees were re-activated, southern communists were placed in many positions of authority, and the main DPRK reforms were applied in the liberated areas.[27]

In September 1950, however, the Korean People's Army was driven out of the South (after the Inchon landing) and the Liberation administration there collapsed (though a large guerrilla movement survived for some time). In early October the US-UN-ROK forces invaded the North, and within a few weeks had reached the River Amnok/Yalu, the border with China; between October and December 1950, they occupied 90 per cent of the North. In late October 1950 Chinese forces entered Korea and the US-UN troops were driven back across the 38th Parallel around New Year 1951. Seoul was briefly reliberated for two months in January–March 1951. Thereafter the war stabilised roughly along the 38th Parallel until an armistice was signed at the end of July 1953.

The war period raises numerous vital issues – here I shall only touch on its effects on the North, which were devastating materially, humanly and politically.

The material destruction can best be understood from the fact that by November 1950, five months after the war had started, the US grounded its bomber force because there were no targets left to hit (something which never happened in Vietnam). By the end of the war, much of the North's industrial and communications facilities had been destroyed. It was reported that in Pyongyang, formerly a city of nearly half a million inhabitants, only two buildings were left intact.

Human losses were enormous, not only from bombing. The DPRK is the only post-revolutionary country ever occupied by the US. Gangs of thugs and vigilantes, as well as dispossessed landlords, returned to the North with the US-UN-ROK forces. It is likely that at least 12 per cent of the population and possibly 15 per cent were killed. Many of these were Party cadres and military, but many were women and children. It is impossible to apportion losses between bombing and other causes. The DPRK claims that extensive massacres were carried out during the occupation of the North; this is probably true.

Politically, the war was a major setback in several ways. The failure to liberate the South and protect southern supporters against the return of US imperialism and the Rhee régime caused serious strains between the southern population and the DPRK régime, massively aggravated by Kim's decision to execute much of the southern communist leadership immediately after the end of the war. Likewise, Kim's failure to make adequate preparations, either military or political, for the US-UN-ROK invasion of the North in October 1950 put great strain on the army, the Party and the society. Moreover, during the occupation of the North, the Party was put under tremendous pressure. Cadres appear to have thrown away their Party cards or fled; many were killed. When the DPRK administration was finally re-established in December 1950, there was a very tough purge and other social measures, including forms of house arrest and isolation affecting large numbers of people. The reimposition of DPRK rule appears to have been extremely fraught, with material misery compounded by political insecurity. It is during this period that it was decided to give a major boost to the cult of Kim by turning his birthplace, Mangyongdae, into a shrine; this coincided with the reconstitution and expansion of the Party with large numbers of new cadres on a flimsy ideological and political base.[28]

Economic Policy and Self-Reliance

Overview

In view of the DPRK's generally poor international reputation, it is worth noting that many western observers rate its economic achievements highly. Harrison Salisbury, who visited it in 1972, wrote of 'a tremendous technical and industrial achievement', and called it 'on a per capita basis . . . the most intensively industrialised country in Asia, with the exception of Japan'. René Dumont claimed (in the late 1960s) that 'In agriculture and probably industry, too, North Korea leads the socialist bloc'. Joan Robinson wrote

Table 4 *Share of industry and agriculture in national income (%)*

	1946	1965	1970
Industry	16.8	64.2	65
Agriculture	63.5	18.3	20

after a visit in 1964: 'All the economic miracles of the post-war world are put in the shade by these achievements.'[29]

The overall extent of socio-economic transformation can be seen from Table 4.[30]

This has been accompanied by a big shift in the balance of rural and urban population. Generally accepted rough estimates for urban population are:[31]

	(%)
1953	17.7
1965	47.5
1975	c.65–70

There has been a policy of spatial decentralisation (partly related to strategic-military concepts of local self-reliance) and controlled urbanisation; and there seems to be a strict system of passes and residence permits.

General figures and claims

By the end of the 1970s, the DPRK claimed to have built 'an excellent independent economy which is well-rounded, equipped up-to-date, fed with our own raw materials, operated by our own cadres and technicians'.[32] It claims high figures for both agricultural and industrial growth, and maintains that it is possible to sustain uninterrupted high growth.

In industry, the régime claims that gross output rose by an average of 23.5 per cent per annum between 1954 and 1970, with the shares of heavy and light industry (idiosyncratically defined) almost constant (59:41 in 1949; 62:38 in 1970). It states that industrial growth slowed in the decade 1961–70 to 12.8 per cent per annum average (from 36.6 per cent per annum in 1957–60), but rose again in the 1970s to an average of 15.9 per cent per annum.[33]

The most reliable western sources, such as Chung, provide

somewhat lower estimates for industrial growth. There have been serious slowdowns and even negative growth in 1966, at which point there is a total statistical blackout. However, after a bad stretch in the late 1960s (unsatisfactorily attributed to greatly increased defence expenditure by some sources), there appears to have been sustained high growth in the 1970s. The US CIA in 1978 stated that 'a reconstruction of official . . . statistics indicates' 14 per cent per annum average industrial growth between 1965 and 1976.[34] This claim is supported by the figures for output of basic items in Table 5, showing per capita output in 1976 roughly double that in the ROK, then in the middle of its industrial boom. No hard analysis is available of later claims, but the *Asia 1981 Yearbook* writes that in the late 1970s 'industrial output appeared to continue to rise strongly'.[35] Industrial growth targets are just over 12 per cent per annum for the 1980s.

In agriculture, which has been the problem area in most post-revolutionary societies, the claims are equally extensive: that output rose by 10 per cent per annum in the 1950s, and by 6.3 per cent per annum in the 1960s. It is also claimed that total grain production in 1979 reached 9 million tons, and self-sufficiency in food was achieved some time ago. In 1976 the US CIA reckoned that the DPRK was 'nearly self-sufficient in grain supplies'. It also writes of 'dramatic increases' in grain output in the mid-1970s after a sharp decline in the early 1970s. It is hard to be absolutely certain about the agricultural situation. There clearly is a very extensive irrigation system, and the régime claims a very high level of mechanisation and use of chemicals: seven tractors per 100 *chongbo* in the plains and six per 100 *chongbo* in other areas in 1979; 97 per cent of all rice fields weeded by chemical means, and 1.5 tons of chemical fertiliser per *chongbo*. The CIA seems to agree: 'fertilizer application is probably among the highest in the world, and irrigation projects are extensive'. By 1980 the claimed yields were 7.2 tons of rice and 6.3 tons of maize per *chongbo*.

These claims are hard to verify, or to disprove. The yields are hard to check since the DPRK mixes in some tubers under the category of 'grains', and also weighs grain unhusked (which needs to be deflated by about 25 per cent to get the unhusked weight). The self-sufficiency claim, if

Table 5 Production of selected products

		1970		1976[1]	
	Units	North Korea	South Korea	North Korea[1]	South Korea
Electric power	Billion kWh	16.5	9.2	21.8	23.1
Coal	Million metric tons	27.5	12.4	39.5	16.4
Crude Steel	Million metric tons	2.2	0.5	2.75	2.7
Fertilizer	Million metric tons (nutrient content)	0.3	0.6	0.6	0.8
Cement	Million metric tons	4.0	5.8	5.0	11.9
Textiles (excluding yarn)	Million square meters	418	329	450	936
Refined petroleum products	Million metric tons	0	9.0	1	17.8
Fish catch	Million metric tons	0.7	0.9	1.2	2.4
Machine tools	Thousand units	10.0	7.5	24	8.4
Trucks	Thousand units	4.0	5.5	10	19.5
Zinc	Thousand metric tons	83	3	125	27
Lead	Thousand metric tons	61	3	80	8
Television sets	Million units	Neg	0.1	Neg	2.3

[1] Preliminary estimates.
Source: CIA. *Korea*, 1978, p. 11.

true, would be a remarkable achievement, with only 17 per cent of the land cultivable and a very harsh climate. The DPRK issues selected (and spasmodic) figures for its food exports, mainly rice. It issues no figures for food imports, but it clearly imports wheat; but the balance of imports and exports is hard to calculate. In my own estimation, the DPRK is virtually self-sufficient, but at a lower level than it claims; fluctuations in crops have been more acute than it acknowledges, but there has been marked growth in output well ahead of population increases; the rice component of overall diet is lower than the régime suggests, and there is strict rationing.

Self-reliance (*juche*)

The DPRK attributes its developmental successes to the 'wise leadership' of Kim Il Sung and to the strategy of *juche*, which is usually and erroneously attributed to Kim.

The starting-point was a severely battered and distorted economy, virtually totally isolated from the world capitalist economy, in the climatically much harsher half of a divided country, but with exceptional resource endowment. As Gordon White noted:

North Korea ranks among the top ten countries in the world in both available deposits and production of such crucial minerals as gold, tungsten, magnesite, molybdenum and fluorite. It also has substantial deposits of asbestos, aluminium, chromium, copper, lead, silver, zinc, nickel, iron ore and coal.[36]

The only two crucial raw materials it lacks are oil and bituminous coal for coking. As White notes, this puts it in a most unusual position compared with most Third World (or any) countries.

The DPRK has promoted self-reliance (not self-sufficiency) to the level of a strategy applicable not only to Korea but to the whole of the Third World. Vast sums of money and countless working hours are expended in pushing *juche* and 'Kim Il Sungism' round the world. The *juche* strategy is comprehensive, embracing political, military and cultural as well as economic independence. At the economic level, it is defined as:

a line of economic construction for meeting by home production the needs for manufactured goods and farm produce necessary for making the country rich and strong and improving the prople's livelihood ... to build one's country with one's own people's labour and one's own national resources.

The aim should be 'an all-embracing economic system in which every branch ... is structurally interrelated'.[37] Official policy is that if possible 70 per cent of all raw materials should be provided from domestic resources.[38] To achieve this, the régime developed a multi-pronged approach: prospect and promote extractive industries to the maximum; where a given raw material was not available, produce a substitute wherever possible; if, as in the case of oil, total substitution is not possible, then minimise dependency on a structural, long-term basis. Transformation was made possible by building a high technology chemical industry. The best-known case of substitution is that of vinalon, a synthetic textile produced from limestone. Synthetic rubber is produced from carbide, and fertiliser from coal.

The central lesson of the Korean experience is the long-term structuring of the entire economy systematically to minimise external dependence and vulnerability. The most striking example of this is the building of what must be the least oil-dependent industrialised economy in the world. The CIA estimated that in 1976 oil accounted for only 5 per cent of primary energy consumption in the DPRK, with coal accounting for 77 per cent and hydroelectric power for 18 per cent (63, 35 and 2 per cent, respectively, for South Korea).[39] If even roughly correct, this would be a remarkable achievement for an economy where industry accounts for a higher proportion of GNP than Japan (45 and 44 per cent, respectively).[40] But what makes it truly astonishing is that minimal oil usage has been achieved at the same time as a level of energy consumption which is the second highest in Asia, as Table 6 shows. Until the early 1970s, Korea was almost entirely dependent on the USSR for its oil. In January 1976 a new pipeline from north-east China was opened, and the DPRK was able to balance supplies between the two countries. More recently, it has diversified its sources of supply to the Middle East and Indonesia. But it is still vulnerable in the military sector, where there is no substitute for petroleum (e.g. for planes).

Much the same picture emerges in industry as a whole.

Table 6   *Energy consumption per capita
(kg of coal equivalent)*, 1976[41]

North Korea	3072
South Korea	1020
Japan	3679
Singapore	2262
China	706

The régime has placed great emphasis on building up the
machine-tool industry, which is the central sector of a
self-reliant economy, and claims 98 per cent self-sufficiency.
It can produce most of the heavy machinery it needs: in
1975, it could make 6000-ton presses, 100-ton lorries, 300-hp
bulldozers, 3000-hp high-speed engines; it is particularly
advanced in heavy earth-moving and digging equipment for
both mining and underground construction. By 1977, it
could also produce most of the advanced military equipment
it required:[42] T-59 tanks, armoured cars, 107mm rockets,
mobile 152mm cannon, 1500ton 'R' class submarines,
anti-submarine destroyers and high-speed gunboats. It is
reported to have initiated moves to produce its own fighter
planes. This impressive range of military equipment, which
no other Third World country of comparable size can
produce, is essentially made possible by the development of
the machine-tool sector.

Foreign aid and domestic accumulation

Many outside observers have suggested that foreign aid must
have played a big role in North Korean development. The
official figure for all foreign aid received is $550 million,
which is impossibly low. Other estimates go up as high as
Salisbury's 'probably ... about $5 billion'.[43] The official
position is that foreign aid was relatively unimportant.
However, though the country did substantially raise itself
by its own bootstraps, foreign aid played a crucial role,
both economically and militarily. It saved the DPRK from
being wiped off the map in 1950 and, in my opinion, was
much more important both in the 1940s and in the post-
Korean War period than is officially acknowledged. More-

over, Korea is still receiving aid from both the USSR and China (while itself giving aid to other countries). The real lesson is not that it developed without foreign aid, but that it made good use of foreign aid and fought hard against its being used by foreign countries for political leverage (which was tried).

Undoubtedly, the key to the country's growth lies in a combination of exceptional mass mobilisation and high domestic accumulation. The DPRK publishes an annual budget but issues only very vague figures about revenue. Outside observers have put the domestic savings rate at 25–35 per cent of GNP, with the higher figure more widely accepted.[44] At the formal level at least, taxation was abolished in April 1974. However, there is no sign that the rate of extraction of the surplus fell at that point and it could be argued that the state in fact extracts a high proportion of the surplus – and does not always use it well ('blowing' large parts of it on grandiose prestige buildings which make the capital seem more like a stage set than a living city; and on discredited propaganda).

Labour is recompensed by a combination of cash wages and subsidies (roughly 50:50, nationwide). The economy functions on a complex system of transfers and subsidies. The régime claims that growth has been fairly balanced between rural and urban areas and between heavy and light industry. It also claims that agricultural tax, which was 25 per cent after the land reform, was abolished by 1966 and that thereafter the cities subsidised the countryside, particularly through high state payments for rice and subsidised inputs.

These claims are impossible to verify. Chung and others have queried the régime's claims for balanced growth (soundly, in my view).[45] Moreover, no clear picture is provided of how hard the peasantry was squeezed. The 25 per cent agricultural tax was on planned, not actual yields, and only top quality rice was accepted. Moreover, during at least part of the period when the tax was in operation, there were serious problems in agriculture.

The government claims that real income (cash and subsidies) is about the same in urban and rural areas. Most foreign observers acknowledge that they are close: there is more housing space per person in rural areas, but amenities must be superior in the towns. The real extent of transfers and subsidies can not be pinned down, because the regime only releases some figures (e.g. the subsidy on rice) and not others (the subsidy on fertiliser, for example).[46] Fairly detailed information is given for cash incomes, but very little for subsidies and only very vague information about the lowering of prices, which may play a role roughly equal to that of wage increases. The régime does not help by stating that certain items are distributed to the people as 'gifts from the Great Leader' – which can only be the fruits of the people's toil reallocated (fairly?) through disguised taxation. In addition, there are areas of unpaid or unwaged labour about which little is known: domestic labour, prison labour, children working, overtime (probably frequent, given the recurrence of special campaigns).

However, exaggerations must not be allowed to obscure some major achievements. On the question of balance, a Japanese economist summed up a comparison with China as follows:

Compared with the First Five-Year Plan period of China [1953–7], the Three-Year [1954–6] and Five-Year [1957–61] Plan periods of Korea comprised less gap between industrial investment and agricultural investment, less difference in investments between heavy industry and light industry and a higher rate of increase of consumer goods production.[47]

In 1980, Kim Il Sung claimed that per capita national income had reached $1920. Most outside observers questioned the figure; one western source put the figure at $1300; another at $950.[48] Quite apart from problems of the exchange rate, no one has devised an acceptable way to compare GNP or national income in capitalist and non-capitalist countries. If one takes the figures for output of basic items in Table 5, plus the indisputably high mechanisation of the society, plus fairly decent housing (many with refrigerators and a few with television), clothing, good social services, education and health, it is hard not to accept a figure over $1000. But visual observation, such as that of Harrison Salisbury who in 1972 put the real standard of living 'at least as good as in Western Russia', seems to me of more value than doubtful statistics.[49]

International economic relations and the CMEA

Korea's achievement has to be measured not only against its domestic starting point, but also against the international context in which it had to develop. It was forcibly delinked from the world capitalist economy right from the start; its early foreign trade was overwhelmingly with the USSR, and it had no counterbalance in the world capitalist economy. The Korean War brought a total embargo by western countries (and the USA still has its toughest trade embargo with any country in the world with the DPRK). It was in this context, and before China could provide much 'counter-vailing power', that the DPRK struck out on its untested path.

As regards the international economy, the main elements in the *juche* strategy were: keep all foreign capital out; keep foreign trade low – and, especially, subordinate it to the interests of a comprehensive domestically-oriented (auto-centric) economy (for example, manufacture tractors rather than import them from the USSR, even if this was not 'cost beneficial'). The DPRK has publicly stated that it was put under great pressure by the USSR to accept subordinate integration into the Soviet economic bloc and its apparent success in controlling the extent of its integration while maintaining high growth is impressive.

The often-repeated statement that the DPRK did not join the CMEA needs qualification. When the CMEA was originally formed, non-European states could not join as full members.[50] Subsequently, the DPRK did join all the next three sub-organisations established as a full member but, unlike Mongolia (and later Cuba and Vietnam), it rejected full membership. Unlike Albania, it never withdrew completely. It adopted a new, middle path. Its option was one of *selective participation*, both as regards which CMEA bodies to join and when to attend meetings. It seems to have been able to gain most of the advantages of the CMEA (barter trade, no need for convertible currencies) while avoiding the major disadvantage, which would have subverted the entire *juche* strategy, *viz.* the loss of economic and therefore political independence involved in the 'socialist international division of labour'.

No less interesting than the DPRK's selective participation in the CMEA was its relinking with the world capitalist economy in the early 1970s. Just before the onset of the world recession, trade with OECD countries (especially with Japan) rose sharply, from about one-fifth to about one-half of DPRK foreign trade. Much of this trade was financed by credits from the OECD countries (as was normal). The reasons for the DPRK switch have not been spelt out, but among them must be the limitations of the CMEA in most high technology fields; economies of scale in high technology sectors; relative prices for exports (especially minerals like zinc, tungsten, lead, molybdenum) as against imports, plus the lure of large credits which were then being pushed by capitalist banks

Among Korea's claims (in 1975) was that it was 'free from any world's economic fluctuations'. This is patently not true. But a modified version of this claim is true: *viz*. that Korea although running a serious trade deficit with Japan and the West in the 1970s, and getting heavily into debt (including default), held off the world capitalist system in a way which no other Third World country has. Pyongyang did not let the IMF in to examine the books; it did not cut social services; it did not (so far as can be seen)[51] devalue its currency. It got itself a bad name, and was blackballed on the Baltic Exchange in London. The debt (mainly normal credit, with perhaps a maximum of US $400m in overdue principal and interest)[52] was given extensive coverage in the OECD and South Korean press; and it was large, if measured by conventional standards, such as debt service ratio (estimated at 30–35 per cent of hard currency export earnings over 1981–5). But it was less serious if related to the underlying strength of the economy, and this is reflected in the way the OECD banks rolled over the credits (although Pyongyang made concessions on interest rates and repayment terms).

In mid-1981 it was revealed that the DPRK had defaulted again on scheduled repayments to Western banks. Pyongyang reportedly offered to allow Western firms to set up joint ventures in the DPRK, an unprecedented step. The *Financial Times* (17 June 1981) reported that the DPRK had even offered equity shares in Korean mining concerns. This major shift by Pyongyang indicates either serious problems in repaying its debts and/or an imperative desire to acquire more advanced Western technology. In any case, Pyongyang's weakness gives the capitalist banks some undoubted leverage. The *Financial Times* (*ibid.*) quoted an official of Morgan Grenfell, one of the British banks on which Pyongyang has defaulted, as saying: 'It is a question of forcing the North Koreans to change their priorities.'

In his 1979 New Year speech, Kim Il Sung proclaimed that the economy had to give 'precedence to the production of export goods' and this was repeated at the sixth Party Congress in October 1980. Such a formulation was itself unprecedented: it implies that important parts of the economy are now working with their priority aim not the satisfaction of internal needs but to pay off debts. The sixth Congress set the target of raising foreign trade by 4.2 times during the 1980s, far more than the growth target for the economy as a whole. This must mean greater integration with the world (especially capitalist) economy, and some lessening of isolation.

Although Pyongyang is not *unaffected* by world economic fluctuations, as it claims, its domestic economy is relatively protected. If CIA estimates are even roughly correct, the DPRK maintained high growth rates through the world recession.[53] If so, then the government was successful in protecting the domestic economy from external pressure and maintaining planned growth targets. The world economic fluctuations existed, but the régime kept them *external* instead of letting them become *internal*.

Korea's experience with both socialist and capitalist international economies is of great interest, yet curiously its material on both aspects is very poor. It has published interesting critical remarks on the CMEA and on Soviet pressure, but in the form of limited remarks and pot-shots.[54] There is no published critique sufficiently systematic to be useful to other developing countries, many of which are now faced with a fundamental issue: how does a small or medium-sized Third World country establish a viable relationship with the CMEA and the USSR if it breaks with the world capitalist system? Likewise Pyongyang has not been forthcoming on how it handled its debt problems.[55]

The reasons behind the DPRK's remarkable economic success are both political and economic. Among the political reasons one must include: the political stability of the régime;

planners and bureaucrats have had reasonable assurances that neither the top leadership nor the political line would change in mid-stream (unlike in, say, China); second, the para-military mobilisation of the population, gaining strength from the strong desire to eliminate the vestiges of Japanese colonialism and overcome the Korean War as well as competition with the South; third, high educational levels (the country now claims over 1 million technicians and engineers).

Among the economic reasons: first, the exceptional resource endowment in industrial raw materials; second, an initial core (admittedly small) of skilled industrial workers; third, sizeable foreign aid at crucial moments; fourth, the integration of an exceptional proportion of the population into the industrial workforce via mechanisation of agriculture; fifth, a sensible investment pattern, managing to achieve both high industrial growth and high agricultural output from a most unpromising start, agricultural success being the core of self-reliance; sixth, the contstruction of a minimally oil-dependent industrialised and mechanised economy.

Korean Actual Existing Socialism

The Party and the Great Leader

The 1972 Constitution claims (Articles 1, 5 and 6) that the DPRK is a socialist state, which has not yet achieved the 'complete' victory of socialism, but in which class antagonisms, exploitation and oppression – and therefore class struggle – have been *definitively and irreversibly* eliminated. The Constitution also gives a principled socialist description of who is really responsible for the country's achievements: 'The working masses are the makers of history. Socialism and communism are built by the creative labour of millions of working people' (Art. 27). But almost all official propaganda claims that the achievements of the Korean people are mainly, or even exclusively, due to one person, Kim Il Sung.

The political system is highly *dirigiste* in two ways: first, from the centre to the 'periphery', and second in terms of the role of Kim Il Sung, who is head of both Party and state apparatus. Cumings suggests that, 'if Mao's mass line reads "from the masses, to the masses", Kim's might be "to the masses, from the masses, to the masses."[56]

The Korean Workers' Party is a large party, with just over 3 million members, about one-third of the adult population. Almost the entire Party leadership is male, and it can safely be assumed that its membership is mostly male. The Party was expanded very fast immediately after Liberation and the criteria for membership were apparently very broad. In 1946, Kim said 'We think that anyone can be a member of the Workers' [i.e. Communist] Party, if he [sic] gives play to his patriotic zeal and initiative in the construction of the democratic fatherland and plays a leading role, even if he is not familiar with Marxism-Leninism.'[57] These loose criteria appear to have been maintained. During the Korean War, after the Party was deprived of many of its best cadres in the early months, it was brought back up to strength within one year. Contemporary propaganda seems to imply that everyone can become a 'communist' as the whole society is 'modelled after the *juche* idea', but the Party's success in achieving this political transformation is impossible to assess.

The main specific feature of DPRK politics is the role, real and/or alleged, of Kim Il Sung. Though the DPRK is not the only 'socialist' country to have had a cult of the personality, there are certain features specific to the Korean case. There are undoubtedly Korean traditions of male authoritarianism. The current dictator of South Korea, Chon Doo Hwan, is having himself called the 'wise and trusted helmsman' – not an appellation that could be used anywhere. The cult of Kim is distinctive for its sheer size and level of hyperbole. It is also centred more than usual on the leader personally and his family, both past, present and future. His mother is given special prominence and an ancestor is alleged to have led the resistance to the first US intrusion into Korea in the nineteenth century; uncles and others are also given prominent historical roles. Kim's son, Kim Jong Il, was, in effect, designated his successor at the sixth Congress and already holds several key positions in the KWP apparatus. Kim's birthplace, Mangyongdae, is by far the main icon now, outnumbering pictures of Kim by about 3:1 (almost everyone wears a small Kim badge).

The cult is also highly exclusive, involving a series of

interconnected eliminations. The history of the Korean revolutionary movement is heavily censored and falsified. Marxism-Leninism is given short shrift; Kim has stated that Marx, Lenin and Stalin were important thinkers in their day, but they do not have the answers to Korea's contemporary problems.[58] As a result, no one need read anything except Kim, and there are credible reports that it is a serious offence to read, for example, Engels's *Anti-Dühring*. The cult also eliminates the role of other people now: apart from anonymous texts, virtually every publication emanating from the DPRK is signed by Kim. Official propaganda tends to ignore not only the role of any Party or state body, but also any democratic process of decision-making, as well as the hard work and day-to-day initiatives of the Korean working masses. These exclusions go far beyond those prevalent in the USSR or China at the peak of the cults of Stalin and Mao.

Such practices are possible only because of the exceptional degree of isolation of the DPRK, compounded by exceptional (and unusually efficient) manipulation of information. The country is isolated geographically, having land and air links only with the USSR and China – hardly the most 'open' societies. It is also largely cut off from its own past, since the language reform after 1945 means that only the literate older generation can read most texts written before 1945 (using Chinese characters). DPRK citizens are not allowed to listen to foreign or ROK radio or television. A Japanese correspondent who visited Pyongyang for the world table-tennis championships in 1979 found the dials on the radios fixed immovably to the state stations.[59] The society is cut off from Marxism and Leninism, and even material from other post-revolutionary countries (for example, there are credible reports of penalties for reading Soviet material in Korean). News hardly exists: if a typhoon hits Vietnam, it only becomes news when President Kim sends a telegram of sympathy. Important events like the DPRK debt seem to be unknown to the mass of the population, who seem to have little idea whatsoever of the outside world, even visually.

Within this exceptional isolation, exceptional falsification is possible. As we have seen, this covers the history of the revolutionary movement, the role both of the Soviet Army in liberating Korea from the Japanese and the Chinese in saving the DPRK from the US in 1950; and the situation in the outside world, especially in South Korea. Citizens of the DPRK are regularly told that the population of the South is living in slums (in 1974, an official DPRK publication claimed that per capita income in the South was $50, the 'lowest in the world'[60]) and that it is eager to be admitted to the bosom of Kim Il Sung. The régime places advertisements in the foreign press extolling Kim; these are then reported in the DPRK press as 'straight' news. Kim is thus portrayed not only as the 'Great Leader' of the DPRK and a world-famous figure, but as *the leader of the entire world revolution*.

The negative effects of these practices are many. Apart from depriving the DPRK masses of the information they need to exercise their democratic rights in a principled manner, it means the population is appallingly misled about the DPRK's place in the world, and especially about the situation as regards support for the DPRK's revolution and its position on reunification (see below). Moreover, by centralising foreign 'communication' through the person of Kim, these practices *deprive* the Korean people of much international support which they and their struggle might otherwise receive.

Göran Therborn rightly states that as 'mechanisms of a kind of politico-ideological mobilization', 'cults' in non-capitalist societies differ from 'cults' in capitalist countries.[61] But they should be considered *particularly* offensive in societies which claim to base themselves on socialist principles, which give special place to *collective* action and democratic decision-making (not to mention important human qualities such as modesty and honesty). Sebastiano Timpanaro, writing on the cult of Mao in the late 1960s, noted that

its function . . . is not just one of reinforcing rational adhesion to a political line with 'emotive' elements. It is not just a question of a revolutionary content expressed in encomiastic form. When the form reaches certain levels of paroxysm, it ends up devouring the content![62]

Any complete study of the cult of Kim would require a detailed history of the *construction* of the cult. Contrary to what DPRK officials claim, it is not a 'natural' growth. It was *manufactured*, especially during the Korean War. It is integrally related to both low politicisation in the KWP (of which it is the other face) and to the need to construct myths and scapegoats to compensate for setbacks. Some features in Korean history do explain *some* aspects of the cult. The fragmentation of the revolutionary movement in the past helps account for centralisation; the imposition by outside powers of their policies and personnel helps account for nationalism. However, none of these explains, much less justifies, the present rampant phenomenon.

The régime's claim to be 'monolithic' is another way of saying that dogmatism prevails. However, as Henri Lefebvre has pointed out, dogmatism is not just an ideological phenomenon; it needs *police*.[63] There are many signs that the 'cult' is not only bureaucratic, not only expropriates the hard work and inventiveness of the masses, but is also highly repressive. The control and manipulation of information is itself a form of repression. Undoubtedly, monolithism has been a factor in the maintenance of a unified political line, which, unlike in China, has provided bureaucratic stability and assisted economic growth. On the other hand, both *juche* as an ideology and the present state of the economy demand more inputs than can be provided by one man. In fact, *juche* must in some way combine these two strands: releasing the creativity of the masses and ensuring tight control from on top. But it is not clear exactly how these two strands are combined.

A militarised society

The DPRK probably has more of its citizens under arms than any country in the world, except Israel. Not only is there the guerrilla background to some of the country's (now ageing) top leaders, but the war of 1950–3 and the uninterrupted confrontation with the heavily-armed South and with the US forces there has kept the North in a state of permanent militarisation.

In mid-1980 an official stated that the armed forces were 'about 350,000–400,000'.[64] This is much lower than the usual western estimates which range between something over 500,000[65] (up to late 1978, when U.S. estimates rose to 778,000 on extremely flimsy grounds). Perhaps about 7 per cent of the adult workforce is in the armed forces, and since the majority of the forces are male, perhaps 10 per cent of the male work force. Officially, there is no military service, but organisational and social pressures are of such intensity that conscription may not be necessary. The armed forces must be, along with the family and the educational system, a major instrument of socialisation, through which the vast majority of young people pass for periods of two to five years. On the other hand, life in the armed forces may not be particularly different from that in civil society, in which there is also a militia of perhaps 1–2 million people. In fact, the entire society is organised along lines which might seem quasi-military to outsiders. The armed forces also play a regular part in every sector of the non-military economy, being mobilised to bring in the harvest each year and work in industry and construction.

Repression and justice

The 1972 Constitution endorses the dictatorship of the proletariat and actions 'against the subversive activities of hostile elements at home and abroad' (Arts 10, 11). This is a standard formulation in any post-revolutionary state. But very little is known about how justice really works in the DPRK. The official position is that there is almost no crime, but the definition of 'crime' is not clear. Women reportedly account for 5–10 per cent of the prison population. One foreigner imprisoned in the DPRK put the total prison population around 1970 at about 150,000, which would be very high (about 4 per cent of the adult male population).[66]

Justice seems to rest on the proposition that social pressure should be the first instrument for controlling wayward behaviour. The society is so highly organised, with every single person, except for babies, enrolled in one or more organisations, that social control may be nearly water-tight. If the formal judicial system comes into action, justice is administered by a combination of professional judges (of whom the majority are women) and 'people's assessors', a kind of social worker from the community in which the accused lives or works. For those condemned to some sort of isolation, there is a system of 'education labour' as well as formal prisons (in which inmates also work full-time). Acknowledgement of guilt and repentance, as in China, seem to be considered essential elements in reform. The régime talks openly of 're-educating' and 'remoulding' people.

The régime boasts that the society is 'monolithic'. This could mean either that there is no disagreement, or that dissenters are harshly dealt with—or both. Given the extraordinary history of the DPRK, the socio-political changes of 1945–53 and the tightly meshed network of social control, the former may be somewhere near the truth. The division of the country and the constant threats from military attack and infiltration have contributed to creating a general attitude of conformity. However, past treatment of opponents offers little evidence of tolerance for alternative views, of whatever kind. In 1961 Kim told educational workers that satire was 'unfit' for the DPRK: 'For a nation with such a strong moral sense, influencing by positive examples is much more effective.'[67] Such remarks, taken together with the manifest absence of self-criticism on the part of Kim and the state apparatus, inspire little confidence that it is possible to question the régime's policies and practice, whether on principled grounds or not.

The position of women

Men have dominated Korean society for centuries, and still do. Apart from historical factors, there are several specific features which contribute to the continued oppression of women by men, in spite of the régime's claims that equality has been achieved (and, sometimes, that the 'women's question' has been entirely 'solved').[68] First, the high level of militarisation has reinforced male control. Second, rapid industrialisation, especially the growth of heavy industry, has meant more men in industry, proportionately, and more women in agriculture. Third, the fact that the South has twice the population of the North has led the régime to put pressure on women to have more than two children (after late marriage). With this goes a whole gamut of male-decided attitudes and laws, including strong hostility to abortion and birth control.

The régime will not reveal what proportion of Party members are women; there appear to be almost no women in senior Party positions, and the most important woman in the country is Kim Il Sung's wife, Kim Song Ae. The régime has developed a comprehensive system of social services, from kindergartens to home food ordering and delivery, in order to get more women into the workforce of which they now make up 48 per cent. Most work in the home is still presented as 'women's work',[69] and there is an unmistakeable emphasis in official culture on 'femininity' in everything from dress through attitudes towards smoking and drinking. Undoubtedly, there have been real advances in the position of women, but the overall picture is one of a thoroughly male-dominated society, in which official complacency leaves little room for a principled stand by either women or men against continued male dominance.

At the sixth Party Congress, Kim Il Sung devoted exactly fourteen lines to the position of women in a five-hour speech. Moreover, this passage made no mention of the enormous under-representation of women in the Party (manifest in photographs of the Party Congress where, one foreign observer estimated, women made up less than 10 per cent and probably nearer 5 per cent of the delegates); and Kim mentioned the subject only as part of the 'technical' revolution ('freeing women from heavy burdens of household chores'). In 1971 Kim told the Korean Democratic Women's Union:

'We have a very small number of women cadres today ... the overwhelming majority of them [cadres] are men. ... And even this small number of women cadres are working mostly in the fields of secondary importance. ... If the working women account for one half of the total working population the women cadres should naturally make up one half of the total number of cadres.'

There is no sign that this situation has changed, basically – and yet Kim did not seem to feel obliged to comment on it at the Party Congress. The situation appears to be one where the regime has proclaimed that women are now 'equal' and all discussion is terminated, in the face of manifest inequality.

Conclusion: The Best and The Bleakest?

A Japanese economist has estimated that between 1946 and 1974 real per capita income in the DPRK rose twenty times.[70] Behind the barrage of depressing propaganda lies a remarkable achievement – an achievement of the Korean people. Because the régime systematically indulges in political distortion, one is led to doubt its economic claims too. Yet no one who has been in the DPRK can fail to be impressed by the economic achievements, making every allowance for selected tours and Potemkin villages.

The combination of exceptional social homogeneity and a divided country has produced an extraordinary level of mass mobilisation. The siege mentality of the government undoubtedly contributes to this. Yet one senses in the DPRK a level of commitment and participation which transcends mere 'top-down' organisation. The society has moved mountains. Paradoxically, if, as Oguri Keitaro suggests, the isolation plus economic advance has actually convinced many people that they really are living in a paradise, then *demobilisation* may soon be on the cards.[71]

The Korean revolution is a real revolution – a massive transformation of the entire society, with extraordinary material advance. Yet, there is an element of tragedy involved, too. This nation fought heroically against US imperialism and has accomplished great deeds. Yet, it is isolated from the sympathy and understanding of much of the world. This society, which has struggled hard to build a better world, deserves our understanding. But, as Isaac Deutscher wrote, 'Solidarity ... does not in any way demand that [the] truth be concealed.'[72]

The truth is, in this case, unpleasant. Kim Il Sung is a redoubtable figure who has played a major role in the Korean revolution. But he is crucial to *both* its failure *and* its success. His leadership has helped bring the DPRK to where it now is, but it has also isolated this revolution from world sympathy. By his grotesque expropriation of the toil of the Korean masses for his own glory, Kim has deprived them of the international solidarity they so richly deserve.

At the sixth Congress in 1980, Kim called on the Party to move ahead into a high technology future. Among other things, he called for work on genetic engineering. But by installing his son, Kim Jong Il, as his successor, he also tried to foist genetic socialism on the Party. I once asked a Peruvian writer and militant who visited the DPRK many times, wrote a laudatory book about it, talked at length with Kim several times and played an active part in the 100 per cent solidarity movement, why he did it. He answered: 'They fought the North Americans; they have done incredible things in the economy; it's the only Third World country where everyone has good health, good education and good housing.' So I asked him what he really thought about it. His reply: 'It is the saddest, most miserable country I've ever been in in my life. As a poet, it strikes bleakness into my heart.'[73]

Notes

1 I would like to thank Perry Anderson, Fred Halliday, Robin Murray and Gordon White for comments on an earlier draft; and Bruce Cumings, Aidan Foster-Carter, John Gittings, Gavan McCormack and Suzanne Paine for input on a related paper and many of the issues discussed here. © Jon Halliday, 1981. This is a revised version of an article in *New Left Review*, no. 127 (1981).

2 Shannon McCune, *Korea's Heritage: A Regional and Social Geography*, Vermont, Tuttle, 1956. These ratios have remained the same.

3 Robert Ante, 'The transformation of the economic geography of the DPRK', *Korea Focus* New York I, 3, (n.d. [1972]), p. 36; cf. Chul Won Kang, 'An analysis of Japanese policy and economic change in Korea', in Andrew C. Nahm (ed.), *Korea Under Japanese Colonial Rule: Studies of the Policy and Techniques of Japanese Colonialism*, Center for Korean Studies, Western Michigan University, 1973, p. 84; and Kwan Suk Kim, 'An analysis of economic change in Korea,' ibid., p. 103. An outstanding new source on the colonial period and the early postwar years in Bruce Cumings, *The Origins of the Korean War: Liberation and the Emergence of Separate Regimes 1945–1947*, Princeton, Princeton University Press, 1981; this work integrates and supersedes much of the earlier literature on many issues discussed below.

4 Takashi Hatada, *A History of Korea* Santa Barbara, ABC–Clio, 1969, p. 125.

5 Hatada, ibid., pp. 122–3, 119; a useful synopsis is also to be found in the basic book on the DPRK economy, Joseph Sang-hoon Chung, *The North Korean Economy: Structure and Development* Stanford, Hoover Institution Press, 1974, pp. 57–9.

6 McCune, *op. cit.*, p. 109; Kwan Suk Kim, *op. cit.*, p. 111; Ante, *op. cit.*

7 Hatada, *op. cit.*, pp. 116ff; cf. Shiota Shobei, 'A "ravaged" people: The Koreans in World War II', *The Japan Interpreter*, Tokyo, 7, 1, 1971.

8 According to Ante (*op. cit.*, p. 36) Japanese owned 80 per cent of the forests (which covered three-quarters of the country) and 25 per cent of the arable land; *The Historical Experience of the Agrarian Reform in Our Country* Pyongyang, Foreign Languages Publishing House (henceforth: FLPH), 1974, pp. 7ff; Ellen Brun and Jacques Hersh, *Socialist Korea: A Case Study in the Strategy of Economic Development*, Monthly Review Press, 1976, pp. 43ff.

9 Hatada, p. 126.

10 McCune, *op. cit.*, p. 84; cf. Hatada, *op. cit.*, p. 130; the urban population had been only 4.4 per cent in 1925 (Ante, *op. cit.*, p. 55).

11 Compiled from information in Kang, *op. cit.*, p. 84; cf. McCune, p. 225, for breakdown by branches of industry and size of factory. I have not attempted discussion of growth rates for GNP and per capita income, partly because these lie outside the focus of the article, partly because gross statistics are misleading, as the data in the text (I hope) show, both because of the privileged position of the Japanese and because of the level of extortion from the Korean workforce, as well as because of outright falsification and inaccuracies.

12 Unforgettable material in Nym Wales (Helen Foster Snow) and Kim San, *Song of Ariran: A Korean Communist in the Chinese Revolution* San Francisco, Ramparts Press, re-issue of 1941 original, n.d. [1973?]; This is one of the great books about revolutionary struggle; significantly, it is completely dismissed by the DPRK. For an excellent assessment of it, see the review by Bruce Cumings in Bulletin of Concerned Asian Scholars (henceforth *BCAS*), 6, 3, 1974; see also Dae-Sook Suh, *The Korean Communist Movement 1918–1948*, Princeton, 1967.

13 Hatada, *op. cit.*, pp. 124ff; Kim, *op. cit.*, Ronald Toby, 'Education in Korea under the Japanese: attitudes and manifestations', in James B. Palais (ed.), *Occasional Papers on Korea*, no. 1, rev. edn, 1974. Older Koreans have told the author they feel physically sick when they have to speak Japanese now.

14 Ante, *op. cit.*, pp. 55–6; cf. Shiota, *op. cit.*; and Hatada, p. 126; useful information also in Chong-sik Lee, *The Korean Workers' Party: A Short History*, Stanford, Hoover Institution Press, 1978, pp. 53ff.

15 Saburo Ienaga, *The Pacific War: World War II and the Japanese, 1931–1945*, New York, Pantheon, 1978, p. 159; cf. p. 184.

16 This is conclusively demonstrated in Suh, *op. cit.*, pp. 198, 137, 132, which also shows that the communist movement was not isolated from the mainstream of nationalism, but the key part of the movement and *contiguous* to the old Nationalist movement; Suh's book is basically unsympathetic to the communist movement, though well-documented: I have given my criticisms of it in 'The Korean Communist Movement', *BCAS*, 2, 4, Fall 1970.

17 See Suh for a useful account; cf. E. H. Carr, *The Bolshevik Revolution 1917–1923*, Pelican, 1966, vol. 3, pp. 488–9; information below from Wales and Kim, *Song of Ariran*.

18 Among the many heroic Koreans involved was a woman general, Yi Hong-kwang (Suh, p. 284). She, along with countless other militants, has now been expunged from the official history, as has Korean participation

in the Canton Commune. When I raised this in Pyongyang in July 1977, I was told that these events were 'not part of the Korean Revolution'.

19 Some official DPRK texts do not even mention that the Soviet Army was in Korea, much less the role it played. Conversely, Soviet sources virtually ignore Korean participation; a standard Soviet work such as *Finale: A Retrospective Review of Imperialist Japan's Defeat in 1945*, Moscow, Progress Publishers, 1972, does not mention either Korean guerrillas or Kim Il-Sung once.

20 Estimated at 'almost one-quarter' of budget revenue in the pre-Korean War years (from all sources, but mainly Soviet) by Rinn-Sup Shinn *et al.*, *Area Handbook for North Korea*, (Washington, DC, 1969), p. 389; I have also discussed the controversial role of aid in 'The North Korean model: gaps and questions', *World Development*, vol. 9, no. 9/10 (1981).

21 'On the work of the organizations at all levels of the Communist Party of North Korea', *Selected Works*, Pyongyang, EPLH, I.

22 Full texts are available in *On the Socialist Constitution of the Democratic People's Republic of Korea*, Pyongyang, FPLH, 1975, pp. 304ff.

23 J.S-h.Chung, pp. 5–10; *The Historical Experience of the Agrarian Reform. . .*; Brun and Hersh, 128ff.

24 *Socialist Transformation of Private Trade and Industry in Korea*, Pyongyang, FPLH, 1977, pp. 19, 21.

25 Chin-Wu Kim, 'Linguistics and language policy in North Korea', *Korean Studies*, vol. 2, Hawaii, 1980, p. 166, from DPRK source.

26 Robert A. Scalapino and Chong-sik Lee, *Communism in Korea*, University of California Press, 1972, part I, p. 416.

27 On both the liberation of the South and the occupation of the North, see my essay, 'The Korean War: Some notes on evidence and solidarity,' *BCAS*, XI, 3, 1979. Sources and argumentation for controversial issues discussed below are provided in this article.

28 Scalapino and Lee, pp. 427ff; cf. Suh, p. 261, who notes that the first official publication on Kim dates from the same month, April 1952.

29 Harrison E. Salisbury, *To Peking – and Beyond: A Report on the New Asia*, New York, Quadrangle, 1973, p. 199; Dumont, *The Hungry Future* London, Deutsch, 1969, p. 137, cited in Aidan Foster-Carter, 'North Korea: development and self-reliance: a critical appraisal', in Gavan McCormack and Mark Selden (eds), *Korea North and South: The Deepening Crisis*, Monthly Review Press, 1978, p. 124; Joan Robinson, 'Korean miracle', *Monthly Review*, January 1965.

30 1946 and 1965, from Chung, *op. cit.*, pp. 146–8; 1970 figure from G.V. Gryaznov, *Stroitel'stvo material'no-tekhnicheskoy bazi sotsializma v KNDR* [The Construction of the material-technical base of socialism in the DPRK] Moscow, Nauka, 1979, p. 190; cf. Jun Nishikawa, 'El desarrollo económico de Corea del Norte', *Estudios de Asia y Africa*, Mexico City, vol. 12, no. 2, 1977, p. 243.

31 Nishikawa, ibid., p. 243, for 1975; 1953 and 1965 from Chong-sik Lee, 'Social changes in North Korea: a preliminary assessment', *Journal of Korean Affairs*, vol. 6, no. 1, 1976, p. 18.

32 Kim Il Sung (to a visitor from Benin), *Pyongyang Times* (henceforth: *PT*), 4 August 1979; cf. *Our Party's Policy for the Building of an Indepen-*

dent National Economy, Pyongyang, FPLH, 1975, which is an excellent basic source.

33   Earlier figures discussed in detail in Chung, and Foster-Carter; later figures from Kim's report to the Sixth Congress, *PT*, 11 October 1980. Agricultural figures below are from the same sources.

34   US, CIA, National Foreign Assessment Center, *Korea: The Economic Race Between the North and the South*, January 1978, p. 2.

35   *Far Eastern Economic Review*, Hong Kong, p. 173.

36   Gordon White, 'North Korean *Chuch'e*: the political economy of independence', *BCAS*, April–June 1975, p. 49; cf. Shannon McCune, *Korea's Heritage*. p. 101, and Appendix F; Ante, *op. cit.*

37   *Our Party's Policy for the Building of an Independent National Economy*, pp. 3–4. Two clarifications on *juche*: first, contrary to what Chung (p. 143) and others have suggested, the strategy does not call for 'self-sufficiency' (autarky): this is explicitly rejected in *Our Party's Policy*, p. 10; the real goal is autarchy – i.e. all-round independence. Second, contrary to the claims of Korean propaganda and foreign sycophants, Kim Il Sung did not 'invent' *juche*, as he himself acknowledged in an interview with the *Mainichi Shimbun* (17 September 1972), in Kim Il Sung, *Answers to the Questions Put by Foreign Journalists*, Pyongyang, FPLH, 1974.

38   In 1980 the régime claimed 75 per cent self-sufficiency, *PT*, 9 August 1980.

39   In my view, this 5 per cent estimate is too low; the size of the armed forces plus the level of mechanisation in agriculture alone would suggest at least 10 per cent. See *North Korea Quarterly*, VI, 3/4, Hamburg, pp. 27ff, for a good survey of the oil situation.

40   *Asia 1981 Yearbook*, p. 10.

41   *Asia and Pacific Annual Review*, 1980, Saffron Walden, p. 56, from World Bank sources. However, energy use is probably also very wasteful.

42   Donald S. Zagoria, 'Korea's future: Moscow's perspective', *Asian Survey*, vol. 17, no. 11, November 1977, p. 1106; on military levels, cf. Stuart E. Johnson with Joseph A. Yager, *The Military Equation in Northeast Asia*, Washington, DC, The Brookings Institution, 1979.

43   Salisbury, *To Peking – and Beyond*, p. 197.

44   CIA, *Korea, op. cit.*, p. 7, give 25–35 per cent; cf. Nishikawa, *op. cit.*

45   Chung, *op. cit.*, pp. 41, 73.

46   The state buys rice at 62 *jon* per kilo, and sells it at 8 *jon* (100 *jon* = 1 *won*).

47   Atsushi Motohashi, 'Comparison of the socialist economies in China and Korea', *The Developing Economies*, vol. 5, no. 1 Tokyo, 1967, p. 78.

48   'American experts', cited by Philippe Pons, *Le Monde*, 18 February 1981, for the $1300 figure; *Asia 1981 Yearbook*, p. 173, for the $950 figure. The most detailed attempt to work out a comparison between North and South is that by Gerhard Breidenstein, 'Economic comparison of North and South Korea', *Journal of Contemporary Asia*, vol. V, no. 2, 1975.

49   *To Peking – and Beyond*, p. 205.

50   On DPRK – Comecon relations, see George Ginsburg, 'North Korea and partners practise regional self-reliance', *Pacific Community*, vol. 8, no. 1, Tokyo, October 1976; chs 4 (by Horst Brezinski) and 5 (Rainer Wiechert), in Youn-Soo Kim (ed.), *The Economy of the Korean Democratic People's Republic 1945–1977: Economic Policy and Foreign Trade*

Relations with Europe, Kiel, German–Korea Studies Group, 1979; Robert Owen Freedman, *Economic Warfare in the Communist Bloc*, New York, Praeger, 1971, pp. 141–9; Gordon White, *op. cit.*, pp. 47–9.

51 Since the DPRK currency, the *won*, is not convertible, there could be a form of 'devaluation' through price adjustments, but there is no sign of this.

52 Pyongyang cut its total trade with the OECD in half in two years in the mid-1970s, which (i) demonstrated discipline, and (ii) was exactly what the capitalist countries did not want. Any attempt to set DPRK actions in perspective cannot ignore verified tales of appalling mismanagement and waste by the Korean authorities.

53 The US CIA appear to accept an average industrial growth rate of 14 per cent from 1965–76 (with fluctuations); while they signal a slowdown in agriculture in the early 1970s, they do not identify any such slowdown in industry in the 1970s.

54 See White, *op. cit.*, for citations on this.

55 Official DPRK explanations for the debt were that the world recession led to a decline in demand for Korean exports, but Pyongyang did not want to cut back on planned imports and thus slow domestic growth; and that shipping chartered for expanded trade proved expensive (for example, Kim Il Sung, interview with Oda Makoto, *Mainichi Shimbun*, 27 November 1976). Much DPRK trade was done in sterling, which fell badly; prices for raw material exports also fell steeply (see Ellen Brun and Jacques Hersh, 'North Korea: default of a model or a model in default?', *Monthly Review*, vol. 29, no. 9, February 1978; cf. Foster-Carter, *op. cit.*, Appendix A).

56 Bruce G. Cumings, 'Kim's Korean Communism', *Problems of Communism*, March–April 1974, p. 33; this article is still the best single overview of the DPRK.

57 Baik Bong, *Kim Il Sung: Biography*, Tokyo, Miraisha, 1976, vol. 2. p. 154, cited by Cumings, *op cit.* 40.

58 See Kim's talk with the Department of Science and Education of the CC of the KWP, 30 December 1963, in Kim, *On Juche in Our Revolution*, vol. I. Pyongyang, FLPH, 1975, pp. 378–80.

59 Oguri Keitaro, 'Naked face of North Korea', *The Korea–Scope*, June–July 1979.

60 *Korean Review*, Pyongyang, FLPH, 1974, p. 149.

61 Göran Therborn, *What Does the Ruling Class Do When It Rules?* London, NLB, 1980, p. 120.

62 Sebastiano Timpanaro, 'Intervento su "Il materialismo e la rivoluzione culturale cinese"', *Nuovo Impegno*, Pisa, nos 9–10 August 1967–January 1968), p. 61.

63 Henri Lefebvre, 'Marxism exploded', *Review*, IV, 1, Summer 1980, p. 20.

64 Information given to Gavan McCormack, May 1980, who kindly made it available to the author.

65 See Johnson and Yager, *op. cit;* Kiwon Chung, 'The North Korean People's Army and the Party', *China Quarterly*, no. 14, 1963; Scalapino and Lee, *op. cit.*, part II, ch. 12; *Far Eastern Economic Review*, 5 March, 1982. Military expenditures are estimated to have fluctuated between about 15 and 30 per cent of the budget.

66 Author's interview, Pyongyang, July 1977. The prison population estimate is given in Ali Lameda, *A Personal Account of the Experience of a Prisoner of Conscience in the Democratic People's Republic of Korea*, London, Amnesty International, 1979, p. 19, but is an extrapolation based partly on second-hand information.

67 'On the duties of Educational Workers in the Upbringing of the Children and Youth', 25 April 1961, Pyongyang: FLPH 1970, pp. 20–21.

68 See, for example, *PT*, 15 March 1980, p. 1. Most texts on the 'women's question' are by a man, Kim Il Sung; most of the rest are by his wife.

69 The drive to provide better social services, more refrigerators, etc., aims to 'free women from the burden of housework' – i.e. women do the bulk of this work; but it is not suggested that men should do more. The Korean Democratic Women's Union (KDWU) is officially described as a 'transmission belt' for the KWP (see, e.g. Kim Il Sung, 'On the Revolutionisation and Working-classisation of Women', speech to Fourth Congress of the KDWU, 7 October 1971, Pyongyang, FLPH, 1974, p. 29).

70 Nishikawa, p. 239.

71 Oguri, *op. cit.*, p. 15.

72 Deutscher, '22 June 1941', *New Left Review*, 124, p. 88. The DPRK completely rejects critical solidarity. It thus ends up with almost no active solidarity except that of discredited sycophants.

73 The late Genaro Carnero Checa; his book, *Korea: Rice and Steel*, Pyongyang, FLPH, 1977, was put out by the DPRK in many languages. He also told me that when he had asked how the DPRK managed to produce enough propaganda about Kim to flood the remotest corner of the world he was taken to a city whose entire economy was devoted to the manufacture of official hagiography.

North Korea: Country Profile

(*indicates officially released figures)

Official name:	Democratic People's Republic of Korea, established on 9 September 1948.
Population:	Almost 18 million* (mid-year 1980).
Capital:	Pyongyang, c.1,250,000–2,500,000 (estimates vary greatly).
Land area:	121,200 sq km, of which forest 75 per cent, arable land 17 per cent.
Official language:	Korean.
Membership of international organisations:	Observer in the UN since 1972; Selective participant in CMEA.
Political Structure	
Constitution:	27 December 1972 (supersedes that of 1948 as amended in 1954 and 1955).

Highest legislative body:	Supreme People's Assembly, with 572 members on a 4-year term.
Highest executive body:	Administrative Council, as of 1980.
Head of state:	President Kim Il Sung, assumed office in 1972.
Prime Minister:	Li Jong Ok, assumed office in 1977.
Ruling Party:	The Korean Workers' Party, established in October 1945.
General Secretary of the Party:	Kim Il Sung (primary Party leader since 1945), assumed this office in 1966.
Party membership:	Just over 3 million, or about one-third of the adult population (according to Soviet source V. Moiseyev and N. Shubnikov, 'Sixth Congress of the Workers' Party of Korea: Results and Perspectives', *Far Eastern Affairs*, no. 2, 1981, p. 39).
Armed forces:	350–400,000 (official source); western estimates around 778,000 or about 12 per cent of the total labour force.

Population
Population density:	148 per sq km.
Population growth (% p.a.):	No official figures; possibly 2–2.6 and declining around 1970–75[e1].
Population of working age (15–64, %):	56(1978).
Urban population (%):	65–70 (1975).[II]
Ethnic groups:	The population is homogeneous, with ethnic Koreans making up 99 per cent.

Education and health
School system:	Universal education for 11 years, including one pre-school year.
Primary school enrolment (gross ratios, %):	Both sexes 113, females 112.
Adult literacy:	100 (official claim; a close to 100 per cent figure is generally accepted in the West).
Life expectancy:	73* (1980)[d]; 63 (1978).[18] (Official DPRK figures: f:76; m:70.
Child death rate (per 1000):	5 (1977).
Population per physician:	429* (1980).

Economy
GNP/national income:	US$ 34 billion (national income 1979, implied from official per capita below); a low western estimate: US$ 14 billion (1979).[1]

GNP/national income per capita:	US$ 1920* (1979), (national income),[III] western estimates range from US$ 750[i] for 1976 to 1300.
State budget (expenditure):	18.8 billion *won** (1980)[h IV].
Defence expenditure as % of state budget:	14.6* (1980)[h].
National income by sector (%):	Agriculture 20, industry 65, construction, transport and trade 15 (1970)[c].
Total labour force by sector:	c.6.5 million: tertiary sector (military, administration and services) probably c.30 per cent, agriculture considerably less than half the labour force.[V] The division between agriculture and industry is somewhat imprecise since there are many rural-industrial areas and urban population and military help seasonally with the rice harvest.
Structure of ownership:	*Industry* (per cent of gross industrial product): state owned 91.2, co-operatives 8.2 (1963)[a]. *Agriculture* (per cent of agricultural land): state farms 8, collective farms (including members' private plots) 92 (1963).[a]
Main crops:	Rice, maize, vegetables.
Irrigated area:	'Nationwide' irrigation claimed officially. FAO (6) gives 1 million ha, which is 45 per cent of arable land and more than total area under rice (1978).
Food self-sufficiency:	100 per cent (official claims); disputed to some extent in the West. Source[g] states imports of wheat to be 450,000 tons in excess of rice exports 1972–6. Food exports also include sizeable amounts of vegetables and other products.
Energy balance – Commercial consumption:	(1976).
per capita:	3072 kg coal equivalent.
by type of energy (%):	Oil 5–10, hydroelectric 15–20, coal 70–80[V].
Growth indicators (% pa):	(1970–9).
GNP:	6.7.[6]
Industry:	15.9*[d VI].
Agriculture (grains):	6.8*[j].
Food production per capita:	3.3[6].
Trade and economic integration	
Main exports:	Iron, steel and other metals; magnesite, food products (vegetables, rice).

	Manufactured products probably over half of total.
Main imports:	Industrial machinery, petroleum, grain (wheat).
Main trading partners:	The USSR, Japan, China (c. 17 per cent of total foreign trade is with China).
Debt service ratio:	Estimate for 1981–5; 30–5 per cent[b] (hard currency debt only).

Notes

[I]The World Bank[18] gives 2.6 for 1970–8.

[II]See text.

[III]Given in US$ in source.

[IV]There is no generally agreed exchange rate for the DPRK won. Rates since 1978 quoted in western sources vary from 0.8–2.6 *won* to US $1. For 'purchasing power parity' (PPP) the rate 1.66 *won* is accepted by some scholars, but is based on estimates for early 1960s.

[V]Author's estimates.

[VI]Some earlier official claims appear to be (vaguely) accepted by the US CIA, for example in [i].

Sources

[a]Chung, Joseph Sang-hoon, *The North Korean Economy: Structure and Development*, Stanford, California, 1974.

[b]*Far Eastern Economic Review*, 26 June 1981.

[c]Gryaznov, G. V., *Stroitel'stvo material' no-tekhnicheskoy bazi sotsializma v. KNDR* (The construction of the material-technical base of socialism in the DPRK), Moscow, Nauka, 1979.

[d]Kim Il Sung 'Report on the work of the KWP Central Committee at the Sixth Congress of the KWP', 10 October 1980. BBC, Summary of World Broadcasts, the Far East (daily), 13 October 1980.

[e]Lee, Chong-Sik, 'Social changes in North Korea', *Journal of Korean Affairs*, vol. 6 no. 1, 1976.

[f]*North Korea Quarterly*, Hamburg, various issues.

[g]Palacpac, Adelita C., *World Rice Statistics*, International Rice Research Institute, Los Baños, 1980.

[h]*Pyongyang Times*, 11 April 1981.

[i]US, CIA, *Korea: The Economic Race between the North and the South*, Washington DC, January 1978.

[j]Li Jong Ok on National Economy at the Sixth Congress of the KWP, 12 October 1980. BBC, Summary of World Broadcasts, the Far East (daily), 18 October 1980.

North Korea: Chronology

1910	Formal seizure of Korea by Japan.
1910-	Large-scale emigration of Koreans to China, USSR, Japan.

1919	1 March, uprising in Korea against Japanese rule.
1930s	First Korean guerrilla actions against Japanese in north-east China.
1945	15 August, Japan surrenders; Korea divided at 38th Parallel; August–September, People's Committees established nationwide.
	10 October, official founding of Communist Party (later titled Korean Workers' Party, KWP).
	October (end), Five Provinces Administrative Bureau set up in Pyongyang (embryonic government for northern half of Korea).
1946	March, First Land Reform; March–August, Reforms of Industry, Trade, etc. Law on Equality of Sexes.
1948	April, Haeju Conference (attempt to prevent US-UN division of Korea); May, separate UN-imposed elections in South Korea; August, Republic of Korea established based on Seoul (ROK); 9 September DPRK established, based on Pyongyang, recognises Seoul as national capital;
	end, Soviet troops withdraw from DPRK.
1948–50	Extensive guerrilla war in the South; heavy fighting along 38th Parallel.
1950	25 June, civil war erupts; June–September, 90 per cent of South incorporated into DPRK; October (end), Chinese troops enter Korea; October–December, 90 per cent of DPRK occupied by US-UN-ROK troops.
1953	July, Armistice signed by US, DPRK and China; August, trial and execution of many leading southern communists in Pyongyang.
1953–8	Co-operativisation (collectivisation) of agriculture.
1958	Last Chinese troops withdraw from Korea.
1961	July, treaties with USSR and China.
1963	Public attacks on Soviet Union and policy towards DPRK.
1966	Last agricultural tax abolished.
1968	US ship *Pueblo* seized.
1972	4 July, North-South Joint Communiqué on Reunification; top-level North-South talks (for first time).
	27 December, New Constitution making Pyongyang the capital of DPRK.
1973	Start of 'Three Revolutions' campaign (Technological [or Technical], Ideological and Cultural).
1974	1 April, last tax formally abolished.
1975	Kim Il Sung visits China during collapse of Saigon (April).
1975	DPRK admitted as full member to Non-Aligned Movement (Seoul application rejected).
1980	October, Sixth Congress of Workers' Party; public installation of Kim Il Sung's son, Kim Jong Il (age c. 40), as successor.

CHINESE DEVELOPMENT STRATEGY AFTER MAO

Gordon White

In the Cultural Revolution decade (1966–76), Chinese development experience was the object of widespread admiration in the West and the Third World from a large number of observers covering a wide political spectrum. For socialists – revolutionary, radical or reforming – the 'Maoist' experiment represented a serious attempt to break with eastern European paradigms of state socialism, whether of the Soviet type of hierarchical bureaucratism, or the Yugoslav type of 'market socialism', and to establish a new pattern for the 'transition to socialism' based on original socialist values of equality, participation and collectivism.[1] In the world of 'development studies', the dominant paradigms shifted in the early 1970s: from an emphasis on growth, to considerations of distribution and participation, from assumptions about the positive impact of international integration and interdependence, to the bleak world of 'dependency' theory and corresponding interest in auto-centric development. In such an intellectual climate, Chinese experiments in mass mobilisation, debureaucratisation, educational redistribution, appropriate technology and local or national 'self-reliance' struck responsive chords. The 'Chinese model' was widely cited by development theorists and practitioners alike, as suitable for emulation and transfer to other Third World countries.[2]

However, after the death of Mao Tse-Tung and the *putsch* against the leftist 'Gang of Four' in late 1976, previous policies were repudiated in China in terms so thoroughgoing and vitriolic that they echoed the most strident critics of Maoism in both West and East before 1976. During the late 1970s, a new development strategy emerged under a re-organised leadership which embodied changes so farreaching that they seemed to vindicate the 'two-line struggle' depicted

155

by radical Maoist ideologues. These events pose two sets of crucial questions which I shall address in this article. First, what happened to 'Maoism' and the 'Chinese model'? Why was it repudiated apparently so decisively by a significant section of the Chinese party and people? Did radical Maoism fail mainly because of its inherent weaknesses or the strength of its opponents? Second, what is the sociopolitical basis and policy content of the new course, and how coherent is it as a development strategy? Is it rooted in the ideological and institutional legacy of Mao's era, or has there been a decisive break? How effective has it proved (as of mid-1981) as a spur for China's socialist development and how stable will it be through the 1980s? Hopefully, answers to these questions may prove instructive for socialists involved in the theory and practice of 'undeveloped socialism', and more widely to development theorists and practitioners puzzled by the sudden end of the Maoist experiment.*

The Nature of the 'Maoist Model'

It is important to begin by clarifying the precise nature of the 'Maoist' paradigm of socialist development. It is my thesis that there are *two major streams* of Maoist thought and action which have different historical roots, theoretical assumptions and practical consequences. Though these two streams have much common ground, they can be (and indeed have been) translated into *alternative* programmes of development appealing to different sets of political actors.[3]

The first form, which I call *developmental Maoism*, emerged during the mid-1950s in response to perceived deficiencies in the Soviet model applied during the first five-year plan (1953–7). Some of its basic ideas appeared in Mao's speech 'On the Ten Great Relationships' in April 1956[4] and, after a period of theoretical and practical elaboration, found vivid

*This is inevitably a preliminary analysis; systematic answers are as yet difficult to develop given the flux in policy and politics during the post-Mao years and the fact that the quality of information from China is still distorted by the Manichean requirements of political struggle, producing black and white pictures of 'before and after', which make scientific analysis very difficult.

expression in the Great Leap Forward of 1958–9. The distinctive elements of this new approach to socialist development have been widely discussed, most systematically by Jack Gray.[5] Mao emphasised the need to revise planning priorities and direct greater state attention to encouraging agriculture and light industry where capital-output ratios are lower and economic returns quicker. These sectors in turn would generate funds which could be ploughed back into heavy industry. By following this sequence, investible surplus could be enticed out of the population in a context of rising incomes and growing consumption, not directly appropriated in conditions of strictly imposed austerity. This position resembles Bukharin's arguments in the Soviet industrialisation debate of the mid-1920s and, as Mao himself pointed out, contrasted sharply with Stalin's strategy of 'draining the pond to catch the fish'. In spite of these ideological echoes, however, the innovative elements in Mao's strategy derive from his experience in Yenan during the war against Japan, and his analysis of the distortions caused by the adoption of an alien model of economic development and institutional transformation in the early 1950s which was ill-attuned to Chinese realities. These influences also led Mao to emphasise the need to 'walk on two legs' towards industrialisation, using intermediate and 'native' as well as advanced foreign technology, and encouraging accumulation in local collectives as well as in the state sector. The principle of local initiative in industrialisation reflected a wider emphasis on decentralisation to local units (in Schurmann's terms, 'decentralisation II')[6] within and outside the state sector, with the slogan of local 'self-reliance' and the principle that 'two enthusiasms are better than one'. The notion of 'self-reliance' also applied to international politico-economic relations; as Mao himself remarked in 1962, 'from 1958 on, we decided to make self-reliance our major policy and striving for foreign assistance a secondary aim'. Development was henceforth to be based overwhelmingly on the mobilisation of domestic resources.

While Mao's ideas of sectoral priorities, technology choice and local accumulation have a conventional ring to them and can easily be accommodated within the framework of western development economics, his approach to development as a social process was distinctive. Development was to be generated through popular mobilisation and intense politicisation, a strategy reflecting Mao's confidence in the tremendous potential of the *masses* working within *collective* institutions under the leadership of a *revolutionary party*. But this was revolution in a special sense, the 'uninterrupted revolution' (*buduan geming*), characterised by qualitative leaps in the development of the productive forces, social relations of production and political superstructure but lacking the core element of previous revolutionary movements – class struggle.[7] Yet Mao emphasised (far more than Stalin) the need to recognise the continued existence of social and political conflicts, 'non-antagonistic contradictions', during the period of socialist construction.

During the early and mid-1960s, however, Mao gradually developed a new paradigm of socialist development, which I call *radical Maoism*. Though more broad-ranging and critical than its predecessor, one cannot argue that it was more developed theoretically. Indeed, the analytical quality of Mao's pronouncements in the 1960s lacked the clarity and order of his earlier thinking. His contribution to the elaboration of radical Maoism came in discursive speeches and brief Delphic 'highest directives'. Indeed, already in his seventies, Mao was no longer the dynamic traveller and intervener of the 1950s, and was losing touch with the increasingly kaleidoscopic realities of the early 1960s, thus breaking his own rules about the primacy of 'social practice' as the origin of 'correct ideas'. To the extent that radical Maoism was fleshed out into a coherent body of thought, this was done by other ideologues and politicians, most notably Zhang Chunqiao, Chen Boda, Lin Biao and small groups of radical intellectuals in various areas and institutions.[8]

From the perspective of many Marxist analysts, the radical Maoist paradigm was *theoretically* distinctive in its reevaluation of 'the transition to socialism', the historical period of indeterminate length and character which leads from the initial period of revolutionary transformation to the ultimate phase of 'communist society'. According to radical Maoists, 'socialist' society contains attitudes and material conditions, deriving not only from pre-revolutionary days but also from the new social formation itself, which obstruct genuine socialist transition and threaten a 'reversion to capitalism'. Thus the transition to socialism is not a smooth and stable process based on gradual development of the productive forces, but uneven and riven by deep conflicts. Institutions and people must continually be transformed alongside processes of economic growth and technical modernisation: otherwise 'while the satellite goes up to the sky the red flag falls to the ground'. The future of socialism – particularly the goals of classlessness, altruism, collectivism, egalitarianism and mass participation – must be secured in the present through political struggle. This struggle is to be conducted under the banner of 'the continuation of class struggle in socialist society' in a process of 'continuing re-volution' *(jixu geming)*. Its primary targets are 'those in authority taking the capitalist road' in the Party-state machine, and 'new bourgeois elements' emerging throughout society. The key source of class formation are the élites created by the new statist political economy, politico-administrative cadres on the one hand, and the intelligentsia on the other. Their power and privileges are to be weakened, their processes of reproduction and aggrandisement impeded, and an effective counterweight created by mobilising the 'masses' under the banner of the 'mass line'. The relationship between capitalism and socialism is defined in zero-sum terms: at the motivational level, there is a struggle between the self and the collective, apathy and commitment, resistance and co-operation; at the ideological level, between forms of Marxism which allegedly foster capitalism, notably 'revision-ism', and the 'correct proletarian revolutionary line'; at the institutional level, radical Maoism calls for struggle against such policies as the use of differentiated wage scales and individual material incentives as spurs to productivity, profits as an index of efficiency, markets as methods of circulation, prices as signals for economic behaviour, and expanded links with capitalist economies abroad.

Policy and ideology in the Cultural Revolution decade were a complex mixture of these two layers of Maoism. They had many common elements, notably the commitment to rapid industrialisation, mass mobilisation and national self-reliance and concern for the rural sector. But there were also important differences which tended to be submerged: for instance, the fundamental distinction between two ideas of 'revolutionary' development, the contrast between 'developmental Maoist' emphasis on development through increased consumption and commodity production and the uncompromising attitude of radical Maoists towards material incentives and market relations.

To some extent, these contradictions were muted by the fact that different paradigms tended to be applied in different sectors: 'developmental Maoism' had more impact on rural policy, 'radical Maoism' on the state-run economy, politics, culture and education. But there were basic tensions as the radical variant was imposed in the 1960s. The latter's strictures on private consumption and exchange, its excessive insistence on the predominance of politics over economics, its emphasis on high rates of accumulation in all sectors and its predilection for 'higher' forms of socialist organisation which might be economically unproductive tended to contradict much of the logic of developmental Maoism. When translated into practice, moreover, the principle of 'class struggle' tended to absolutise issues and thwart policy flexibility, so crucial for the success of 'developmental Maoism'. To a certain extent, therefore, the two 'Maoisms' were at war with each other, as their originator gradually retreated from the battlefield.

The complex and contradictory nature of the 'Maoist' model is reflected in the fact that it appealed to foreign observers of different ideological hues. At the practical level, Marxists and other socialists were attracted by the innovations of the Cultural Revolution decade. These were seen not merely as alternatives to Soviet-style socialism but also as fruitful avenues for political struggle in industrialised capitalist societies: the efforts to curb bureaucratisation through administrative decentralisation, 'sending down' (*xiafang*) of cadres to the grass-roots and various forms of mass participation and supervision; attempts to redistribute resources and opportunities through egalitarian wage policies and educational reform; attempts to involve ordinary people in processes of basic-level administration and technical change; the concerted effort to instil collectivist and altruistic attitudes in everyday life; and the principle of self-reliance as a means of insulating nations from the 'sugar-coated bullets' of the international bourgeoisie.

For development specialists in North and South, the

Maoist composite offered distinctive approaches to common problems. As a general strategy, the Maoist path was interesting on several counts. First, it attempted to combine growth with distributive goals, notably the redistribution of social opportunities, the compression of wage and sectoral differentials and programmes to provide for the basic needs of the general population. Second, it set out to involve the mass of the population in processes of capital construction and technological change and tap the developmental resources latent in community mobilisation and collective effort, notably in the rural communes. Third, China offered a model of self-reliance, bootstrap development based overwhelmingly on national talents and resources which contrasted sharply with the dire descriptions of 'dependency' analysts.

More specifically, certain facets of 'Maoist' developmental practice attracted widespread approval: the programme to link formal education more closely to practical problems of industrial and agricultural development, the campaign to settle unemployed urban 'educated youth' in the countryside; the stress on the importance of 'native' and intermediate technology; and programmes to provide basic welfare services through the universalisation of primary education, co-operative medical plans and 'barefoot doctors'.

Despite its internal contradictions, in the late 1960s and early 1970s the 'Chinese model' seemed to open an optimistic page in the depressing annals of Third World poverty, injustice and dependence on the one hand and bureaucratic calcification in the 'socialist countries' on the other. Why was much of it rejected after the death of Mao, and how can we account for these fundamental changes?

The Demise of 'Maoism'

It is common talk of the death of 'Maoism' or the 'Maoist model' after the death of Mao and the removal of the Shanghai radical group. However, the *coup* in late 1976 did not bring the demise of Maoism as a whole, but of *one version* of it, *viz.* radical Maoism and its adherents. Indeed 1977–8 saw a resurgence of 'developmental Maoism', redolent of the late 1950s, under the leadership of Mao's chosen successor, Hua

Guofeng. This in turn was criticised and superceded during 1978–81 by a new approach to development, the 'reform' position, linked to the growing political predominance of Deng Xiaoping, and ratified by the Third Plenum of the CCP Central Committee in December 1978. This retained some elements of developmental Maoism but, as a comprehensive programme, was incompatible with both Maoist traditions.

Repudiation of 'radical Maoism'

After the arrest of the Shanghai group in late 1976, the new leadership took immediate steps to reject the ideological foundations of radical Maoism, vilify its chief exponents, remove or suppress its main supporters at all levels and expunge its practical manifestations. This campaign was carried out without concerted opposition or popular protest; on the contrary, it appears to have been received well by most sectors of the population. Clearly, the radical experiment had already failed before Mao's death. For what reasons?

The radical movement had certain basic political weaknesses. Though radical ideologues attributed a crucial role to revolutionary theory and 'Mao Tse-Tung Thought', their own theory was unsystematic and easily distorted to serve personal, factional or sectional interests. Systematic and authoritative exegeses were few indeed during the Cultural Revolution decade. In fact, the only one with any serious theoretical content was Zhang Chunqiao's article, 'On exercising all-round dictatorship over the bourgeoisie', published in early 1975 – rather too late to make much difference. Zhang did not get round to writing his promised analysis of new class relations in Chinese society. Moreover, for all their emphasis on 'correct thought' and 'proletarian politics', the political behaviour of radical leaders – often dogmatic and authoritarian – contrasted with their democratic and egalitarian message. Their individual political skills were also unimpressive, from Lin Biao's botched attempt at the succession, to the truculent isolation of the Shanghai group in the 1970s. Their personification of ideology and adoption of the leadership cult led them to excessive dependence on Mao and they lost influence as his health declined. Mao's authority evaporated to such an extent that his death was greeted with widespread popular relief, albeit masked by tears. Radical leaders and activists tended to adopt a 'closed door-ist' style of politics; they polarised political relationships artificially, and contravened Mao's own principles of united front politics by antagonising too many people, losing the middle ground, and isolating themselves rather than their opponents. They also ignored or played down issues of great significance for most Chinese citizens, notably the desire for a more rapid increase in material living standards, political and cultural freedom, and social harmony and stability. Their sectarian style led them to dismiss or suppress people or ideas which might have contributed to greater efficiency and consumption *without* compromising radical Maoist values. Though refusing to woo the masses by appeals to material interests, their own political appeals offered little by way of compensation. Notwithstanding the revolutionary rhetoric of the Cultural Revolution, they failed to break with the structural and normative logic of Leninist (i.e. Stalinist) political economy by offering an alternative 'associationist' model of socialism which would have transferred real, not symbolic, power to the population. They used hierarchical methods to foster egalitarianism, authoritarianism to stimulate democracy and attempted to mobilise mass initiative by invoking obedience to the supreme and infallible figure of Mao. Small wonder they could not build a unified and stable following among the masses. At the same time, their radicalism affronted the strategic élites of state socialism: they pilloried cultural intellectuals as 'bourgeois', scientists and technicians as 'white experts', managers and administrators as 'revisionists' and 'capitalist-roaders'.

Inherent weaknesses aside, however, the radicals faced almost insuperable political obstacles. Their policies were often implemented in conservative or hostile contexts, and were subverted by unprincipled factionalism, personal antagonisms and sectional manoeuvring. The original content of policy was dissipated and the resultant gap between ideology and reality, promise and performance, created cynicism and apathy, even among their initial supporters. Most important, however, they faced a formidable array of opponents: most people in dominant positions of the state and economy (with the possible exception of the People's Liberation Army) seem to have resisted radical Maoism from the start. Indeed, the surprising thing is not so much the swift end of the radical challenge, but the fact that it was able to get off the ground in the first place and retain some (fluctuating) power for a decade.

In retrospect, the radical Maoist programme did contain positive elements and have some positive effects. It pinpointed fundamental problems in post-revolutionary Chinese society, raised issues crucial to socialist aspirations and preserved or developed much that was valuable, notably a popular spirit of criticism and potential defiance and a general spread of egalitarian values. In the economic realm, it had some limited success in restraining inequalities between classes and socio-economic sectors, consolidated the rural commune system and utilised it as an effective instrument for local capital construction and technological change, and introduced a more comprehensive network of basic social services in the rural areas.

But radical Maoism was problematic as a strategy of socialist development in at least four ways. As a system of *socialist theory*, it lacked vigour, range and texture. As a set of prescriptions for *socialist practice*, it failed to break with the authoritarian traditions of Stalinism (and, indeed, of imperial China) and formulate a set of productive and democratic policies which generated widespread popular support. As a *political* project, it had many inherent flaws and, in the context of the entrenched constellation of opposing forces, was 'structurally' weak. As a programme of *material development*, it failed to solve basic problems of economic backwardness and inefficiency and deliver the material goods it promised, partly because of deficiencies in the economic system it encouraged, partly because many of the economic problems it faced were so intractable. Mediocre economic performance created a backlog of pent-up consumer frustration, worsening unemployment and political discontent which was to pose a major challenge for the post-Mao leadership.

The survival of developmental Maoism: 1977–8

Though the major elements of radical Maoism were re-pudiated after the removal of the Shanghai group, some themes of the previous decade were retained, even including a residual version of the theory of 'the continuation of class struggle in socialist society', now redirected against its radical inventors. The 'Gang of Four' were now described as 'the bourgeoisie in the Party'. The new leadership did not reject Mao or the Cultural Revolution, nor did they view the previous decade as a disaster. Indeed, they emphasised that, in spite of 'serious interference and sabotage' from Lin Biao and the Gang, development strategy had basically been correct and economic performance generally good. Development was still seen as 'revolutionary', but, in the language of developmental Maoism, was mainly defined in terms of economic and technological change.[9] Development was still seen as a big push, a struggle against backwardness, proceeding through Great Leaps and mass movements organised by an interventionist party. Though political mobilisation was to remain important, however, there was a new sobriety about its developmental impact. Political work was henceforth to serve the economic base directly and respect the 'objective laws' of economic development.[10] The Gang were criticised for allegedly maintaining that 'it is all right for production to go down as long as we do a good job in revolution' and 'we would rather have a low socialist growth rate than a high capitalist one'. Henceforth, politics would not be allowed to 'brush aside or supersede economics'.[11] The Thought of Mao Tse Tung, suitably bowdlerised, was maintained (along with Marxism-Leninism) as the ruling doctrine and Mao's 1956 speech 'On the Ten Major Relationships', was now publicised as providing an overall framework of development policy.[12] Chairman Hua was lionised as Mao's chosen successor, and symbolic figures such as Chen Yongguei, Party Secretary of the model Dazhai brigade, remained in the top leadership. Developmental Maoist slogans of local and regional self-reliance were maintained, as was the political style of setting 'models' for nationwide emulation. The previous models of *Dazhai* (agriculture) and *Daqing* (industry) were retained as was the 'Charter of the Anshan Iron and Steel Company' as a framework for industrial relations. The original 'general line' of the 1958–9 Great Leap Forward – 'going all out, aiming high to achieve greater, faster, better and more economical results in building socialism' – was reiterated, overall accumulation was set at a high rate, speed was identified as a primary objective of socialist construction, and capital construction in heavy industry was still stressed. An overly ambitious new ten-year plan was introduced at the first session of the Fifth National People's Congress in early 1978.[13] The aim was to achieve '85 per cent mechanisation in all major processes of farmwork' and 'the completion of an independent and fairly comprehensive industrial complex' by 1985. Agricultural output was scheduled to rise by 4.5 per cent per annum and industrial output by over 10 per cent. State investment in capital construction in the eight years to 1985 was to be equivalent to the total for the previous twenty-eight years, focusing on 120 large-scale projects. Although the need to increase investment in light industry and agriculture was emphasised, heavy industry was still to receive the lion's share of state funds. The principle of decentralisation of economic management to localities was reiterated, with the specific intention of establishing six relatively self-reliant economic regions. Although Party spokesmen laid greater stress on the need for more accurate macro-economic planning, more competent management, tighter discipline and more responsible accounting in enterprises, the basic principles of material balance planning, directive plan implementation and centralisation of most major industrial decisions remained intact. Although there was greater stress on the use of material incentives to motivate the industrial workforce, moral incentives and 'socialist labour emulation' were still given precedence. In the rural sector, though there were some moves towards the revival of private production and exchange, and criticism of 'egalitarianism' in income distribution, the absolute predominance of collective institutions was emphasised along with the need to 'overcome spontaneous tendencies towards capitalism'.

Though 1977 and 1978 thus maintained much of the content and style of developmental Maoism, in retrospect it was a period of transition. Mao's supporters in the Central Committee were gradually weakened and isolated, eventually to be removed or forced to resign. By early 1981, only Hua Guofeng remained of the major developmental Maoist leaders, and he was finally demoted at the Sixth Plenum of the CCPCC in June of that year, to be replaced as Party Chairman by Hu Yaobang.[14] On the other side, 1977–8 saw the rise of Deng Xiaoping and his allies, rallying under the slogan of 'practice as the sole criterion of truth',[15] counterposed against remaining Maoist leaders whom they dubbed as 'whateverists', i.e. people who thought and did 'whatever Mao Tse Tung thought or did'. These transitional years also saw the public appearance of new policy positions which went beyond a mere attack on radical Maoism to include a thoroughgoing critique of national developmental experience over the past two decades. In the next section, I shall focus on the main elements of this critique and briefly discuss its impact between 1979 and 1981.

The Reform Alternative

The Third Plenum of the CCP Central Committee in December 1978 announced a decisive shift in the Party's purpose to an exclusive concentration on 'socialist modernisation', thereby removing most of the residual Maoist political and ideological themes current during 1977–8. The new strategy embodied a triple critique: of the basic ideas and institutions of radical Maoism, of the Great Leap psychology, mass mobilisation and local self-reliance of developmental Maoism, and of the centralised system of economic planning inherited from the 'Soviet model' of the early and mid-1950s. Though these systems of political economy had brought economic growth, the new leadership and its academic spokesmen argued, with considerable justification, that this had been purchased at excessively high costs within an institutional framework which systematically generated inefficiency, imbalance and waste at all levels. Sectoral reorientation and institutional change were regarded as crucial.

The new strategy* had two major thrusts, 'readjustment' and 'reform' (the latter is often called 'restructuring' in Chinese texts). These two components were initially seen as inter-

---

*To minimise superficiality or inordinate length, I shall simplify this discussion by concentrating mainly on changes in the economic as opposed to the political sphere, and in the state industrial sector as opposed to the collective agricultural sector.

dependent, but they did embody separate programmes and, as we shall see later, proved somewhat incompatible in practice. They also differed in their degree of innovation: while 'readjustment' contained important elements of continuity with the Maoist era, 'reform' struck off boldly in new directions.

Readjustment reflected an attempt to correct certain basic 'imbalances' in the economy which, it was argued, originated in the mid-1950s, under the Soviet model. 'Ultra-leftist' Maoist developmental strategy, beginning with the Great Leap, had ignored, intensified or failed to correct them.[16] For example, critics pointed out, Maoists of different varieties had emphasised speed over balance in economic performance and, through their use of 'teleological' planning whereby 'an unusually high target was set for a particular sector and other sectors were forced to give way to it', had exacerbated economic imbalances.

The main areas of imbalance or dislocation were identified as follows: (i) *the rate of overall accumulation* had been too high: over the twenty-six years, from 1953 to 1978, investment had swallowed up over 30 per cent of GDP for thirteen years, reaching a high point of 43.8 per cent in 1959. In the future, it was to be kept at 25 per cent or below, and more attention paid to raising levels of individual and social consumption.[17] By Chinese reckoning, per capita income was US $253 in 1979 and it was proposed to raise this to US $1000 by the year 2000.[18] (ii) *Investment priorities* were to be changed; the longstanding tendency to 'overextend the front of capital construction' by building projects that were too big, too numerous, too wasteful and too slow in gestation (so-called 'beard-growing' projects) was to be curtailed. Investment in new heavy industrial construction was to be reduced in favour of refurbishing existing capacity and developing sectors which brought quicker returns and stimulated productivity, employment and consumer demand (including light industry and the service trades). Though heavy industry would still retain priority in state investment, the share of investment in light industry and agriculture was to be increased; the previous situation whereby heavy industry had taken 76 per cent of total productive state investment was to be remedied. (iii) *the linkage between production and consumption* was to be strengthened and reoriented. Previously, it was argued, the economy had been overly supply-driven, production for the sake of production rather than demand, for planners rather than consumers, resulting in systematic over-and under-production in both consumer and producer goods sectors. The balance between supply and demand was to be corrected by strengthening the latter as a determinant of production. (iv) In the urban sector, the previous stress on large-scale, capital-intensive forms of industrial production was to be amended to one encouraging more labour-intensive collective industry outside the state sector. This coincided with a more systematic attempt than previously to establish *employment* as a prime consideration in urban economic expansion. (v) a balance was to be set between the demand for imports and capacity to pay for them, either through exports or capital imports. New forms of international economic co-operation were to be established, which could stimulate economic activity without exacerbating balance of payments deficits, provide employment and absorb foreign technology and business knowhow.

These readjustments were to be accompanied by a thorough-going *reform of the economic management system*. 1978 and 1979 were years of reform mania, with members of the newly resuscitated Chinese Academy of Social Sciences playing an important public role, notably key economists such as Xue Muqiao and Hu Qiaomu. A wide range of often farreaching proposals were aired in the media, some authors going so far as to propose a radical shift towards 'self-management socialism' on the Yugoslav model.[19] Let us examine the main elements of the economic reform programme.

(i) There has been an attempt to *change the relationship between politics, administration and economics* in the system of economic guidance and control, to separate the three spheres and define their respective functions more precisely. One thrust was towards the *depoliticisation* of economic administration and management at various levels. *Ideologically*, this embodies an attempt to theorise the areas of politics and economics as separate spheres, with their own priorities and dynamics. Economics operates according to 'objective laws', and thus is to a considerable degree independent of politics and resistant to its manipulation. Politics may still remain 'in command', but in a *parametric* sense, i.e. setting the basic goals of economic strategy. However, in implementing these goals, the role of politics must yield to economic calculation and 'economic mechanisms'. The Maoist conception of development as a directly politicised process of mobilisation, i.e. 'politics in command' in a *pervasive* sense, is thus repudiated. This separation of the economic sphere has legitimised the revival of 'economic science' as an intellectual activity.

At the *institutional* level, this separation implies a more limited role for the Party and political agencies generally in everyday processes of economic administration and management. 'Interlocking directorates' or the 'wearing of two hats' must be reduced, and the concrete spheres of Party, government and economy separated in reality as well as in theory. This calls for greater role-specialisation, i.e. the gradual removal of political generalists in favour of a rational division of labour between professionals: politicians, administrators, managers, financial experts, technicians, academics, and so on.

At the *motivational* level, there is re-emphasis on the importance of material as opposed to moral-political incentives in motivating labour – the former are now given *de facto* primacy as the key determinant of economic action, though official lip-service is still paid to the primacy of non-material motivations and incentives.[20] In practice this meant a move towards individual bonus and piece-rate systems in industry, and in agriculture a repudiation of the relatively egalitarian Dazhai method of income distribution in favour of various kinds of piece-rate system.[21]

The economy, moreover, is to be *de-administered*. In the previous Soviet-derived system, argued the reformers, the economy was run as an administrative system through a complex system of central ministries and local governments – as such, it was prone to the characteristic problems of complex, centralised bureaucracies which systematically impaired economic performance. For example, reformers criticised 'the kind of management mentality that regards the enterprise as an appendage of any administrative organ, as a bead on an abacus that can only be moved at an external command from the upper level'. The problem was exacerbated by the fact that the 'upper level' was often neither uniform nor consistent:

higher organs were multiple and overlapping, functional and regional, with the result that enterprises were subject to 'too many mothers-in-law'. Economic management requires economic means, argued the reformers; where possible, administrative organs should be converted into 'enterprise type' organisations, even including ministries, and greater use should be made, in relations between higher organs and basic productive units, to economic methods such as price, credit, taxation, interest and wage incentives. Accordingly, the economic role of the state was to be partly redefined from directly interventionist to parametric; the process of plan implementation was to be shifted from directive to indicative.

(ii) This redefinition of the economic role of the state set the context for a proposed programme of *decentralisation* of economic decision-making power and a *revival of market-type relations* between basic economic units. Economic decisions within the state sector were to be shifted from superior government organs (both functional and regional) to basic units of production, whether these be single enterprises or various intermediate units such as 'trusts' or 'companies' which amalgamated groups of enterprises, but still operated on economic as opposed to administrative principles. In short, the Maoist emphasis on local decentralisation was largely replaced by emphasis on *basic-level* decentralisation. Local 'self-reliance', it was argued, did generate some initiative from below, but tended to lead to the establishment of irrationally comprehensive local industrial systems which violated the need for specialisation.[22] Decentralisation to the enterprise would avoid this problem, and would be far more effective in alleviating the irrationalities inherent in the over-centralisation of the old system, wherein enterprises were denied, in theory and often in practice, the slightest degree of economic initiative. There was a similar policy shift *vis à vis* rural relations of production with a new emphasis on the need to protect and reinforce the autonomy of the production team, the lowest level within the three-tier framework of the commune. In the past, it was argued, the teams had been subject to excessive pressure and dictation from higher levels, notably the brigade and the commune, and this had restricted their economic initiative, slowed income growth, reduced individual incentives and generally depressed agricultural performance.

In the new system, superior organs were still to be responsible for macro-economic planning but, in the process of plan implementation, were to use fewer precise targets and more flexible guidelines administered by economic inducement and control rather than bureaucratic fiat. This new relationship between state and enterprise would, it was argued, create a better planning system by reducing the scope of direct planning to a level where rational calculation and effective control were feasible.[23] The enterprise was to gain greater power over investment, product mix, payment methods, pricing, material procurement and sales outlets, and was to behave more directly in pursuit of its 'independent financial interests'. The latter two powers implied a *reorientation of economic links*, i.e. a partial substitution of horizontal (market) links between enterprises regulated by contracts for vertical (bureaucratic) links between them and their superior organs. The assumption here is that planning and market are compatible principles – markets can be utilised to serve socialist aims. It is also argued that markets are an objective necessity, reflecting differences in material interests between individuals and productive units. In the words of one reform text, 'the state plan can only reflect the needs of society in totality but not correctly and pliably the kaleidoscopic needs of our economic life'.[24] In consequence, there was greater stress on the need 'to determine production by marketing, supply by production and the integration of production with demand': in short, 'production for customers not for planning statistics'. This exchange component of the 'law of value' would require enterprises henceforth to sell products not merely produce them and would give them more say in fixing supply and sales contracts and negotiating prices (within prescribed limits). These freedoms would in turn create competitive pressures which would feed back into the production process itself, ideally reducing the amount of 'socially necessary labour time' to produce a given unit of output. Henceforth, profitability was to serve as the key index of economic performance and, to this end, the production process was to be rationalised through professionalisation of management, stricter accounting procedures, tighter disciplinary systems and more effective methods of linking individual labour with remuneration in both agriculture and industry, thus realising more fully 'the socialist principle of distribution according to work'. Previous payment systems, it is argued, had been too egalitarian, encouraging workers to 'use an iron bowl to eat the rice cooked in a single large pan'.

(iii) Liberalisation of the domestic economy was to be accompanied by a *greater openness to the international economy* and a proliferation of forms of international economic linkage. Previous Maoist emphasis on 'self-reliance' was condemned as exclusionist and the beneficial potential of the international division of labour in foreign trade and of the developmental impact of foreign capital infusions have been emphasised. Economic theorists reasserted the 'rational kernel' of Ricardo's theory of comparative advantage and argued that 'the international division of labour drives productive forces forward because it reduces social labour', citing Yugoslavia and Romania as successful examples.[25] This has led to a rise in the ratio of foreign trade in the economy, the acceptance of foreign credits from both governmental and private sources, encouragement of direct foreign investment through joint ventures, and the establishment of special 'economic zones' to foster (and corral) foreign participation in the economy.

The range of 'readjustment and reform' *proposals* was very sweeping, far greater than those actually translated into *policy*. Moreover the *impact* of policies, once enacted, was often superficial. Progress was made in key areas of readjustment, though it was slower than the new leadership would have liked. The scale of capital construction was reduced (the number of large and medium-sized state construction projects falling from 1624 in late 1978 to 663 in 1981) and the ratio of overall accumulation, which was reduced from 36.5 per cent in 1978 to under 30 per cent in 1981. There was also a reallocation of state investment funds in 1979–80 in favour of light industry and agriculture: of total investment in capital construction, the share of heavy industry dropped from 50.9 per cent in 1978 to 40.3 per cent in 1981 while light industry's share rose from 6.1 to 10 per cent. The ratio of 'productive' to 'non-productive' investment also changed, the latter (for housing, public facilities etc.) rising from 17.4 to 41.3 per cent of total state investment over the same period. Light industry's share in total industrial output value increased from 42.7 per cent in 1978 to 51.4 per cent in 1981.[27]

In the area of economic reform, various experimental schemes were introduced to increase enterprise autonomy. The initial trial began in Sichuan province in October 1978. During 1979, about 3300 enterprises took part, and this rose to 6600 by June 1980 (about 16 per cent of the total number of state-run industrial units, but accounting for 60 per cent of total output value). The basic thrust of these reforms was to grant enterprises the right to retain a share of profits for three 'enterprise funds',[26] i.e. for bonuses, welfare facilities and investment, to produce and market goods outside plan targets; and to have greater freedom in material procurement, wage policies and labour recruitment. These changes involved greater use of market relations between enterprises and a (restricted) deregulation of prices.[28] At the macro-level, there has been an attempt to expand the active role of money by partially replacing budgetary allocations to enterprises with credit dispensed by the People's Bank.[29] On the international side, by the end of 1980 twenty joint ventures had been approved with a total investment of US $210 million, of which over US$170 million came from foreign sources. It was also decided to establish four 'economic zones' for foreign investment on preferential terms: Shenzhen, Zhuhai and Shantou in Guangdong province and Xiamen in Fujian province. Construction of the first zone, Shenzhen (bordering Hongkong), began in August 1979 and by mid-1982 it had 330 projects under way. Local authorities and enterprises were also granted limited powers to deal directly with foreign concerns.[30]

In general, the process of readjustment between 1978 and 1981 kept its momentum but was far less smooth than hoped. On the other hand, the economic reform programme ran into stormy weather and its impact was disappointing – certainly there was no decisive move towards 'market socialism'. Indeed, a backlash against the reform process had set in by late 1980 which threatened the limited progress already achieved.

In the next section, I shall examine the reasons for this deceleration and the prospects for economic reform in the early 1980s. This discussion will, it is hoped, open the way towards a deeper analysis of the causal dynamics of change and continuity in China's political economy.

The Reform Programme: Problems and Prospects

According to official statistics,* the overall economic impact of the new policy strategy between 1978 and 1981 was very positive in terms of improvements in growth, income and productivity. Though the rise in grain output was modest (6.7 per cent between 1978 and 1981) output of industrial crops increased (cotton, for example, increasing by 37 per cent). Industrial output value increased by 8.5 per cent in 1979 and 8.4 per cent in 1980, with light industry registering a 14 per cent annual increase between 1978 and 1981. Between 1977 and 1980, it was claimed, urban jobs were found for 26.6 million people and net per capita incomes (unadjusted for inflation) increased from 117 to 170 *yuan* in the country-side, and from 602 to 781 *yuan* in the cities.[31]

As to reforms in the economic management system, official sources claimed they had brought about significant improvements in the output and profitability of participating industrial enterprises. But the period of reform was too short to justify such optimism, and, as Lockett points out, the results cited are very similar to those claimed by Soviet reformers in 1966, but the Soviet reforms later lost much of their initial impetus.[32]

Indeed, one common feature of the Soviet and eastern European economic reforms is their *reversibility*. Events in China in late 1980 and early 1981 suggest a similar pattern, which one Chinese source describes as follows:

Centralism leads to rigidity, rigidity leads to complaints, complaints lead to decentralisation, decentralisation leads to disorder, and disorder leads back to centralisation.[33]

1979 and 1980 did indeed bring some economic 'disorder'

---

*These should be treated with caution: they vary considerably from report to report, and the bases of calculation are often unspecified.

and disequilibrium which prompted an official decision in late 1980 to stop or slow down reforms in the management of the state sector.[34] In January 1981, it was announced that 'the scope of the reforms will not be expanded for the time being', mainly on the grounds that effective reforms could not be introduced in a context of economic instability and structural imbalance:

Readjustment will be the central task in the next few years which will of course hold back the reforms. It is common knowledge that large-scale reforms are inadvisable and may end in failure when the financial and economic situation is not stable.[35]

This policy shift was accompanied by a widespread reimposition of political and economic controls in late 1980, 1981 and early 1982: including campaigns against unauthorised price rises, and "economic crimes" such as corruption speculation and black markets; partial recentralisation of economic controls in the state sector (notably a reduction of the number of commodities subject to 'negotiated', i.e. partially deregulated, prices and a restriction of the autonomy of local authorities and enterprises to commit funds for capital projects or conduct economic relations with foreign concerns);[36] and moves to strengthen Party leadership and ideological education, notably through a reaffirmation of the 'four principles [the socialist road, the dictatorship of the proletariat, Party leadership and Marxism-Leninism–Mao Tse Tung thought] and a call for the establishment of a 'socialist spiritual civilisation' and 'the dominance of communist ideals'. As of mid-1982, the economic reform programme still lies in the doldrums.

The official line from early 1981 onwards claimed that the reform process had in fact been successful and was merely being postponed until circumstances were more propitious. However, it is likely that the reforms themselves contributed to the 'disorder' which eroded the commitment of the Party leadership to thoroughgoing institutional change. For example, limited price deregulation in a context of excess demand allowed enterprises to boost profits and thereby bonuses by raising prices. Across-the-board urban wage rises and increased procurement prices for farm produce both fuelled inflation. Official sources admit there was an average retail price inflation of 6 per cent in 1980 with the price of non-staple foods rising by 13.8 per cent, and these estimates were probably on the conservative side.

Moreover, successful implementation of the post-Third Plenum strategy was also hampered by two inherent contradictions. First, the basic aims of 'readjustment' and 'reform' were incompatible: the former implies the ability of the central authority to impose structural changes and reduce disequilibria in the economy, while the latter undermines that capacity by decentralising important areas of economic decision to localities or productive units.

Two examples help to clarify this contradiction: first, the clash between micro and macro, state and enterprise rationality is demonstrated by the case of the Sichuan Province No. 1 Textile Mill. The mill's management planned to use their new freedom to invest by buying 3000 more spindles with their own funds. This decision was vetoed by the provincial authorities on the grounds that, while it made sense from the enterprise's point of view (by providing more jobs for the unemployed children of workers and releasing equipment to turn out more profitable products), from the provincial point of view, spinning and weaving capacity already surpassed printing and dyeing capacity so more spindles were not required.[37] Second, the clash between central restriction and uncontrolled local initiative in the field of capital construction is reflected in the case of the wine industry. Before 1980, there were about 1500 wine factories above the county level with a total production capacity which was, according to central estimates at least, sufficient to meet domestic and external markets. In 1980, however, provinces and counties set up over 12,000 small-scale factories – an eight-fold increase.[38] Similar tendencies towards 'over-investment' were visible in other industries, notably cigarettes, soap, silk fabrics, plastics, fur and leather, and household electrical appliances.

Second, there is a basic problem involved in the introduction of partial, piecemeal reform in the context of a basically unreformed system. The prerogatives of the central economic authorities and the methods of administrative control have remained basically intact; there has been no overall price reform to blow life into market stirrings, and competitive pressures have not developed to a level necessary to prevent monopoly pricing by enterprises. The Soviet reforms of the mid-1960s shared this basic contradiction and, as Lavigne points out, it was one of the major reasons for their eventual loss of impetus.[39]

These contradictions and the specific economic problems which emerged during 1979–80, notably inflation and budgetary deficits, embody basic problems of *political* economy. First, much of the new development programme reflects the political priority of gaining and consolidating popular and élite support rather than a 'rational', comprehensively integrated development strategy. Second, the Party leadership is operating within tight political constraints; the success of their strategy depends not merely on policy redefinition but also on redistribution of power. If we consider public expenditure, for example, policy-makers have been caught in a political vice. On the one hand, the readjustment programme entailed faster increases in urban and rural living standards, and was in part a response to a backlog of consumption pressures which had built up over the past two decades. In the short run, however, higher wages for urban workers and higher procurement prices for farmers were not accompanied by an increase in production sufficient to avoid inflation and generate public revenue. Given the potential for discontent among the urban population, moreover, the leadership did not follow the rise in the procurement price of grain with a rise in its retail price, resulting in an annual subsidy of 7–8 billion *yuan* by late 1980. These and other food subsidies (notably for meat and vegetables) had reached 20 billion *yuan* by that date, nearly one-fifth of the entire state budget revenue.[40] On the other hand, the logic of readjustment also required the government to cut back on capital construction, notably in heavy industry. But this meant taking on the big spending ministries, ambitious local governments and the armed forces and proved very difficult in the short run. As a result of these conflicting pressures, public financial commitments became overextended and the shortfall was financed by printing money. Thus, in 1980, the Central People's Bank increased its planned issue of currency from 3000 million *yuan* to 7600 million *yuan*.

Taking our analysis of political forces one step further,

the basic thrust of both readjustment and reform, at the declaratory level at least, threaten to undermine the Leninist nature of the Chinese political economy, specifically the dominant role of the Party and the government bureaucracy in the system of economic policy-making and management. The readjustment strategy seeks to restrain the rate of accumulation and to redistribute resources out of key state sectors, notably heavy industry – the realm of planned allocation – into light industry and agriculture, where *collective* relations of production are dominant and the force of market relations is greater. At the practical level, this shift in priorities entails reallocation of power and has run into heavy resistance. At the ideological level, the strategy of readjustment questions the maintenance of very high rates of accumulation, the primacy of heavy industry and the logic of a supply-driven economy; thus it implicitly questions the legitimacy of the Party-state as an historically necessary force of accumulation and ultimate arbiter of economic priorities. Economic reform has similar consequences by shifting economic initiative to the basic level, undermining the power and legitimacy of the state bureaucracy. Moreover, by attempting to distinguish and defend the 'economic' sphere the notion of 'politics in command' and the interventionist role of the Party is further brought into question. It is likely, therefore, that the reforms have encountered resistance from middle- and upper-level Party cadres and from officials in ministries and regional-local governments. If we add the fact that many lower- and middle-ranking cadres in the Party-government system and large numbers of Party members in all sectors of society were recruited or promoted during the Cultural Revolution decade and thus, to varying degrees, susceptible to Maoist appeals, the social basis for an effective reform programme may be tenuous indeed, and the forces of reversion overwhelming.

Economic problems aside, moreover, opponents of the economic reforms and liberalisation in general could point to many phenomena during 1979 and 1980 as signs of social degeneration and 'anti-socialist' tendencies. The officially sponsored attacks on 'the ultra-leftist ideology of the Gang of Four' exceeded their intended purpose by damaging the general credibility of Marxist-Leninist concepts and genuine socialist values such as equality, altruism, collectivism and mass initiative. The new policy strategy also encouraged a trend towards the privatisation and materialisation of personal motivation; it opened Chinese society to the dazzling glare of western consumption styles spreading 'unhealthy' social values, raising consumer aspirations to unrealistic heights, and setting in motion various forms of corruption, smuggling and black marketing. The Party leadership was concerned about this dramatic decline in social morality and political commitment, and responded in early 1981 with a call for the creation of a 'socialist spiritual civilisation' and 'the dominance of communist ideals'.[41] There was even an attempt to revive the discredited moral models of the 1960s such as the PLA hero Lei Feng. That Chinese youth viewed the latter figure with widespread cynicism and ridicule is hardly surprising. Such signs of socio-political 'degeneration', suitably magnified for propaganda purposes, provide opponents of reform with another powerful weapon.

Conclusion

What does the fall of Maoism and the rise of the Chinese reform movement tell us about the basic dynamics of Chinese state socialism? The failure of the Maoist approach, particularly its radical version, illustrates the ineluctable pressures of economic scarcity and mass poverty. Any Chinese leadership, however ideologically virtuous or politically 'correct', must grapple with the underlying constraints posed by shortage of land and capital and population pressure in such a way as to deliver on its promises of higher economic welfare. It is an undeniable fact that Maoists of both varieties were unable to meet this challenge well enough to gain and retain widespread support and compensate for the costs to individual liberty and social stability embodied in their programme. On the other hand, the record of the reform programme in the late 1970s suggests that even when a strategy of socialist development is designed overwhelmingly in terms of maximising economic growth and efficiency, and attains considerable initial success on these indices, it is difficult to introduce it without causing serious economic problems which, together with its impact on other long-term goals of socialist development – notably equality and collectivism – make it problematic if subjected to cost-benefit analysis.

However, this type of policy analysis only takes us part way towards an analysis of Chinese development strategies. There is need for a multi-level framework which allows us to go beyond ideological alignments and policy programmes to consider the structural conditions which shape policy alternatives, set the rules of the game, and favour certain sides in the process of debate and conflict. At the political level, the fulcrum of power in China, as in many other state-socialist societies, is the 'Leninist centre', a system of cadres whose strength is concentrated in the Party-government apparatus and whose programme, indeed *raison d'être*, embodies the principle of one-party dominance and the centrally planned and administered economy. This centre defines the basic parameters which make or break individual leaders, structure policy agendas and establish the limits of reform, whether from the Left or the Right. It was the main bulwark against the radical attacks of the Cultural Revolution in 1966–8 and successfully drew the fangs of radical Maoist policy initiatives between 1966 and 1976.

This centre must ensure material progress to buttress its political authority. Amid the manifold pressures for economic changes in the late 1970s, the ideas of the reformers were attractive, particularly their promise to raise real incomes more rapidly and reduce unemployment. However, when the reform programme threatened to go 'too far', in both political and economic realms, and when the effects of reforms threatened to elude the Party's control, the basic logic of Leninist political economy, embodied in the 'four principles', had to be reimposed *even if this had adverse economic consequences*. To this extent, political and economic logic are warring principles.

Political analysis of this kind should in turn be situated within a wider structural analysis of Chinese society. One can hypothesise that the groundswell of support for economic reform, like its conterparts in eastern Europe, reflects the presence of important new social forces and represents their attempt to rearrange society according to their own vision and their own interests. These new strata – professional administrators, economic managers, scientists, technicians and educators – are 'technocratic' in so far as their power is rooted in skills and knowledge crucial to material production and social reproduction. They have emerged as a product of the statist political economy established in the 1950s. To the extent that the reform programme was actually implemented, it marked a shift of power to these groups, at the expense partly of those members of the 'masses' given authority in the institutions of radical Maoism and partly of the older generation of 'revolutionary cadres' holding administrative posts without the capacity or training necessary for the job. This new 'socialist intelligentsia' has benefitted from the policy initiatives of the late 1970s, notably cultural and political liberalisation, new policies on science, technology and education, the moves towards a new system of cadre recruitment based on expertise and greater power to professional managers. To the extent that these strata are a crucial component of effective development, there is a basis for accommodation between them and members of the dominant politico-bureaucratic élite. But accommodation does not mean harmony and unanimity: the bases of power of these two class constellations are different, as are their social interests, developmental programmes and methods of social reproduction. They may share a common interest in the decentralisation and domestication of the working classes, achieved through a familiar combination of carrot, stick, co-optative participation and ideological hegemony, but they are ready to bid for worker-peasant support in their mutual competition. The 'masses' can thus play an important role in determining the balance of power and the content of development strategy, a fact visible in the force of pent-up consumer pressure in the 1970s which provided so much impetus for the fall of Maoism and the initial popularity of reforms.

Of course, to equate these broad class forces with specific political programmes in a mechanical way would be too crude. It seems likely, for example, that many industrial managers prefer the old system of economic management and are resistant to reforms; on the other hand, many supporters of the reforms may be found in the central ministries, particularly those whose role will be enhanced if the reforms are implemented (for example, the Ministries of Finance,

Foreign Economic Cooperation and Foreign Trade). Nor can the call for market forces simply be equated with 'technocracy', since the latter is perfectly compatible with a comprehensively-planned economy, suitably rationalised by greater information flows, more sophisticated techniques and better trained planners.[42] Structural analysis of classes must be linked with that of strata and substrata, of geographical regions and levels of government, and vertical divisions within the state apparatus – such a comprehensive analysis is a task for the future.

The above analysis of conflict and cooperation between statist, technocratic and 'mass' forces will be familiar to students of state-socialism in eastern Europe. A comparative perspective would lead us to predict that the relationship between these three forces will be at the roots of policy debate and political conflict in the 1980s. However, the Maoist experience has made China distinct from the Soviet Union and eastern Europe. The heritage of the radical and developmental Maoist attempts to incorporate the mass of the population more directly into the development process through a strategy of mass mobilisation led by a militant party has left a lasting imprint on Chinese institutions and patterns of thought. This heralds a pattern of 'three-line struggle' for the future, between the competing projects of Maoism, reformism and the conservative Leninist centre. The interaction between these political forces and between them and the intractable pressures of economic backwardness, social discontent and the international political economy will define the dynamics of Chinese development strategy for the rest of this century.

Notes

1 The most articulated form of western 'Maoism' was the work of Charles Bettelheim, notably his debate with Paul Sweezy, in P.M. Sweezy and C. Bettelheim, *On the Transition to Socialism* (2nd end), New York, Monthly Review Press, 1971; and his *Cultural Revolution and Industrial Organisation in China: Changes in Management and the Division of Labour*, New York, Monthly Review Press, 1974. For a posthumous paean, see P. Corrigan, H. Ramsay and D. Sayer, *For Mao*, London, Macmillan, 1979.

2 For discussion of this issue, see N.B. Scott, 'The development path of China', in U.G. Damachi, G. Routh and A.E. Alitaha (eds), *Development Paths in Africa and China*, London, Macmillan, 1976; Neville Maxwell (ed.), *China's Road to Development*, Oxford, Pergamon Press, 1976; Sartaj Aziz, *Rural Development: Learning From China*, London, Macmillan, 1978; Jonathan Unger (ed.), 'Chinese rural institutions and the question of transferability', *World Development*, vol. 6, no. 5, May 1978; R.F. Dernberger, 'The relevance of China's development experience for other developing countries', *Items*, New York, Social Science Research Council, 1977, pp. 25–33.

3 In making this argument, I agree substantially with several scholars in Australia who have done excellent work in clarifying the distinction between the Maoist theories of 'uninterrupted' and 'continuous revolution': for example, see Graham Young and Dennis Woodward, 'From contradictions among the people to class struggle: the theories of uninterrupted and continuous revolution', *Asian Survey* XVIII, 9, September 1978, pp. 912–33; Michael Sullivan, 'The politics of conflict and compromise', in Bill Brugger (ed.), *China Since the 'Gang of Four'*, London, Croom Helm, 1980, pp. 20–50.

4 For an interesting analysis of CCP thinking in the mid-1950s, see Steve Regler, 'The development of Chinese approach to socialism: Chinese reforms after the denunciation of Stalin', *Journal of Contemporary Asia*, 10, 1/2, 1980, pp. 181–214.

5 'The two roads: alternative strategies of social change and economic growth in China', in S.R. Schram (ed.), *Authority, Participation and Cultural Change in China*, Cambridge University Press, 1973, pp. 109–57.

6 In Schurmann's words, 'decentralization can take two different paths: either decision-making powers are put into the hands of the producing units themselves (decentralisation I) or they are put into the hands of lower-echelon administrative units (decentralization II)'. *Source*: Franz Schurmann, *Ideology and Organization in Communist China*, Berkeley, University of California Press, 1968.

7 For a discussion of Mao's different views of 'revolution', see Young and Woodward, *op. cit.*

8 For the two classic documents of radical Maoism in the 1970s, see Yao Wenyuan, 'On the social basis of the Lin Piao anti-party clique', *Peking Review*, 10, 1973, pp. 5–10; Zhang Chunqiao, 'On exercising all-round dictatorship over the bourgeoisie', *Peking Review*, 14, 1975, pp. 5–11.

9 Hua Guofeng stated that 'revolution means liberating the productive forces', in his 'Speech at the Second National Conference on learning from Dazhai in agriculture', *Peking Review*, 1, 1 January 1977, p. 41. For a statement of Hua's ideological position, see the political report to the eleventh National Congress of the CCP, 12 August 1977, *Peking Review*, 35, 26 August 1977.

10 The eminent economist Hu Qiaomu later argued against those 'who take the will of society, the government and the authorities as economic laws which can be bent to political expediency . . . politics itself cannot create other laws and impose them on the economy; 'Observe economic laws, speed up the four modernisations', *Peking Review*, 45, 10 November 1978, p. 8.

11 Chi Wei, 'How the "Gang of Four" opposed socialist modernisation', *Peking Review* 11, 11 March 1977, p. 8; Lin Kang, 'Is it necessary to develop the productive forces in continuing the revolution?', *Peking Review*, 14, 1 April 1978, pp. 6–10.

12 This was made public for the first time on 25 December 1976, Mao's birthday. See *Peking Review*, 1, 1 January 1977, pp. 10–25. For approving commentaries on this speech, see Chu Chin-ping, 'The basic policy for socialist revolution and construction', *Peking Review*, 12, 18 March 1977, pp. 10–13; Chung Chin, 'China's road to industrialisation', *Peking Review*, 14, 1 April 1977, pp. 12–15.

13 For a programmatic statement of this strategy, see the State Planning Commission, 'Great guiding principle for socialist construction', *Peking Review*, 39, 23 September 1977; for a discussion of the plan, see Hua Guofeng, 'Unite and strive to build a modern powerful socialist country', 26 February 1978, *Peking Review*, 10, 10 March 1978, pp. 7–40.

14 For the 'resolution on Hua Guofeng's errors', issued at the Sixth Plenum, see Xinhua News Agency, *Daily Report*, 30 June 1981.

15 See 'Practice is the only criterion for verifying truth', *Guangming Daily*, 11 May 1978; and 'One of the fundamental principles of Marxism', *People's Daily*, 24 June 1978. The article by Hu Qiaomu, *op. cit.*, *Peking Review*, 45, 46 and 47, 1978, helped to set the intellectual scene for changes in thinking about development strategy before the Third Plenum.

16 For a general analysis of these imbalances, see Jin Ping, 'Make a success of comprehensive balancing; advance in the course of making adjustment', *Guangming Daily*, 25 March 1979, p. 3, translated in *Foreign Broadcast Information Service*, China Report (hereafter *FBIS*), 4 April 1979.

17 For example, see Zhong Renfu, 'Inquire into the reasonable rates for accumulation for our country from historical experiences', *People's Daily*, 15 May 1980, translated in *FBIS*, 20 May 1980.

18 Yu Youhai, 'US $1000 by the year 2000', *Peking Review*, 43, 27 October 1980, pp. 16–18.

19 In an important article, Jiang Yiwei cited the Polish economist Bogdan Glinski, who classifies reform models into three types: (i) a combination of central government planning with partial autonomy for basic economic units (present-day Soviet Union); (ii) a combination of central government planning with a high degree of autonomy for basic economic units (Hungary); (iii) central government planning plays hardly any role and economic units have the highest possible degree of autonomy, interacting through market relations (Yugoslavia). Each of these three reform positions has its supporters in China, with majority opinion concentrated on (i) and (ii). *Source*: Jiang Yiwei, 'The theory of an enterprise-based economy', *Social Sciences in China*, no. 1, 1980, p. 53.

20 For example, see 'Integrating moral encouragement with material reward', *Peking Review*, 21 April 1978.

21 For a discussion of changes in rural policy, see Peter Nolan and Gordon White, 'Distribution and development', *Bulletin of Concerned Asian Scholars*, vol. 13, no. 3, July–September 1981, pp. 2–18.

22 Local decentralisation still has its adherents in China. Jiang Yiwei, for

example, notes that those who support greater power for the enterprise were only one among three groups with proposals on the issue of centralisation and decentralisation. The other two proposed the following: (i) greater centralisation (Jiang comments that 'although such a view has not appeared in print, it is supported by many more people than one may expect'); and (ii) greater decentralisation to provincial and municipal authorities. *Source*: Jiang Yiwei, *op. cit.*, pp. 53–4.

23   For an authoritative exposition of such arguments, see Xue Muqiao, 'A study in the planned management of the socialist economy', *Peking Review*, 43, 26 October 1979.

24   Liu Guoguang, Wu Jinglian and Zhao Renwei, 'Relationship between planning and market as seen by China in her socialist economy', *Atlantic Economic Journal*, no. 31, 1979, p. 15.

25   Yuan Wenqi, Dai Lunzhang and Wang Linsheng, 'International division of labour and China's economic relations with foreign countries', *Social Sciences in China*, 1, 1980, p. 30. For an opposing analysis, see Yao Xianhao, 'The international division of labour and the foreign economic relations of a socialist state', *Jingji Kexue* (Economic Science), no. 4, 1980.

26   For a discussion of enterprise funds, see Wu Jinglian, Zhou Shulian and Wang Haibo, 'Establish and improve the system of retaining earnings for enterprise funds', *People's Daily*, 2 September 1978. For a discussion of the Sichuan experiment with enterprise autonomy, see *Peking Review*, 14, 6 April 1981, pp. 21–9.

27   *Peking Review*, 30, 27 July 1981, p. 6; 35, 30 August 1982, pp. 13–17.

28   Li Zhisheng, 'Commercial reforms: smooth circulation of goods', *Peking Review*, 22, 1 June 1981, pp. 20–9.

29   Zhang Enhua, 'On banking reform', *Peking Review*, 29, 20 July 1981, pp. 24–7.

30   For general discussions of international economic policies, see Ji Chongwei, 'China's utilisation of foreign funds and relevant policies'; and Bu Ming, 'China's financial relations with foreign countries', *Peking Review*, 16, 20 April 1981, pp. 15ff.

31   For an official retrospective review of the period, see Zhou Jin, 'Further economic readjustment: a break with "leftist" thinking', *Peking Review*, 12, 23 March 1981.

32   Martin Lockett, 'Self-management in China?', in *Economic Analysis and Worker's Management*, Belgrade, Yugoslavia, 1981.

33   Jiang Yiwei, *op. cit.*, p. 55.

34   For an example of the official rationale, see Yao Yilin, 'Report on the readjustment of the 1981 National Economic Plan and State revenue and expenditure', *Peking Review*, 11, 16 March 1981.

35   'Economic reform and readjustment', *Peking Review*, 4, 26 January 1981, p.3.

36   For the 'eight fields of centralisation and unification' in economic management, see *Peking Review*, 11, 16 March 1981, p. 18. For a specific discussion of price stabilisation, see Liu Zhuofu, 'Can China's prices be stabilised?', *Peking Review*, 20, 18 May 1981, pp. 21–2.

37   *Peking Review*, 14, 6 April 1981, p. 29.

38 *People's Daily*, 25 December 1980. I am indebted to Noriko Yamamoto
    for drawing this to my attention.
39 Marie Lavigne, *The Socialist Economies*, London, Martin Robertson,
    1974, p. 65.
40 Interview with Wang Renzhong, Secretary of the CCP Central Commit-
    tee, on 11 September 1980, reported in *Politika*, Belgrade, 5 October 1980
    (translated in *FBIS* 200, 1980).
41 For example, see Zhou Jinwei, 'On spiritual civilisation', *Peking Review*,
    10, 9 March 1981, pp. 18–20.
42 For example, while the distinguished economist Sun Yefang recognises
    the importance of the 'law of value', he does not necessarily equate it with
    markets – its functions can be replicated through the calculations of
    planners: 'What is the origin of the law of value?', *Social Sciences in
    China*, 3 September 1980, pp. 155–71.

China: Country Profile

*Denotes official figures released by the State Statistical Bureau of the PRC.

Name of the country:	People's Republic of China, established 1 October 1949.
Population:	1032 million* (1982 census)
Capital:	Peking, population c. 8 million (1977).
Total land area:	9.3 million sq km, of which arable land 11 per cent, pastures 24 per cent, woodland and forest 12 per cent.
Official language:	Mandarin Chinese (putonghua).
Membership of international organisations:	UN since 1971, IMF since April 1980.

Political structure

State Constitution:	March 1978, superseding the 1954 and 1975 Constitutions; revised draft circulated in April 1982.
Highest legislative body:	National People's Congress, with delegates elected for a 5-year term, and sessions once a year.
Highest executive body:	State Council.
Prime Minister:	Zhao Ziyang, succeeding Hua Guofeng in September 1980.
Head of State (nominal):	Chairman of the Standing Committee of the National People's Congress, Ye Jianying, who assumed office in March 1978.
Ruling Party:	The Chinese Communist Party, founded in 1921.
Party Chairman:	Hu Yaobang, succeeding Hua Guofeng in June 1981; became General Secretary in September 1982

when the post of Chairman was
abolished.

Party membership:

35 million (5–6 per cent of adult
population, 1977); about 39 million
by 1981.

Armed forces:

4.5 million regular troops in the
People's Liberation Army (PLA) (c.1
per cent of total labour force) based
on selective military service, plus a
people's militia.

Population
  Population density: 106 per sq km.
  Population growth (% p.a.):   2.0 (1970–7); 1.3* (1978–80).
  Population of working age   61 per cent (1978).
  (15–64):
  Urban population: 25 per cent (1980).
  Ethnic and linguistic groups: Ethnic Chinese (Han) 94 per cent;
                                     55 ethnic minorities 6 per cent (in-
                                     cluding Chuangs, Uighurs, Tibetans,
                                     Manchus, and Mongols). The Chinese
                                     language includes a large number of
                                     mutually incomprehensible dialects;
                                     Mandarin is taught in schools.

Education and health
  School system: Five years of universal primary educa-
                                     tion from the age of six, and five
                                     years of secondary.
  Primary school enrollment:[I]   c.94 per cent of school-age children
                                     enrolled (mid-1970s).[d]
  Secondary school enrollment:[II]   60–75 per cent of rural children,
                                     80–90 per cent of urban children
                                     continue to secondary school (mid-
                                     1970s).[d]
  Higher education enrollment   0.6 per cent (males 0.9 per cent;
  (gross ratios):   females 0.4 per cent) (1977).
  Life expectancy: 70 (1978).
  Child death rate (per 1000):   1 (1978).
  Population per hospital bed: 496* (1980).[k]
  Population per physician:[III]   853* (1980).[k]

Economy
  GNP: US $517 billion (1979).[16]
  GNP per capita: US $510.
  Capital construction   15, of which for non-productive pur-
  investment as % of national   poses 34 per cent, for investment for
  income:[IV]   production 66 per cent (1980).**[k]

State budget (expenditure)	112 billion *yuan*[*][v] (1979 plan).[a]
Defence expenditure–	
% of state budget:	18 (1979 plan).[j]
% of GNP:	5–10 (1978–9).[j]
GNP by sector (%):	Agriculture 27, industry 55, service 19 (1975).[b]
Relative value of industrial and agricultural output:	3:1[*] (1980).[k]
Total labour force by sector (%):	400–50 million (1978–80)[l,f] agriculture 62, industry 25, service 13 (1978).
Structure of ownership:	*Industry*: dominated by the state sector. Rural People's Communes produce 9 per cent of total industrial output value,[l] the collective urban sector is currently being expanded. *Agriculture*: (per cent of total output value): state-owned units 4, people's communes 80, individual production by commune members 16 (1978).[e] Private plots represented c.5 per cent of a production team's arable land until the late 1970s; moves to increase this have taken place in 1979–80 (up to c.15 per cent). *Commercial services and handicrafts*: a small urban sector of private business is emerging. Employment by sector (in millions, 1980): State sector 80, collective urban sector 24, private urban sector 0.8,[*][k] collective rural sector 300–50, with 9 per cent working in industry).[l,f]
Main crops:	Rice, wheat, maize, soybeans, vegetables.
Irrigated area:	48 million ha, or 49 per cent of arable land (1978).
Grain self-sufficiency (%):	97.8 (1978).[h]
Energy balance–	
a. commercial energy consumption per capita:	805 kg coal equivalent.
liquid fuels (% of a):	18.
b. primary production by type of energy (%):	Liquid fuels 19, solid fuels 79, natural gas 1, hydroelectric 1.
net exports (% of b):	2.1.

Growth indicators (% p.a.)–	(1971–8)[h]	(1979–80)[*][k]
GNP:	7	7
industry, *of which*	9	9
heavy industry	—	14

light industry	—	5
agriculture	3	6
food per capita production	2[VI]	—

Foreign trade and economic integration

Trade balance–	(1979).
exports:	US\$ 13.5 billion.
imports:	US\$ 14.7 billion.
Exports as % of national income[IV]:	7.5 (1980).[k]
Export products (%):	Food products 19, crude oil and products 16, other crude materials 14, textile products 24, metal manufactures and machinery 10 (1979).[i] 1980: heavy industrial and mineral products 52.*[k]
Import products (%):	Single-item equipment and raw materials for heavy industry 35, raw materials for the textile and light industries 24, consumer goods (including food) 21, complete sets of equipment 13, means of production for rural use 7 (1980).*[k]
Destination of exports (%):	Industrialised countries 42, developing countries 46, socialist countries[VII] 12 (1979).[i]
Main trading partners:	*Exports*: Japan, Hong Kong (1977–9)[i]; *imports* Japan, West Germany, the US, Canada, Australia.
Foreign debt:	US\$ 1.3 billion.[h]
Debt service ratio (%):	8.1 (1977).[h]
Foreign aid extended to other countries:	To non-socialist countries: 4.9 billion (1954–79); 135 million (1979).[16] Estimate of total aid 6.7 billion (1953–78).[5]
Foreign investment:	During 1980, first full year of allowing foreign investment: over US\$1 billion.[c]

Notes

[I] Gross ratios (1977, %): 112 (males 111, females 114).
[II] Gross ratios (1978, %): 79 (males 92, females 65).
[III] With 'barefoot doctors' included, the figure is 285.
[IV] For definition of national income, see appendix B.
[V] Market rate as of December 1979: 1.51 *yuan* per US\$.
[VI] FAO 1969/71–9.
[VII] The USSR, eastern Europe, Kampuchea, Mongolian Republic, Laos, North Korea, Vietnam and Cuba.

Sources

[a]*Peking Review*, no. 28, June 29, 1979.

[b]R. Dernberger and David Fasenfelt, 'China's post-Mao economic future', in US Congress, Joint Economic Committee, *Chinese Economy Post-Mao*, vol. I. Washington DC, November 1978.

[c]International Monetary Fund, *Survey* (weekly), 6 April 1981.

[d]Frederic M. Kaplan, Julian M. Sobin and Stephen Andors, (eds), *Encyclopedia of China Today*, London, 1979.

[e]Qi Wen, *China: A General Survey*, Foreign Language Press, Peking, 1979.

[f]Thomas G. Rawski, *Economic Growth and Employment in China*. World Bank, Washington DC, 1979.

[g]US, CIA, *China: The Continuing Search for a Modernization Strategy*, Research paper, Washington DC, April 1980.

[h]US, CIA, *China: Economic Indicators*, Research paper, Washington DC, December 1978.

[i]US, CIA, *China: International Trade Quarterly Review*, Research paper, Washington DC, 2nd quarter 1980.

[j]US, CIA, *Chinese Defense Spending 1965–79*, Research paper, Washington DC, July 1979.

[k]'Communique on fulfilment of China's 1980 national economic plan', Xinhua News Agency (Peking), *Daily Bulletin*, no. 8398, 29 April 1980.

[l]Xue Muqiao, *China's Socialist Economy*, China Knowledge Series, Foreign Language Press, Peking, 1981.

China Post-Mao: Chronology

4–5 April 1976	The Tiananmen incident.
9 September 1976	Death of Chairman Mao Tse Tung.
7 October 1976	Hua Guofeng becomes Chairman of the Chinese Communist Party; arrest of the 'Gang of Four' (Wang Hongwen, Zhang Chunqiao, Jiang Qing and Yao Wenyuan).
16–21 July 1977	The Third Plenum of the CCP Tenth Central Committee, meeting in Peking, confirms the appointment of Hua Guofeng as CCP Chairman, restores Deng Xiaoping to the posts held in early 1976 and expels the 'Gang of Four' from the Party.
12–18 August 1977	Eleventh National Congress of the CCP: the Political Report delivered by Hua and the Congress approves a new Party Constitution.
12 September 1977	The State Planning Commission publishes a comprehensive analysis of China's development strategy: 'Great guiding principle for socialist construction'.
26 February–5 March 1977	The Fifth National People's Congress. Hua Guofeng delivers the report on the work of the government; a draft ten-year plan is submitted for discussion and a revised state constitution approved.
11 May 1978	Publication of the article 'Practice is the only criterion for verifying truth', which provides a theoretical frame-

	work for attacking remaining Maoist leaders in the so-called 'whateverist' group.
June 1978	Vice-Premier Li Xiannian informs a visiting British parliamentary delegation that China would now borrow directly from British banks.
July 1978	Important speech by the prominent economist Hu Qiaomu before the State Council entitled 'Observe economic laws, speed up the four modernisations'. This lays the theoretical basis for later reforms in the system of economic management.
4 July 1978	Report on the newly-issued 'Draft decision of the CCP Central Committee concerning some problems in accelerating the development of industry' (known as the 'thirty points').
October 1978	Experiment with greater enterprise autonomy begins in Sichuan province.
18–22 December 1978	The Third Plenum of the eleventh CCP Central Committee held in Peking.
January 1979	CCP Central Committe decides to remove class labels from 'remoulded' former landlords, rich peasants, 'counter-revolutionaries' and 'bad elements' – they are now to be treated as ordinary citizens.
18 June – 1 July 1979	Second Session of the Fifth National People's Congress, held in Peking, announces a three-year programme of economic readjustment.
July 1979	The State Council issues 'Five Documents' on economic reform in the state sector.
25–8 September 1979	Fourth Plenum of the eleventh CCP Central Committee approves a set of important measures designed to accelerate agricultural development.
23–9 February 1980	Fifth Plenum of the eleventh Central Committee. Hu Yaobang is elected as CCP Central Secretary and former President Liu Shaoqi is formally rehabilitated. Key members of the 'whateverist' group resign.
30 August – 10 September 1980	Third Session of the Fifth National People Congress: issues regulations on joint ventures with Chinese and foreign investment. Hua Guofeng resigns as premier to be replaced by Zhao Ziyang.
2 September 1980	State Council approves the State Economic Commission's 'Report on the experimental expansion of enterprise self-management and opinions on future work'.
December 1980	Working Conference of the CCP Central Committee decides to deepen economic readjustment and slow the pace of reforms.
27–9 June 1981	Sixth Plenum of the eleventh Central Committee. Hua Guofeng resigns from the post of Party Chairman and is replaced by Hu Yaobang. Official evaluations of Mao's historical role and of the Cultural Revolution are made public.
September 1982	Twelfth Party Congress takes place in Peking.

CUBA IN THE SEVENTIES

Ricardo Carciofi

Introduction

The first twelve years of the Cuban revolution (1959–70) attracted the attention of many writers for two basic sets of reasons: first, Cuba – a poor and underdeveloped island in the Caribbean – emerged at the beginning of the 1960s from a social revolution the leadership of which decided to direct the country along a socialist road.[1]

The repercussions of that decision were immense; Cuba became the first socialist country in the American continent, and that simple fact was 'destabilising' for the intra-continental order dictated by the US. In launching a socialist strategy, the Cuban leaders were implicitly pointing out to the rest of Latin America that there might be an alternative route to social and economic development. At this time, Latin American countries were following a variety of development policies, but the socialist path was simply not on the agenda. The Cuban experience thus introduced a new element to prevalent political and academic discussions. Additionally, socialist Cuba posed an overt challenge to US domination within the continent, and, given the geographical location of the island, the events that culminated in the overthrow of Batista's régime represented a direct threat to the US defence system.[2] The Cuban revolution carried important consequences for the future of the continent: Latin American countries would have a 'socialist model' to look at, and the US was forced to recognise that its foreign policy towards the continent required major revision.[3]

The second powerful reason for debating Cuba during the 1960s was its implications for left-wing movements throughout the world. From the socialist perspective, Cuba was interesting on several counts. First, at the political level, the new-born revolution represented a victory for a social alliance whose main strength came from an over-exploited rural proletariat, in a country with a very small industrial base. Second, the use of guerrilla warfare and its success were a novelty in Latin America. The support of the rural masses for the revolution and the deployment of guerrilla tactics raised an obvious question about the feasibility of similar political strategies in other Latin American countries with analogous economic structures. Third, the discussion that surrounded the economic strategy of the sixties – the role of the market v. planning, and especially the operation of the labour market – had significant theoretical implications. On the one hand, the Cuban debate on economic strategies between 1960 and 1965 resembled the Soviet industrialisation debate of the 1920s. On the other hand, in tackling the questions of economic planning and the role of exchange relations in socialism, the Cubans contributed to a set of discussions which have been a source of bitter and long-standing disagreement amongst socialist writers. But there was a pronounced tendency to generalise the issues and ideas deriving from the Cuban case to other scenarios. In consequence, a great deal of the literature on Cuba in the first decade of the revolution tended to stress the *general* validity of particular arguments which were originally framed to deal with the concrete historical circumstances that Cuba was facing at the time. Even when such analyses were valuable in understanding the issues at hand, they tended to relegate to the background a more basic problem: why was the socialist revolution confronted with those questions?

It is against this background that I intend to discuss Cuba's experience during the 1970s in this paper. From one aspect, concentration on the 1970s reflects a simple attempt to balance quantities: the 1960s have been intensively studied, but the 1970s much less so. But my focus also reflects more substantive considerations. Cuba has been neither a de-stabilising factor in the Latin America scenario of the 1970s, nor the subject of deep theoretical debates on the construction of a socialist society. Such features might appear to make Cuba in the 1970s less interesting, but one can turn the argument on its head: Cuba's lower profile in Latin America and its already maturing revolutionary experience require analysis also. The fact that there is a second decade suggests the need to look within Cuba, rather than trying to analyse the implications of the Cuban revolution *outside* Cuba. The 1970s is also an appropriate period of analysis since the turn of the decade brought a shift in the strategy of socialist development. The importance of that change is not primarily related to the general line of economic development, but rather to the strategy of labour mobilisation and the organisation of internal politics. Given the situation that Cuba faced at the end of the 1960s, however, any attempt at introducing substantial changes in the policy of labour mobilisation was bound to have significant effects on the pattern of economic growth. Thus, the 1970s raise the issue of explaining the dynamics of Cuban society utilising different strategies of labour mobilisation.

Though the context of the 1970s is different, it still throws light on the crucial issue of how to construct socialism at a given level of development of the productive forces. The different approaches attempted by the Cuban revolution cannot be understood unless one realises how the level of development of the country represented a permanent constraint that determined the results achieved at each stage. Thus, before dealing with Cuba during the second decade, we must first draw a picture of the late 1960s and the overall meaning of the first decade of revolutionary experience.

The Background: The late 1960s: Imbalanced Growth and Economic 'Failure'

1970 was a turning-point in Cuban economic strategy. After the failure of the 1970 harvest, when despite enormous efforts the output goal of 10 million tons was not achieved, emphasis on sugar was reduced. At the same time, Cuba seemed to give up the approach to moral incentives characteristic of the late 1960s and the political life of the country entered another stage as new institutions and participatory structures were created.

Two important questions must be clarified here. First, to the extent that a shift took place in 1970, why was this necessary, and what was it a reaction against? Secondly, who recognised the need for and implemented the change in direction? The answer to the first question directs our analysis to the main trends of the late 1960s. This was a decade when the revolution was trying to find the best road towards industrialisation. After 1966 the leadership decided that, in order to overcome the difficulties associated with the strategy of import substitution launched during the first half of the decade, the economy could (and should) rely upon its 'comparative advantage' in sugar production as the basis for a steady process of industrial growth and structural integration.

Industrialisation of a sugar economy

Before going into the implications of the sugar strategy and the policy of the late 1960s, it is important to discuss the industrialisation question in general. Was it wise to set an absolute and relative increase in industrial output as a revolutionary target? What was the rationale behind the decision to achieve industrial growth?

The first element in the stress on industrialisation derives from the socialist orientation adopted by Cuban leaders. To the extent that it was socialist, the new economic strategy could not neglect industrial growth. Cuba's sugar production had given rise to an agricultural proletariat which had provided the main support to the revolutionary movement. But this class could not constitute the basic support of a socialist state. Its prevailing standards of living were below any measure of socialist standards and it was a primary responsibility of the revolution to improve them. This task required industrialisation.

Second, there is an important political element stemming from the tradition that grew up during the pre-revolutionary period. According to this view, US domination had always constituted a fetter on Cuba's economic and social progress. Though Cuba had escaped from Spanish domination in 1898, the post-colonial period had brought little advance towards 'independence'; it was rather a substitution of one imperial power for another.[4]

Foreign economic relations, many believed, were the most serious hindrance to the potential capabilities of a country whose resource endowments constituted a fairly good basis for a more industrialised and democratic society. This evaluation was of course not in relation to the US, but to the tiny sugar economies of the Caribbean. In the latter context, Cuba's actual socio-economic performance seemed to contrast sharply with its potential. Since the real problem was seen as the issue of imperial domination, any position favouring national development was bound to have a strong anti-imperialist flavour.

To the extent that these external constraints could be removed, the central task would then be to establish the basis for a sustained process of economic development. Beyond any doubts, that task meant industrialisation which was necessary to 'restore the balance' of an economy systematically sabotaged first by Spain and later by the US. Therefore, at the dawn of the revolution, these nationalistic sentiments were strong because the victory belonged to a movement based on anti-imperialist struggle. They were intensified by US policy during the post-revolutionary period. The discussion on industrialisation which followed reflected this ideological framework.

At this point it might be argued that, if external constraints were removed, industrialisation was not in fact necessary as a precondition for economic development. If 'exploitation through the sugar trade' had been the main economic hindrance, it would seem that its removal would lead almost automatically to a better position.[5] In other words this is not a matter of industrial growth, but of internal distribution of a surplus previously pumped off through trade relations.

But this point misses a central feature of the pre-revolutionary period: the technology of sugar production. This provides a third element in the rationale for industrialisation. Sugar production in Cuba was based upon a labour intensive technology. The harvest required a vast mobilisation of labour, but there was equally vast unemployment during the dead season.[6] Though this was a very efficient allocation of resources from the point of view of capitalists interested in profits from the sugar business, it was not suitable for a socialist revolution which has a radically different approach to the relative importance of private v. social efficiency and welfare. This political orientation made industrialisation necessary.

Though these factors provided a rationale for industrialisation, they did not lead automatically to a precise strategy for building industry. Import substitution was attempted first (1961–4), and given the difficulties that it produced, the decision was taken to adopt an 'export-led' strategy by 'leaning' the economy on sugar (1965–70). Let us examine this latter stage.

The sugar strategy

Though the weaknesses of an industrial strategy based on sugar specialisation are obvious – and were well-known in 1965 in Cuba – there were some positive factors which played a major role in supporting the policy. First, most of the land devoted to sugar production was in the hands of the state as a result of the second agrarian reform.[7] Second, the sugar mills had already been nationalised after the bitter US–Cuban exchanges of the early 1960s. Third, as a consequence of the nationalisation process and the current line in economic theory, mechanisms of economic management became increasingly centralised. Fourth, despite the US embargo, Cuba had already made some progress in working out bilateral agreements with the USSR to commercialise her sugar exports.

These four factors fitted neatly with an export-led strategy. Sugar output (and exports) could be planned to the extent that the state provided the bulk of cane production, the operation of the mills was centrally controlled, and trade arrangements helped to avoid dependence on cyclical demand. Moreover, foreign exchange earnings could be used to finance an industrial expansion consistent with the plan. However, sugar proved to be more resistant to planning than expected. Without major improvements in agricultural technology, the problem of labour mobilisation for the harvest remained an insurmountable difficulty. Thus, the 1970 target of 10 million tons of sugar was based on the assumption that technical change would be forthcoming, specifically the introduction of labour-saving techniques in harvesting, rearrangement of the transportation system, better coordination and operation of the mills, and modernisation of mill equipment. The other response to the problem was social rather than technological. The sugar harvest was to be conceived as a national campaign for the construction of socialism. The main incentives were to be moral, and the verbal framework embodied a conception of guerrilla war applied to sugar. If the battle was won, the basis for socialist construction was laid. As Fidel Castro put it:

The question of a sugar harvest of 10 million tons has been something more than an economic goal; it is something that has been converted into a point of honor for this Revolution; *it has become a yardstick by which to judge the capability of the Revolution.* (emphasis added).[8]

It is important to take a closer look at the stress on moral incentives to pave the way for the analysis of the 1970s. They were not chosen as a mere pragmatic response to problems of labour mobilisation. Choice of incentives raises deeper theoretical issues of the construction of socialism which were the focus of the 'Great Debate' during 1963–4, two years before the adoption of the sugar strategy.[9] The emergence of the distinctive stress on moral incentives can be explained in terms of the strong commitment to egalitarianism and social justice demonstrated by the Cuban leaders, rather than by the necessity of implementing an economic policy. These commitments reflect the political background of the Cuban leadership, and the practice of guerrilla warfare that they developed.[10] But use of moral incentives also seemed to make good economic sense, particularly as a response to the failure in other areas considered essential for a successful sugar policy. In particular, the more difficult it proved to introduce technical change and to organise the entire operation of the sugar harvest, the more intensive had to be the use of moral instruments.

The 1970 harvest and the origin of policies in the 1970s

Although 1970 was a year of a record production, the planned goal of 10 million tons was not achieved. Furthermore, the negative side-effects of pursuing that target had become clear. The process of labour mobilisation caused many disruptions in other sectors of the economy which faced labour shortages and lack of appropriate inputs.[11] The poor results of this economic strategy are usually considered by the literature on Cuba as the source of explanation of the shift started in the 1970s. While it is true that continuation of the same line would have been unwise and a fundamental shift was necessary, the real problem lies in assessing the reasons behind the 'failure'. Investigation of this will help explain what the policies of the 1970s were reacting against. Let us consider the different explanations advanced to account for the shift.

The 'Sovietisation thesis'

One common interpretation of the relationship between the 1960s and the 1970s is the thesis raised by Mesa Lago and others.[12] According to this view, the failure of the economic strategy of the 1960s brought increasing dependence on the USSR (in terms of foreign aid and trade relations) which led to a significant intervention of the USSR in moulding the strategy of the 1970s.

This approach has certain difficulties which make it less than convincing. Though it is indisputable that Cuban–Soviet relations have been increasing during the last decade, the meaning of those relations needs investigation. The Sovietisation hypothesis argues that these relations involve an increasing degree of economic dependence and the imposition of a Soviet model on the Cuban society. But this begs more questions than it answers. In the first place, there is a prior need to specify a theory of dependency applicable to underdeveloped socialist countries. Dependency theory has faced many difficulties when applied to capitalist countries and its utility has been the focus of bitter disagreement amongst social scientists. Secondly, one of the central ingredients of established dependency theory is the concept of exploitation through trade relations. But this cannot be transferred to the analysis of socialist societies without further elaboration. In the Cuban case, moreover, it is not easy to document the existence of exploitative trade relations with the USSR, as we shall see. If one cannot prove that such a transfer of surplus exists, it is difficult to establish a plausible basis for the notion of political and ideological dependency.

Although relations amongst socialist countries may involve means of extra-economic domination, it is not clear what these are and whether opposing tendencies exist. Proponents of the 'Sovietisation' hypothesis have tended to disregard these theoretical problems, thereby weakening the analytical force of their arguments.

This approach also tends to over-emphasise the role of external factors in the determination of Cuban development. Thus, the real dynamics of the Cuban experience during the 1970s are attributed to the Soviet desire for domination. In consequence, important internal elements are missed and there is insufficient attention to the relative influence of external *vis à vis* internal factors and the nature of interactions between them. As the next section shows, the policy shift of the 1970s can be better understood by taking a closer look at the complex internal problems produced by the strategy of the late 1960s. Such an approach does not deny that Soviet interests may have influenced Cuban assessments of sugar strategy; but it argues that the issue involves more than a simple shift from a sino-Guevarist to a Soviet line and that the economics and politics of the 1960s created contradictions which deserve attention in their own terms.

Mobilisation strategy and the cost of 'conciencia'[13]
Authors like Ritter and Silverman tend to point out that the difficulties of the first decade of the Cuban revolution lay in the method of labour mobilisation. Though mass mobilisation was relatively successful in achieving egalitarian goals, it could not secure economic growth.[14] Since such methods embody a system of labour allocation that makes very little use of efficiency calculations – through prices and wage differentials – it is very difficult to monitor the growth process because there are no 'effective signals' to identify successes and mistakes. This led to systematic misallocation, waste and disorganisation, which created cynicism among the workers and undermined the moral basis of mobilisation – *conciencia*. In this approach, the main framework of analysis concerns the relationship between the plan and the market or, as Silverman argues, between the 'forces of production' and the 'relations of production'.[15]

Working-class democracy as an instrument of self-control
MacEwan goes beyond such arguments about 'the cost of *conciencia*', and posits that moral incentives and non-market

mechanisms in general can only be effective if applied in a situation where the workers have participatory institutions which involve them in the process of production.[16] Thus, he sees the high rate of absenteeism during the crucial year of the 1970 harvest not as a manifestation of 'cynical attitudes' or lack of popular support for the strategy, but the almost unavoidable result of applying moral incentives, while at the same time applying an 'inhibition on the exercise of power by the working class'.

MacEwan thus develops a more interesting alternative to the dichotomy of plan v. market. If centralised planning is applied and labour is mobilised through moral means (collective incentives as MacEwan would prefer) it is the working class who determine the effectiveness of the strategy. If the workers lack political control or the power of participation, this leads to a disorganisation of the social labour process and absenteeism. Such a massive strategy of labour mobilisation requires a check-and-balance mechanism, but this is not a matter of cadres and trained administrators but working-class organisations.

MacEwan's view provides a useful insight that is lacking in the Ritter/Silverman approach. He raises the question of the preconditions for applying a certain method of labour allocation and its implications for the design of a socialist economic strategy. He thus overcomes the problem of calculating efficiency in a system of moral incentives, for, in his framework, working-class organisation would provide the device of self-control that non-market allocation requires. His point about the preconditions is quite different from the position taken by Charles Bettelheim at the time, *viz.* that 'moral incentives' were infeasible because they infringed the necessary relationship between the forces of production and the relations of production. Resulting inefficiencies, argued Bettelheim, impeded achievement of the primary target which was capital accumulation. The use of market instruments was more appropriate to that level of development of the productive forces.[17] However, Bettelheim's position was unacceptable in the Cuban context because it amounted to a negation of the Cuban revolution itself, since it had taken place at an historical moment when the development of productive forces did not allow a leap forward towards socialism. The experience seemed to be the voluntaristic result of the ideology of the Cuban leaders!

Sierra Maestra and the struggle for economic and social development[18]

However, MacEwan's explanation would seem to leave a fundamental question unanswered. If working-class organisation was so essential for a successful non-bureaucratic strategy of moral mobilisation, why did it not come about?

It is easy to point out the fact that the planning machinery developed to control the strategy created bureaucratic forces, but why, in the event, did bureaucratic planning preclude workers' organisation and not the other way around? A much more solid explanation can be constructed if one recalls the situation of the Cuban economy prior to 1959, the type of working-class organisation that emerged from that process, and the economic difficulties at both national and international levels which confronted the Cuban revolution during the 1960s.

All these conditions, and the need to develop an industrial base in spite of them, made it virtually impossible to construct an egalitarian socialist society in the context of working-class democracy. In fact, the working class had to be created along with the moulding of the new society. In consequence, the 'mistakes' usually attributed to Cuba in the 1960s – inefficiency associated with a certain method of labour allocation, lack of working-class democracy, bureaucratism, etc. – should be primarily understood as a reflection of the constraints which economic and social underdevelopment imposed upon the revolutionary experience. This is not to say that the problems emerging from the strategy of the 1960s were necessarily bound to appear. In fact, greater success could have been achieved if certain limiting factors had not been present. For example, had the introduction of technical change in sugar production been easier, some of the problems raised above could have been avoided.

It is my contention that the situation of underdevelopment inherited by the revolution was the main constraint on the economic strategy of the 1960s. But the problems which emerged pointed to a critical *political* question. Though the strategy had been conceived and implemented by the Cuban leadership, by the end of the decade it was clear that they had lost contact with the real potential of the working class they were leading. In consequence, they did not notice the failures until it was too late. It was against this lack of transmission-belts between the leaders and the masses that the reaction of the 1970s took place.

After 1970 it was apparent that guerrilla warfare had been a useful method for overthrowing Batista's régime, but its application to the fight for economic and social development was of dubious efficacy. For that reason the changes during the 1970s took two main directions. On the one hand, the use of non-market mechanisms for labour mobilisation and allocation was abandoned to a significant extent in view of the negative experience of the 1960s. On the other hand, it was clear that 'investments' had to be made in developing institutions which provided for working-class participation. If we view the 1970s from this point of view, the arguments of the Sovietisation hypothesis – that the 1970s reflect a retreat of the Cuban revolution based on concessions to the Soviet Union – are highly misleading. Our explanation does not need such external elements. It was the internal events of the first decade which acted both as a constraint and stimulus of subsequent alterations of that previous pattern in the following decade.

The 1970s and the New Economic Strategy

This section will deal with three issues: first, the question of the general direction of Cuban economic growth and the degree of reliance upon sugar; second, trade policy and commercial relationships; and, third, the new system of economic management.

Economic strategy and the productive structure, 1970–8

Information on Cuba's economic evolution has always been scarce, making systematic analysis difficult. Fortunately, a recent report produced by CEPAL (ECLA) provides a great deal of statistical data on trends in the 1970s which help us to understand the movement of the Cuban economy

Table 1 *Gross material product by sectors of economic activity*[a]

	1970	1971	1972	1973	1974	1975	1976	1977b	1978
	Millions of constant pesos								
Total material product	5566	5904	6478	7328	7900	8868	9210	9555	10,353
Rural sector	1230	1153	1216	1271	1328	1394	1468	1565	1675
Industry	4000	4177	4458	4988	5393	6067	6250	6337	6914
Construction	436	574	804	1069	1179	1407	1492	1653	1767
	Composition (%)								
Total material product	100.0	100.0	100.0	100.0	100.0	100.0	100.0	100.0	100.0
Rural sector	21.7	19.5	18.8	17.3	16.8	15.7	15.9	16.4	16.2
Industry	70.6	70.8	68.8	68.1	68.3	68.4	67.9	66.3	66.8
Construction	7.7	9.7	12.4	14.6	14.9	15.9	16.2	17.3	17.0
	Growth rates								
Total material product		4.2	9.7	13.1	7.8	12.3	3.9	3.7	8.4
Rural sector		6.3	5.5	4.5	4.5	5.0	5.3	6.3	7.0
Industry		4.4	6.7	11.9	8.1	12.5	3.0	1.4	9.1
Construction		31.7	40.1	33.0	10.3	19.3	6.0	10.8	6.9

[a]Gross Material Product equals the gross output of the "productive" sectors: rural sector, fishing, mining, manufacture, construction and electricity.

Source: CEPAL, *Cuba: Notas para el Estudio Económico de América Latina: 1978*, 1980.

as a whole.[19] During the 1970s, Cuba experienced relatively rapid but very uneven expansion. As Table 1 shows, the average rate of growth in gross material product (GMP) was 9.4 per cent during 1970–5, and slowed down to 6.0 per cent over the next three years. The dynamics of this process can be better grasped if the productive sectors are related to their sources of demand. Thus, the bulk of the agricultural product represents export earnings whereas industry and construction are oriented towards the internal market.[20]

Taking into account the fact that external restrictions have always been a fetter on growth in Cuba, it is easy to see that domestic expansion has been possible when foreign exchange has been abundant. In other words, the cyclical pattern of growth is tightly connected with the evolution of exports and these, in turn, depend on the revenue of sugar sales abroad.

As Table 2 illustrates, 1971–2 were very bad years for sugar production and exports (due to a severe drought). 1972–5 saw an acceleration of overall economic growth (Table 1) because the excellent price conditions in the international market provided the revenue to finance industrial growth.[21] The next two years saw a drastic drop of sugar prices that could not be offset through higher levels of production. In 1978 external conditions were again easier to the extent that the record harvest for the decade was mainly traded with the USSR at prices four times higher than world market levels. The performance of the other two sectors – industry and construction – clearly reflect the impact of the sugar cycle (Table 1).[22] Thus, 1972–5 was a period of sustained growth and so was 1978 when the supply of foreign exchange was again able to finance internal expansion.

This analysis suggests that the Cuban economy is still highly sensitive to the quantum and value of sugar exports and that it is not possible to isolate the national economy from general trends in the world market. In that sense, it is an export-led economy of a special type because it is dependent on a single crop.

In spite of the heavy reliance on sugar, the figures on sugar production and export (Table 2), and the evolution of the industrial and construction sectors, show no evidence

Table 2 *Sugar: production, exports and export prices*

	Thousands of tons		US$ per pound	
			Prices paid	Prices paid
	Sugar	Sugar	by the	by the
Year	production	exports	USSR	world market
1950	6039	4951	–	2.97
1960	5943	5634	–	3.14
1961	6876	6413	4.09	2.75
1962	4882	5132	4.09	2.83
1963	3883	3520	6.11	8.34
1964	4475	4176	6.11	5.77
1965	6156	5316	6.11	2.08
1966	4537	4435	6.11	1.81
1967	6236	5683	6.11	1.92
1968	5165	4612	6.11	1.90
1969	4459	4799	6.11	3.20
1970	8538	6906	6.11	3.68
1971	5925	5511	6.11	4.50
1972	4325	4140	6.11	7.27
1973	5253	4797	12.02	9.45
1974	5925	5491	19.64	29.66
1975	6314	5744	30.40	20.37
1976	6151	5764	30.91[a]	11.51
1977	6485	6238	35.73[a]	8.14
1978	7328	6900	40.78[a]	7.80

[a]ECLA, *Report on Cuba*, (English edn).
Source: CEPAL, *Cuba: Notas para el Estudio Económico de América Latina: 1978*, 1980.

of a 'big push for sugar' in the 1970s. The variation in levels of sugar production seems to have diminished; and, even in gloomy international market conditions, sugar production has steadily increased. Both these features would tend to suggest that the level of sugar production has approached a new level of minimum output. This has allowed the Cubans to increase internal demand, seeking both a more balanced economy and an increase in consumption.

The outstanding importance of the sugar economy and the growth of some branches of light industry and construction do not square with the idea that Cuban economy in the 1970s resembles the Soviet approach to industrialisation. Instead, it seems more reasonable to understand the shift towards a more balanced economy as a consequence of changes in the agricultural sector and a policy that has softened restrictions on consumption. The following analysis of the sectoral evolution confirms that view.

(i) New features in the sugar sector

The figures on yields and mechanisation in Table 3 provide evidence that the 'big push' policy has ceased. First the average area harvested between 1971 and 1979 has remained

Table 3 *Cane-area harvested, total cane production, yields per hectare, state and private sector, and percentage of harvest cut by combines, 1961–2/1978–9*

Year	Cane area harvested (000s ha)	Cane production (millions of tons)	Total (tons)	State (tons)	Private (tons)	Harvested by combines %
1961–2	1117.0	37.1	33.2	35.7	31.7	–
1962–3	1074.9	32.0	29.8	31.0	28.9	–
1963–4	1033.9	37.8	36.5	37.4	35.0	–
1964–5	1054.5	51.5	48.9	48.9	48.8	2
1965–6	937.7	37.4	39.9	39.1	42.0	3
1966–7	1081.1	51.6	47.7	47.9	47.3	2
1967–8	987.9	43.6	44.1	42.4	49.2	3
1968–9	944.4	42.9	45.4	43.6	50.9	2
1969–70	1464.3	84.4	57.6	56.0	63.5	1
1970–1	1255.7	54.0	43.0	42.1	46.7	3
1971–2	1211.9	45.9	37.9	37.4	39.9	7
1972–3	1072.9	48.2	44.9	44.4	47.5	11
1973–4	1105.6	50.4	45.6	45.0	48.6	18
1974–5	1181.4	52.4	44.3	43.6	48.0	25
1975–6	1226.1	53.8	43.9	42.7	50.3	32
1976–7	1137.5	60.4	53.1	51.1	62.8	36
1977–8	1236.8	69.7	56.3	55.3	61.2	38
1978–9	1304.1	73.1	56.0	–	–	42

Cane area, production and yields, 1961–2 to 1977–8, *Anuario Estadistico de Cuba*, 1978, ch. v, table 7, p. 68. For 1978–9, *Guida Estadistica, 1979*, p. 8. Percentage of mechanised harvest, *Memorias*, Ministerio de Agricultura, 1980 for 1971–2 to 1978–9. For 1964–5 to 1970–1, 'Algunos Aspectos sobre el Desarrollo de la Agricultura Canera en Cuba', O. Grande Balbona, Paper given at the Annual Conference of the Jamaican Association of Sugar Technologists, Kingston, Jamaica, November 1975, MINAZ doc. no. 1897, ATAC.
Source: Pollit, *Revolution in the Mode of Production in the Sugar-Cane Sector of the Cuban Economy, 1959–1980*, 1981.

at a level 20 per cent less than the year of the record harvest (1970). Moreover, the government has followed a more stable policy of land allocation which has avoided the yearly changes of the 1960s. Second, the relatively constant area harvested contrasts with the steady introduction of machinery. If the previous insistence on output targets had prevailed, the labour freed by mechanisation could have been devoted

Table 4 *Basic indicators of the sugar industry production*
(thousands of tons)

	Cane processed at the mills	Crude sugar production	Industrial yield (%)
1951	44,938	5821	12.95
1952	59,538	7298	12.26
1953	40,812	5224	12.80
1954	39,295	4959	12.62
1955	34,819	4598	13.20
1956	37,039	4807	12.98
1957	44,714	5742	12.84
1958	45,716	5863	12.82
1959	48,051	6039	12.57
1960	47,492	5943	12.51
1961	54,325	6876	12.66
1962	36,686	4882	13.31
1963	31,413	3833	12.36
1964	37,196	4475	12.03
1965	50,687	6156	12.15
1966	36,840	4537	12.32
1967	50,880	6236	12.26
1968	42,368	5165	12.19
1969	40,476	4459	11.02
1970	79,678	8538	10.71
1971	51,548	5925	11.49
1972	43,545	4325	9.93
1973	47,459	5253	11.07
1974	49,562	5930	11.95
1975	50,769	6315	12.44
1976	60,400[a]	6151	10.20
1977	69,700[a]	6485	9.30
1978	73,100[a]	7328	10.00

[a]Source, Table 5.
Source: CEPAL, *Cuba: Notas para el Estudio Económico de América Latina: 1978*, 1980.

to expand the area under cultivation. To the extent this has not been the case, the non-sugar economy has greatly benefited from mechanisation of the harvest. This is one of the reasons underlying the expansion of industry.

Increased mechanisation has also brought an increase in average yields: while yields remained at 42.4 tons/ha between 1961 and 1970, they increased to 47.2 tons/ha in the next decade. Although this increase of 11 per cent may look rather meagre, it should be added that variation in yields has been lower during the last ten years, and the averages seem to have reached a higher plateau of 54 tons/ha during 1977–9.[23]

Though harvesting operations have changed quite drastically, serious bottlenecks remain in the sugar sector. As shown in Table 4, 'recovery rates' – the ratio between sugar production and the total weight of cane processed by the mills – have averaged 11 per cent during the 1970s, and there was an apparent downward trend. This decrease cannot be explained by losses in milling time (Table 5) which have remained fairly constant. The most important constraint on improvement of recovery rates is the productive age of mill

Table 5 *Milling time lost in sugar harvests through rain, cane shortages and other causes (hours, %, 1971–8)*

Year	Total hours (000s)	Total %	Shortage of cane from fields	Rain	Other[a]
1971	–	35.77	12.84	1.88	21.05
1972	184.9	38.23	13.34	6.65	18.24
1973	127.1	28.51	8.46	2.99	17.06
1974	100.5	23.18	6.72	1.37	15.09
1975	78.2	18.24	3.31	0.64	14.29
1976	98.6	22.01	6.10	3.52	12.39
1977	124.3	24.84	4.22	8.65	11.97
1978	164.4	27.28	4.56	11.71	11.01

[a]Includes cane shortage attributed to railroad deficiencies; cleaning mill-equipment; interruptions in milling process, and breakdowns or deficiencies of machinery and equipment; and miscellaneous. Breakdowns and operative interruptions fell from 15.47 per cent of total hours lost in 1971 to 6.04 per cent in 1978.
Source: *Anuario Estadistico de Cuba*, 1978, ch. VI, from Tables 12 and 13, pp. 91–2, quoted in Pollit, op. cit.

equipment. Thus, even when yields per hectare are higher, and the harvest is better coordinated, total sugar production may not increase if mill productivity is not improved.[24] Since recovery rates are a function of time – both in harvesting and processing – since the sucrose content of the cane tends to diminish after cutting, operating speed of the mills is crucial for increasing production.

Though the Cuban economy remains dependent on sugar and thus prone to the weaknesses associated with it, there has been a significant change from the situation of the 1960s. Cuba exploited her comparative advantages in sugar in both decades, but with very different results. Though part of this change can be attributed to the more favourable influence of 'uncontrolled' variables (weather and world prices) and a more sensible political strategy, we must recognise the crucial influence of the mechanisation and consequent increases in productivity (per ha, and per person)

Technical progress in sugar has also brought a vast change in the allocation of labour in the economy as a whole and the organisation of the labour process in general. In relation to the first, the evolution of the volume of sugar production during the late 1970s is quite encouraging. While it is too soon to say that the Cuban economy has definitively approached a new level of minimum production, the positive effects on macro-economic growth are clear. There is thus reason to believe that the economy has been freed to some extent from the main constraint on its performance in the 1960s (and before). On the second point – the social labour process – one should realise that a level of mechanisation of 50 per cent implies a diminished demand for labour supplied by the non-sugar economy. This means a more stable supply of workers to other sectors which allows better planning of their activities. It also means that the period of acute seasonal demand for workers does not need to mobilise 'non-sugar skills'.

To summarise the argument so far, though the basic development strategy shows a relative continuity over the 1960s and 1970s – in the sense that the economy is using sugar as a lever for development – certain key structural changes have taken place in the latter decade. But why did it take 10–15 years before these changes were introduced?

MacEwan argues that, for a socialist economy, it may well be that a prior stage of redistribution lays down better conditions for further growth. In the Cuban case, he identifies the 1960s as a distributionist stage when major political and economic decisions paved the way for the 1970s, but growth and technical improvements were impeded. This analysis of 'distribution first – growth later' explains the delay in achieving better results in sugar production. On the other hand, Pollit argues that the structural conditions inherited from the pre-revolutionary period were not easy to remove or modify. In other words, the failure to get quicker results does not reflect a lack of attention towards the sugar sector but the intrinsic difficulties of 'dominating' sugar.

Any complete analysis should combine both of these arguments, i.e. structural changes during the 1970s were delayed because of longstanding objective constraints and the economic policy of the 1960s.

However, in attributing a role to economic policy, we should widen the scope of the term. Without neglecting the existence of a certain opposition between distribution and economic growth, the strategy of the 'big push' in the later half of the decade was also an important contributing factor, as we have argued in the previous section.

(ii) The non-sugar economy: the impact of economic expansion on consumption

As Table 1 indicates, rapid economic growth during 1970–5 gave rise to a significant rebalancing of the productive sectors oriented towards the internal market. After 1975, the industrial sector – constrained by the import capacity of the economy – slowed down during 1976 (3 per cent) and 1977 (1.4 per cent) but picked up again in 1978 (9.1 per cent). If the structure of GMP is observed, the non-sugar economy gains several points in terms of its contribution to total output. The most remarkable case is construction, its share of GMP growing from 7.7 per cent to almost 15 per cent between 1970 and 1975. In terms of growth rate, this was the most expansive economic sector (27 per cent), given the importance attached to housing and educational construction. In turn, due to 'multiplicative' effects, construction has boosted other industrial branches. But it should also be noted that manufacturing grew at a much higher rate than population growth: for example, manufacturing of leather goods and textiles grew at a rate of 12.3 per cent.

Derationing and expansion of consumer goods

The introduction of new final goods, and an increased supply of those existing before, allowed changes in policies on rationing and wages. It was unnecessary to keep the low levels of consumption that had prevailed during the late 1960s. By the turn of the decade there existed one year of wage funds immobilised in savings accounts, i.e. the total demand for consumer goods was significantly higher than the level that could be supplied. In order to provide an outlet for this frozen purchasing power, the number of rationed items was reduced, and norms of price control on certain products (cigarettes, alcohol, petrol and restaurant services) were abolished. These measures, and increased supplies of final goods, greatly expanded the consumer market and previously suppressed demand was transferred from (forced) savings to effective demand. The consequence of these new policies was a steep increase in some prices – sometimes referred to as 'socialist inflation' – which was particularly acute for the liberalised goods. On the other hand, they were beneficial in that they eliminated black markets. But we must consider the issue of the extent to which they contributed to a widening of wage differentials.

If one looks at the consumer market during the late 1960s, it is not easy to decide whether or not the distribution of consumption approached equality. Scarcity and rationing had reduced the possibilities of realising the purchasing power of wages in the market. In other words, nominal wage differences existed, but the possibility of transferring these differentials into the market was significantly reduced. The 1960s brought about income redistribution from rich to poor, but also, and just as important perhaps, from town to country. In consequence, the scarcity of consumer goods meant a relative loss for the urban sectors (including industrial workers) in relation to wage labourers in the countryside – though urban workers *were* better-off than before. These modifications in the pattern of income distribution were deliberately introduced by the revolution to remedy the sharp inequality between town and countryside inherited from the pre-revolutionary period, and to strengthen the political alliance between urban workers and rural labourers. The 1960s wrought a remarkable change in the pattern of income distribution which favoured the working class in general. But one should not assume that this radical equalisation of consumption was necessarily socially desirable. In so far as the situation of market scarcity did not allow wage differentials to be reflected in actual purchasing power, those who were above the average, including many workers, were compelled to forgo a portion of their potential consumption.

It is impossible to analyse changes in consumption patterns in the 1970s in any systematic way, given the dearth of statistical information on wages and prices. According to the ECLA study, wages in agriculture which in 1966 were 66 per cent of the national average wage had increased to 94 per cent by 1975. On the other hand, industrial wages which in 1966 were 29 per cent above the national average rose only slightly, (by 3 per cent). In consequence, it would seem that while the increased supply of consumer goods might have affected the workers receiving the lower wages, the nominal structure of wage differentials also changed in order to make them better-off in relation to the average. This evidence suggests that, in relation to the distribution of final goods, the revolution seems to have maintained its commitment to preserve equality and to enhance the transfer of income from urban to rural areas in the 1970s.

International trade and commercial policy

The evolution of Cuba's international trade during the 1970s is interesting on two major counts. On the one hand, the general picture is favourable though detailed analysis suggests that trade relations still constitute a constraint. On the other hand, the issue of commercial and trade policy raises the question of Cuba's relations with the Soviet bloc and the capitalist world.

Trade balance
As Table 6 shows, the trend of trade balances during the 1970s is not very favourable, though it is an improvement on

Table 6 *Exports, imports and trade account (millions of Cuban pesos)*

	1970	1971	1972	1973	1974	1975	1976	1977	1978
Total exports	1050	861	771	1153	2237	2947	2692	2912	3427
USSR	529	304	224	477	811	1661	1638	2066	–
Other socialist countries	248	261	197	268	472	341	452	378	–
Rest of the world	273	296	350	408	954	945	602	468	–
Total imports	1311	1387	1190	1463	2226	3113	3180	3433	3557
USSR	691	731	714	811	1025	1250	1490	1858	–
Other socialist countries	226	239	200	224	328	354	374	467	–
Rest of the world	394	417	276	428	873	1509	1316	1108	–
Trade account	– 261	– 526	– 419	– 310	11	– 166	– 488	– 521	– 130
USSR	– 162	– 427	– 490	– 334	– 214	411	148	208	–
Other socialist countries	22	22	– 3	44	144	– 13	78	– 89	–
Rest of the world	– 121	– 121	74	– 20	81	– 564	– 714	– 640	–

Source: CEPAL, Cuba: Notas para el Estudio Económico de América Latina: 1978, 1980.

the previous decade. It has clearly not been easy to arrive at a trading equilibrium. All years but one show a deficit, although the absolute size of the deficit is quite variable. Following the trends in the sugar market, 1971–2 and 1976–7 were years of peak deficits. The figures also suggest that there have been attempts to control imports when the economy faced difficulties with export revenues. During 1971–2 and 1976–7 the value of imports tends to remain at levels previous to the downturn; this suggests that it has been difficult to impose controls on imports sufficient to counter fluctuating export receipts.

One of the most interesting features of the trade statistics is the shift in commercial policy and in the financing of trade debts. Between 1970 and 1974, Cuba increased its deficit with the USSR; in the following years trade with the Soviet bloc began to produce a surplus, but a deficit appeared in relation with the capitalist countries.

To explain this policy shift, we should consider two different sets of circumstances. First, Cuba made new trade agreements with the USSR and the socialist bloc after joining CMEA in 1972. We shall examine the impact of those agreements later when discussing terms of trade. Second, there was a change of attitude towards Cuba on the part of capitalist countries. The 1970s brought a significant decrease in Cuba's economic isolation after the US embargo of the 1960s. A wide range of countries in Europe, Asia and Latin America were now willing to sign commercial agreements with Cuba and, in most cases, also provided credit facilities. Spain, Japan and Argentina are notable examples of countries which developed more active trade after 1975.

Commercial policy with the USSR
By 1975 Cuba's deficit with the USSR had increased to a cumulative total of 4363 million *pesos*. Three-quarters of this debt was financed through credit, but we have no information on these credit agreements (period of repayment, rate of interest, etc.), nor are there any figures on the magnitude of capital transfers or grants from the USSR. This lacuna makes it difficult to discuss the extent to which these economic relations involve dependency.

Despite the USSR's overwhelming role as a creditor, it

Table 7 *Destination of exports and sugar price variations*

Exports and prices	1970	1971	1972	1973	1974	1975	1976	1977
Exports to socialist countries, % of total	74.0	65.6	54.6	64.6	57.4	67.9	77.7	83.9
Sugar prices paid by USSR/ paid by the world market	166.0	135.8	84.0	127.2	66.2	149.2	268.9	438.9

Source: Tables 1 and 6.

seems that the Cubans have been able to work out favourable terms for their products, as Table 7 suggests. The table shows the proportion of Cuban exports sold to socialist countries compared with the ratio of the sugar prices paid by the USSR *vis à vis* the capitalist countries. The data suggest that in those years when prices for sugar in the capitalist market were better than those offered by CMEA countries, the proportion of exports sold to the socialist market has been lower (notably in 1972 and 1974). Therefore, it seems that export of sugar to the Soviet bloc has followed a counter-cyclical policy which seeks to cushion the negative consequences of variations in the world market. For that reason, the mere fact of trade concentration, especially with the USSR, cannot be immediately interpreted as a weakness; on the contrary, it may be a factor of strength.

Turning to terms of trade (Table 8), it is clear that they have been very favourable during the second decade. Between 1971 and 1977, Cuba's terms of trade almost doubled. As the table shows, trends vary for the USSR and the capitalist countries. In the latter case, the evolution of the terms of trade reflects the situation of sugar prices. Thus the index climbs between 1971 (116.2) and 1975 (283.4); after that year, when sugar prices fell from 20.4 to 11.5, the index of the terms of trade shows the same drastic fall. By the end of the period, Cuba faced neither losses nor gains in her trade relationships with the capitalist countries. The index of terms of trade with the USSR is very different. There is a definite improvement if one compares 1971 with 1977, and the period shows an absence of cyclical movement and its associated negative effects on exports earnings. The index is low for 1971 and 1972 because sugar prices had not yet been adjusted to the world market situation. Once the agreements were implemented the terms of

Table 8 *Main indicators of international trade (Index 1970 = 100)*

	1971	1972	1973	1974	1975	1976	1977
Export price index							
Total average	111.7	130.5	162.4	313.5	372.3	332.8	309.4
USSR	102.0	98.9	162.5	260.0	360.0	362.9	371.7
Capitalist countries	124.0	163.7	162.7	380.6	396.8	271.7	178.1
Import price index							
Total average	105.7	107.3	111.2	136.0	155.3	154.7	170.2
USSR	105.2	108.0	113.2	136.7	179.2	180.0	184.3
Capitalist countures	106.7	105.2	107.6	135.2	140.0	133.5	150.8
Terms of trade							
Total average	105.7	121.6	146.0	230.5	240.1	215.1	181.8
USSR	97.0	91.6	143.6	190.2	200.9	201.6	201.7
Capitalist countries	116.2	155.6	151.2	281.5	283.4	203.5	118.1

Source: CEPAL, Cuba: Notas para el Estudio Económico de América Latina: 1978, 1980.

Table 9 *Oil and by-products: indicators of imports*

	1970	1971	1972	1973	1974	1975	1976	1977	1978
Imports (millions of pesos)	110.1	122.9	144.4	159.2	196.2	307.3	342.0	–	–
Import Index (1970 = 100)									
Value	100.0	111.6	131.2	144.6	178.2	279.1	310.6	–	–
Quantity	100.0	112.5	108.3	122.8	134.5	127.4	–	–	–
Prices	100.0	99.2	121.0	117.6	132.5	218.9	–	–	–
Oil imports as a % of total imports	8.4	8.9	12.1	10.7	8.8	9.9	10.8	–	–

Source: CEPAL, Cuba: Notas para el Estudio Economica de America Latina: 1978, 1980

trade quickly improved, climbing until 1975. After that year the level remained stationary because of the new pricing formula adopted by both countries which essentially indexes Cuban imports from the USSR to the price of sugar. This policy has been particularly beneficial for Cuba by reducing the impact of rising oil prices. As Table 9 shows, oil imports from the USSR were purchased in 1974 at a price level 32.5 per cent higher than 1970. After the adoption of the indexation mechanism, Soviet oil began to be purchased at more 'realistic' prices. This agreement, together with the joint planning of imports and exports by both trade partners and the provision of credit facilities, are the benefits Cuba derived from joining CMEA.

In sum, during the 1970s, the Cuban economy improved its international terms of trade and, in general, has found it easier to cope with the constraints imposed by a relatively rigid demand for imports. In particular, analysis of Cuba–USSR trade relations shows that any hypothesis which argues that this relationship has not been economically favourable for Cuba, faces a significant problem of proof.

Economic planning

Some important changes in the planning system took place during the 1970s. Although the new orientation is often equated with the Soviet planning model, this is not a very helpful analytical approach given that the two economies are so different and their histories of planning so divergent.

During the 1960s, Cuba had a very centralised system of economic planning and management. Individual enterprises were consolidated into aggregates which were centrally planned by the relevant ministry: this was the so-called budgetary system of planning. In this system, most of the transactions between enterprises were considered as a circulation of products within the *consolidado*, thereby making the use of prices unnecessary. In the new system, there is an attempt to expand accounting procedures at the level of each enterprise. Every transaction is recorded in price terms and, in consequence, it is possible to have a profit-and-loss account as an indicator of performance. At the same time, a system of bonuses has been introduced, the level of remuneration depending on the results achieved by the enterprise. Though a process of payments and receipts has been developed, it does not mean that either investment decisions are taken by managers, or that prices are determined on the market. Investment is centrally controlled, and there is very little room for manoeuvre in the allocation of surplus funds at the enterprise level. Prices are also centrally determined, with the exception, discussed earlier, of certain consumer goods which have been allowed to 'float' according to scarcity.

All these reforms have meant that by the beginning of 1977, a complete system of planned prices was introduced whereby every transaction is recorded with the aim of arriving at efficiency indicators. Such a drastic shift has raised the usual theoretical discussion of the role of markets in socialism, the validity of the law of value as the instrument for allocating social labour, and the importance attached to economic calculation. Since this is a wide-ranging topic which exceeds the scope of this paper, I shall concentrate on some aspects of the new system of economic management (SEM) as it operates rather than the theoretical debate surrounding the issue.

Though there are not many detailed accounts of the SEM, the Cuban journal *Economia y Desarrollo* (Economy and Development) has published several papers which clarify some aspects of the new system. The most important elements are: (i) the role attached to prices and planning; (ii) the question of enterprise autonomy; and (iii) the procedure for elaborating the plan. On the first point, Lopez Coll and Santiago – two Cuban economists who commented on the planning process at a time (1974) when the final decisions of the SEM had not yet been taken – state that 'the instrument that regulates the proportions of the Cuban economy is planning'. The basic proportions are those between the size of the investment and consumer goods sectors, and between all 'branches of the economy'.[25] Once the crucial decisions about the volume of production of departments I and II are worked out, the planning board (JUCEPLAN) establishes consistent production targets for the most important branches and enterprises. Decisions about production plans for enterprises of secondary importance are taken at lower levels, provincial and municipal. These targets are the basis of the plan and constitute obligatory norms for enterprises. Each norm is considered as a minimum (legal) target and there are no constraints on either overfulfilment of norms or utilisation of by-products.

Thus, insistence on the point that planning is the main instrument of economic regulation implies that production plans are not decided at the level of the productive unit. However, there is no central or planned allocation of physical products, a fact which implies that enterprises are responsible for organising the production process. Yet the search for supplies of inputs does not strictly mean that the enterprise is confronted with the market since there are no market prices as such.

The method of arriving at a set of relative and absolute prices for the economy follows the rule of 'socially necessary labour time'. This general principle can be modified, notably with regard to different types of prices – industrial, agricultural and final goods. For example, in setting agricultural prices the rent factor is eliminated through taxation, thereby equalising the cost structure of rural enterprises. The price system is ideally dynamic, the actual performance of productive units and the situation in the market for consumer goods providing the basis for periodic revisions.

The second aspect – the autonomy of enterprises – means that there are no central guidelines concerning the internal organisation of the productive unit, the labour process or the direction of technical change. The annual performance of the enterprise, the degree of fulfilment of the norms and allocation of bonuses are matters to be decided by the workers themselves.

The third aspect – the procedure for elaborating the plan – raises the most fundamental issues. This is not first a question of formal planning structures, but rather how the plan can perform its basic function, the satisfaction of needs. In market economy, the procedure for allocating resources – and the process of economic growth in general – is based on the drive for profits and the instruments are prices and markets. On the one hand, there are possibilities for gaining super-normal profits in producing a particular commodity; on the other hand, the structure of relative prices is not independent of the composition of demand. Thus, prices are a device used by consumers in a competitive economy to 'vote' and express their needs. A planned economy is completely different. The allocative function is performed by the plan and in a planned economy of the Cuban type where prices are centrally fixed, there is little opportunity for 'voting' in the market.

There is a 'minor' problem involved in determining relative (and absolute) prices for final goods. The official resolution on the creation of SEM describes the question as follows:

[The prices of final goods] should be fixed taking into account the social use value of those goods and services in relation to the needs that they meet. In turn, [prices] should be oriented to seek a proper correlation between supply and demand, to obtain a financial equilibrium between income and expenditures of the population, and to achieve the realisation in consumption of the law of distribution [labour performance].[26]

This quotation brings up two related aspects of the new planning system. First, there is an explicit recognition of a 'law of distribution', i.e. remuneration according to labour performed. This implies a closer relationship between wages and productivity, and the subsequent need to plan the structure of incomes to meet expenditures. Second, the 'correlation between supply and demand' implies that relative prices should mirror conditions of scarcity and (individual and collective) tastes.

However, it is clear that Cubans do not 'vote' in the market and it is the plan which is expected to capture the entire set of social needs. In economic terms, the crucial difficulty is the extent to which these economic decision – implemented through the plan and its structure of relative prices – respond to the needs of the population. That is the issue of the degree of democracy of the planning system which, in a socialist society, rests on the nature of democracy in society as a whole.

Political Changes and the Advance towards a Democratic Society

In this section I intend to draw on the analysis presented to arrive at some conclusions about the political changes brought about by the shift of the 1970s. I shall focus on one major question: is Cuba advancing towards a democratic form of socio-political organisation?

New institutions and old institutions with new roles

Two important changes took place in the 1970s: (a) the national trade union organ, the *Central de Trabajadores Cubanos* (CTC), held a conference in 1973 which laid down new guidelines for the activity of trade unions; (b) the Party celebrated its first General Congress, and at the same time (1975) the basis for the Constitution of the Republic was decided. This embodied a mechanism to integrate the masses into the planning process.

If one analyses the information available on the role of the trade unions in the formulation of economic policy, and the planning and management of productive units, there seems to have been significant shift compared with the 1960s. In the previous decade, the CTC and its component organisations played a very important role in the process of labour mobilisation. They acted as transmission-belts, but operated only in a downward direction, i.e. contributing to the implementation of guidelines emerging from the planning apparatus. However, they failed to communicate the needs of the workers to higher levels, and they did not take up the task of organising workers' interests at factory level. The general political orientation of the period legitimised these constraints: since the state was an instrument of the working class, there was no room for autonomous trade unions – they had to be an instrument of the state.

At the 1973 Congress of the CTC, held after several years of substantial changes in the constitution of the movement (local elections, new branches at provincial and regional levels, etc.), a different political orientation was adopted which redefined relations with the Party and the state:

It is a type of co-operation where each component has its *own sphere of action* and its *own distinct method* of action to arrive at the common goal. (emphasis added)[27]

It was also decided that the unions should play a role in 'pointing out errors and drawbacks in the work process'. Thus the foundations were laid for partially independent organisations of the working class which might act as a 'check-and-balance' on the planning structure.

Similar tendencies may be detected in the political structures of mass participation. One of the central ideas introduced by the new Constitution that began to be applied in 1977 was the need to create centres of local participation – called Organs of Popular Power (OPP) – to complement the planning function of the state apparatus at provinical and municipal levels. They also have the authority to set production targets for local enterprises and units of distribution. Delegates of the OPPs at district, provincial and national levels are elected.

Have these institutional changes brought greater democracy to Cuban society? Detailed discussion of the structures as such is not too fruitful; in formal terms they may have been well-founded. It is more important to discuss the origin of these changes, the role they play in the development strategy of the seventies and their prospects for success.

Leadership, bureaucracy and workers' participation

Political life in the 1960s embodied a heavy reliance on the major revolutionary leaders. As we have seen, the policy of the 'big push' with its use of moral incentives was an extension of pre-revolutionary methods, especially in its first three years. In the process, however, the leadership failed to lay the foundations for a more integrative process of political participation. Furthermore, the strategy implied the development of a bureaucracy as the agent of policy implementation.

The relationship which developed between the leadership and the bureaucracy during this period is very interesting. On the one hand, the leaders needed the bureaucratic strata because there were no other means to carry out the policy; on the other hand, the leadership conferred a certain degree of legitimacy on the bureaucracy. Its existence was justified by the leadership, but its actions had a clear limit defined by the leadership's exercise of political power.

When the crisis of 1970 demonstrated that the production of sugar and the battle for socio-economic development were more complex than anticipated and that another economic strategy was required, it also provoked a crisis in the leadership. Their role was no longer necessary in facing the new stage. Thus the political problem of the 1970s has implied a process of substituting democratic power for the role performed by the leaders. The new guidelines of the SEM and the institutional framework of the OPP and CTC may be understood as changes aimed at a more effective substitution.

However, there are very serious constraints on this process of democratisation. First, it should be noted that the changes have been designed *from above*, as part of the leadership's retreat from its previous style of political control. Therefore, it is likely that elements of the old system may be carried through into the new institutional structure.[28] The fact that both the crucial congresses of the CTC and the Party were preceded by periods of intense political activity might suggest that there has been a serious effort to shape the new structures according to the needs of the people. But there is no guarantee that, once those institutions are set in motion, they will continue to perform their assigned functions.

Second, the role of the bureaucracy may be *enhanced* by this process of substitution. In so far as the leaders have decided to move one step back, their place may be occupied by the bureaucracy. However, one can argue that such an advance would be difficult for at least two reasons. First, the conditions that gave rise to the strength of bureaucracy are no longer there; Castro and other leading figures can no longer be used to justify the strengthening of bureaucratic power. Secondly, consistent egalitarianism and the historical impact of the 1960s also act as a brake on bureaucratisation. Any process of bureaucratic growth implies a change in the pattern of income distribution whereby privileges can be established. In Cuba, this would be a very difficult task because of the strong tradition of egalitarianism and the nature of the relationship between town and countryside in which the latter tend to be relatively privileged.

A Final Comment

The material discussed in this paper suggests that the Cuban revolution has passed through two distinct stages. During the 1960s the battle was centred on the attempt to dominate the economy, whereas the 1970s brought significant success in the economic struggle, and the question of how to develop a democratic socialist society has become crucial.

It is too early to make a final judgement about democracy

in Cuba. The mere fact of a shift towards more democratic institutions does not mean that these institutions have a solid political foundation. Different tendencies exist, some of them fed by the political style of the first decade. Indeed, the experience of the 1960s – notably the enhancement of the New Man philosophy and egalitarianism – is not just past history. If existing bureaucratic elements attempt to consolidate their power, they will have to remove that experience from the consciousness of the people.

It is in relation to this basic conflict of the 1970s – democracy v. bureaucracy – that we may judge the Soviet–Cuban relationship. This is one crucial way in which foreign interests may find an internal agent to reshape cuban political life.

Notes

1 The remark about Cuba's level of development requires some qualification. Cuba's US$ 500 per capita income (at 1960 dollar values) in the late 1950s was higher than in most Latin American countries; only Venezuela and Argentina were better off. However, in the thirty-five years from 1923 to 1958 the Cuban economy had shown symptoms of premature stagnation, whereas the rest of Latin America recorded a more dynamic performance (see D. Seers (ed.), *Cuba, the Economic and Social Revolution*, Chapel Hill, University of North Carolina Press, 1964, especially pp. 13–19).

2 General Fulgencio Batista had seized the Presidency of the Republic on 10 March 1952 after a military *coup*.

3 This revision took the form of the Alliance for Progress launched by President Kennedy in 1961.

4 For a discussion of US–Cuba relations, see Smith, R. *The United States and Cuba*, New York, Bookman Associates, 1960.

5 Brian Pollit has argued (in a 1981 lecture at the Institute of Development Studies) that Cuban writers of the pre-revolutionary period concentrated heavily on the *external* causes of underdevelopment, with a consequent lack of attention to analysing how the Cuban economy actually worked. Compare Ritter's analysis of economic thinking in the immediate post-revolutionary period in his *The Economic Development of Revolutionary Cuba*, Praeger, London, 1974.

6 According to the US Bureau of Labor Statistics (1957), employment in the sugar sector alone – i.e. excluding ancillary services and public transportation used in sugar production – amounted to 24.7 per cent (547,000) of the total labour force in 1950–5. Of the 470,000 workers involved in the sugar harvest, only a small proportion had employment throughout the year. During the dead season (April to December) most of them had to return to casual jobs in the cities, or simply remained unemployed

in the country. It has been estimated that total unemployment reached a peak of 21–3 per cent and went down to 8–9 per cent during the sugar months.

7   The first step towards the reform of land tenure was taken in 1959, affecting about 30 per cent of all farmland. In early 1961 two major decisions were taken: first 80–90,000 proprietors of small plots not affected by the earlier reform were grouped into the National Association of Small Producers; second, agricultural co-operatives and state-administered farms (both the result of the first reform) were amalgamated into People's Farms.

8   A speech delivered on 13 March 1968, quoted by A. MacEwan, *Revolution and Economic Development in Cuba*, MacMillan, London, 1981, pp. 117–18.

9   For a discussion of the issues of the Great Debate, see Silverman, B. (ed.), *Man and Socialism in Cuba. The Great Debate*, New York, Atheneum, 1971; and Pollit, B., 'Moral and Material Incentives in Socialist Economic Development', *Journal of Contemporary Asia*, 7, 1977, pp. 116–23.

10 On the political experience of the main leaders of the Revolution and their role in it, see Mathews, H., *Political Leaders of the Twentieth Century: Castro*, Pelican, 1969; and Sinclair, A., *Guevara*, Fontana, Modern Masters edn, London, 1970.

11 For a good description of the impact of the economic policy of the 1960s upon growth performance see Ritter, *op. cit.*, ch. 5.

12 See Mesa Lago, C., *Cuba in the 1970s. Pragmatism and Institutionalisation*, University of New Mexico Press, Albuquerque, 2nd edn, 1976; Horowitz, L., 'Authenticiy and autocracy in the Cuban experience', *Cuban Studies*, 6, 1, January 1976, pp. 67–74; and 'Institutionalisation as integration: the Cuban revolution at age twenty', *Cuban Studies*, 9, 2, July 1979; and Dominguez, J., *Cuba: Order and Revolution*, Cambridge, Massachusetts, The Belknap Press of Harvard University Press 1978. For a critique of this approach, see Fitzgerald, F.T., 'A critique of the "Sovietization of Cuba Thesis"', *Science and Society* vol. XLII, no. 1, Spring 1978.

13 The term refers to the revolutionary consciousness that would emerge from wide application of moral incentives.

14 For example, see Ritter, *op. cit.* pp. 348; and Silverman, *op. cit.* pp. 23ff.

15 Silverman, *op. cit*; he is using the concepts of Charles Bettelheim here.

16 MacEwan, *op. cit.*

17 It is interesting how in his discussions with Sweezy in the late 1960s Bettelheim had already developed a critical attitude to his former position on the Cuban debate. See Bettelheim and Sweezy, *On the Transition to Socialism*, Monthly Review Press, New York, 2nd edn, 1971.

18 Sierra Maestra is a region of Oriente province, where Fidel launched the Rebel Army to fight Batista's régime.

19 CEPAL, *Cuba: Notas para el Estudio Económico de América Latina: 1978*, 1980. English edn published by Banco Nacional de Comercio Exterior, SA; see *Comercio Exterior* (English edn, vol. 26, no. 1).

20 The composition of exports by type of products reveals that during the period 1970–4 sugar and its derivatives amounted to 75 per cent of the

total value of exports; minerals and concentrates were the second item. See MacEwan, *op. cit.*, p. 203.

21 1972 was a good year despite the difficulties in sugar because the implementation of a construction plan accelerated the contribution of this sector to total GMP (see Table 1).

22 It should be noted that the annual rates of growth of the agricultural sector in Table 1 do not mirror the cyclical pattern referred to in the text (the exception is 1971, when the rate is negative). This misleading impression results from GMP pricing at constant values; the fall of sugar output in 1976 and 1977 was mainly due to price variations.

23 Local production of combines started in 1976. Soviet and Cuban technicians have jointly designed a model which is particularly suited to Cuban conditions.

24 MacEwan provides an idea of the backwardness of the sugar industrial equipment: 'Except for four new mills which began operation in the 1978 harvest, Cuba is still working with mills the newest of which was built in 1927.... One problem exists in simply keeping the old mills going.' MacEwan *op. cit.*, p. 193. Technical improvements and the transformation of the sugar economy in the last decade are analysed in detail by Pollit, 'Revolution in the mode of production in the sugar-cane sector of the Cuban Economy, 1959–1980', Notes of a paper for the Fifth Annual Conference of the Society for Caribbean Studies, High Leigh, 26–8 May 1981.

25 A. Lopez Coll and A. Santiago, 'Notas sobre el proceso de planificacion en Cuba', *Economia y Sociedad*, no. 29, May – June 1975.

26 Quoted by Ayala Castro and Hidalgo Gato, 'Aspectos teoricos del SDPE', *Economia y Desarrollo* no. 57, May – June 1980.

27 Resolution of the Thirteenth Congress of the CTC, quoted by Perez-Stable, M., 'Whither, the Cuban working class?', *Latin American Perspectives*, issue 7, (supplement), vol. II, no. 4, 1975, pp. 66–7.

28 Valdés, using a Weberian terminology, has labelled this process as 'the institutionalization of charisma': Valdés, N.P., 'Revolution and institutionalization in Cuba', *Cuban Studies* 6, 1 January 1976, pp. 1–38.

Cuba: Country Profile

Official name:	Republic of Cuba, established on 1 January 1959.
Population:	9.77 million (1979).
Capital:	Havana, 2 million (1977).
Land area:	114,500 sq km, of which 22 per cent arable land, 6 per cent permanent crops, 18 per cent pasture, 18 per cent woodland and forest (1978).
Official language:	Spanish.
Membership of international organisations:	UN, Organisation of American States (non-participant), CMEA (since 1972).

Political structure
  Constitution: Effective on 24 February 1976, super-
                                    seding the Basic Law of the Republic
                                    of 7 February 1959.
  Highest legislative body: National People's Assembly with 481
                                    delegates elected on a 5-year term.
  Highest executive body: Council of Ministers.
  Head of state: President Fidel Castro Ruz, assumed
                                    office in December 1976.
  Prime Minister: Fidel Castro Ruz, assumed office
                                    in 1959.
  Ruling party: The Cuban Communist Party, esta-
                                    blished in 1962 (present name since
                                    1965) with earlier origins; first Party
                                    Congress in 1975.
  First Secretary   Fidel Castro Ruz, assumed office
  of the Party: in October 1965.
  Party membership: c. 200,000 (c. 3 per cent of adult
                                    population, 1976).[17]
  Armed forces: 206,000 (c. 7 per cent of total labour
                                    force, 1980).

Population
  Population density: 86 per sq km.
  Population growth (%p.a.):   1.6 (1970–8).
  Population of working
  age (15–64 %):   59 (1978).
  Urban population (%):   65 (1980).
  Ethnic and linguistic groups: c. 51 per cent mulatto, 37 per cent
                                    white, 11 per cent African, 1 per
                                    cent Chinese.

Education and health
  School system: Six years of universal primary edu-
                                    cation implemented; nine years target
                                    for 1990.
  Primary school enrolment:[I]   98.5 per cent of school-age children
                                    enrolled (1980).[a]
  Secondary school   Nearly 90 per cent of 13–15 age group
  enrolment:[II]   enrolled in lower secondary (1980).[a]
  Higher education enrolment   14; males 17, females 12 (1976);
  (gross ratios, %):   17 (1978).
  Adult literacy: Practically 100 per cent (1980).[a]
  Life expectancy: 72 (1978).
  Infant death rate (per 1000):   23 (1976).[b]
  Child death rate (per 1000):   1 (1977).
  Population per hospital bed: 235 (1976).
  Population per physician: 1120 (1974).[12]
Economy
  GNP: US$ 718 billion (1978).
  GNP per capita: US$ 810.

Material product.[III]
by sector: Agriculture 16, industry 67, service 17 (1978).[d]

Total labour force
by sector (%):   3.0 million (1979); agriculture 25, industry 31, service 44 (1978).

Structure of ownership: All sectors except agriculture were wholly nationalised by 1968. Agriculture: 79 per cent of arable land state farms, the rest is worked by individual farmers (1977).[b]

Land tenure: Maximum size of holdings 5 *caballerias* (67 ha) since the second land reform in 1963.

Main crops: Sugar (53 per cent of arable land in 1979), rice, potatoes, tubers, tobacco, coffee, citrus fruits.

Irrigated area: 720,000 ha or 23 per cent of arable land (1978).

Food self-sufficiency   Not self-sufficient in basic foodstuffs.

Energy balance–   (1978).
commercial consumption per capita: 1168 kg coal equivalent.
%liquid fuels: 98.5.
%net imports: 105.3.

Growth indicators (% p.a.)–   (1971–8).[d]
material product: 7.9.[IV]
industry: 7.1.
construction: 19.8.
agriculture: 4.0.[VI]
food production per capita: 1.0.[6]

Foreign trade and economic integration

Trade balance–   (1978).[d]
exports: US$ 4456.
imports: US$ 4687.

Real growth of exports (%p.a.):   13.5 (1970–8).

Exports as % of material product:[III]   33 (1978).[d]

Main exports (%):   Sugar 86, minerals (nickel) 7, tobacco 2, food products 4, (fish 2, citrus 0.7) (1976).[e VII]

Main imports (%):   Food products 22, fuels 10, machinery and transport equipment 24, raw materials and intermediate goods 24 (1976).[e VII]

Destination of exports (%):   USSR 73, other socialist countries 12, rest of the world 15 (1978).[d]

Main trading partners: USSR, Spain, Japan (1977).[d]

Foreign investment: No private direct investment.

Notes

[I]Gross ratios (1976, %): 122; males 125, females 119.
[II]Gross ratios (1976, %): 51; males 50, females 51.
[III]Material product = production value of the agricultural, fisheries, mining, manufacture, construction and electricity sectors, calculated at constant prices; see also Appendix. Note that the latter is likely to cause an under-valuation of the agricultural (sugar) sector (see text).
[IV]World Bank[18]; GDP growth 1970–8: 0.4%.
[V]Manufacturing, mining and electric energy generation.
[VI]FAO volume index of total agricultural production (6), same period: 2.3.
[VII]Preliminary estimates.

Sources

[a]Joseph Casas, 'Education et développement à Cuba', *Revue Tiers Monde*, vol. 22, no. 85, January–March 1981.
[b]Jorge I. Domingues, *Cuba, Order and Revolution*, Cambridge, Massachusetts, 1978.
[c]Arthur MacEwan, *Revolution and Economic Development in Cuba*, London, 1981.
[d]UN, Economic Commission for Latin America, *The Cuban Economy in the Seventies*, Commercio Exterior de Mexico, vol. 26, no. 1, January 1980.
[e]US, CIA, *The Cuban Economy. A statistical review 1968–76*, Washington DC, December 1976.

Cuba: Some Relevant Facts of the 1970s.

1970	Failure to achieve target in sugar production. The policy of the 'big push' is abandoned.
1972	Cuba joins COMECON and makes long-term commercial agreements with the USSR, which includes deferring payments of existing debts until 1986.
1973	Trade unions, *Central de Trabajadores Cubanos* (CTC), held their 13th Congress. The role of unions in socialist Cuba is redefined. The Congress approved a series of measures aimed at guaranteeing the flow of communication between workers and management. Material incentives are re-emphasised.
January 1974	Leonid Brezhnev visits Cuba.
1975	The Organisation of American States – under pressure from Mexico and Venezuela – lifted sanctions against Cuba. The long isolation started in the 1960s comes to an end. As a result OAS's member countries have the individual right to re-establish diplomatic relations. This decision meant the explicit recognition of the fact that many Latin American countries had already established diplomatic relations – Chile (1970), Peru (1972), Argentina (1973), Venezuela (1974), Colombia (1975).

The Cuban Communist Party (PCC), created in 1965, celebrated its First Congress in December. The Congress opened
up the Party and decided to increase membership (there
were 203,000 members at that time). A new Political Bureau,
Secretariat and Central Committee were elected. The compo-
sitions of these organs reflected greater élite diversity. Fidel
Castro and his brother Raúl were elected First and Second
Secretaries of the Party respectively.

Cuban Military Aid to Angola begins to escalate. From
November 1975 to March 1976 between 18,000 and 24,000
Cubans arrived in Angola.

1976   A new socialist constitution is approved by 97.7 per cent of the
electorate. Creation of Organs of People's Power (OPP), a
form of local government which gives substantial responsibility to the province and municipality for the running of
health and education. Decentralisation at the political level:
the six old provinces, dating from Spanish times, became
fourteen new ones, each of a size to make more manageable
and operational OPP's system.

New 5-year Soviet–Cuban agreements on technical and
economic co-operation (oil contracts and sugar price indexing
is agreed).

1977   The Cuban and US governments agree to establish 'interest
sections' on each other's capital with the exchange of diplo-
mats to take place in September 1978.

The first stage of the System of Economic Management is
put into practice: new national accounting systems, national
budget and purchase-and-sale relations among enterprises.

1978   New system of prices, taxation and credit are applied in
selected enterprises. Measures encourage self-financing and
profits as a major indicator of managerial performance.

RECENT DEBATES IN VIETNAMESE DEVELOPMENT POLICY

Christine White

The aim of this paper is to summarise the main lines of Vietnamese development policy, and to situate recent debates and current orientations in international and historical context. My main focus will be on agricultural policy. The paper is not written for specialists in Vietnamese affairs, rather for readers interested in an introduction to socialist Vietnam's approach to development problems.

The Historical International Context of Vietnamese Development Policy

To the extent that Vietnamese policy debates have attracted attention in the western press, the focus for many years was on identifying 'pro-Soviet' and 'pro-Chinese' factions and leanings. The general assumption is still that policy in the Socialist Republic of Vietnam (SRV) is a dependent variable, determined above all by its international orientation. In this section I wish to challenge this conventional view, and argue that the primary causality has been in the opposite direction, i.e. that Vietnam's international orientation has been and continues to be most influenced by its leadership's view of development priorities and possibilities.

Vietnam has been seen as tending toward either the Soviet or Chinese models of socialism, or some strange hybrid of the two. Vietnam is thus seen as a country of the socialist world's 'periphery', determined above all by its orientation toward the larger and wealthier socialist 'centres', China and the Soviet Union.[1] However, this assumption has been challenged by Gareth Porter, who argues that for many years the Sino-Soviet split made it possible for Vietnam to break free of its relegation to the periphery of the concerns of the socialist world, and successfully redefine its own priorities as central. When one of the socialist giants would not support a Vietnamese initiative, backing was available from the other. This provided the Vietnamese leadership with important room for manoeuvre.[2]

The 1954 Geneva Accords had ended the Communist Party-led struggle against French colonial rule by temporarily dividing the country at the 17th Parallel into two regroupment zones (the Viet Minh army in the North, French and Bao Dai forces in the South) pending elections for unification within two years. After Ngo Dinh Diem took over in the South, replacing the French puppet leader Bao Dai with the help of US backing, the division of Vietnam became a *fait accompli* seemingly as fixed as that of East and West Germany or North and South Korea. This posed severe problems for Vietnamese development, as the coal-and mineral-rich North was the primary industrial base of the country, but historically a food-deficit area, whereas the Mekong Delta in the South was one of the great exporting ricebowls of south-east Asia. The division of the country thus posed a major obstacle to the emergence of a strong, integrated national economy with a balance of agriculture and industry. China and the Soviet Union were willing to accept the *status quo* of this division, but the leadership of the Democratic Republic of Vietnam (DRV) in the North and the remnants of the Viet Minh anti-colonial movement in the South, were not.[3]

The problems of achieving national sovereignty, independence and unity have thus dominated considerations of economic development in Vietnam much more thoroughly and obviously than in most Third World countries. However, as many Third World leaders have learned, it is at least as difficult to maintain independence from foreign friends and allies as it is to fight those defined as the national enemy in a war. In its relationship with socialist country benefactors, the DRV experienced the contradiction between the need for foreign aid, both in material goods and training, and the risks of dependency which are endemic in any unequal relationship. The DRV managed to maximise its independence and keep control of relations with its main wartime allies, the Soviet Union and China, primarily by attempts to maintain and maximise diversity of external contact while trying to avoid internal interference by limiting the number of foreign personnel in the country. DRV institutions of higher education quickly dispensed with foreign teachers (except in language schools), and offers of 'international brigades' as in the Spanish Civil War were refused. For over a decade and a half after the Sino-Soviet split, Vietnam refused to take sides, and received aid from both China and the Soviet bloc. In terms of intellectual orientation, a surprisingly large number of senior-and middle-level government officials and researchers with foreign training have studied in *both* the Soviet Union and China, while the number with western training (primarily overseas Vietnamese with French education) is exceptional within the communist bloc.

Following the Paris Agreements of January 1973, and during the first post-war years, Vietnam surprisingly was at pains to stress its openness to western aid, trade and even investment. In 1974, DRV officials expressed interest in joint-venture agreements with both western governments and private companies. Foreign observers at the time were amazed that after fighting 'western imperialism' for two long wars, Vietnam was actually trying to attract western capital. But, as one American visitor wrote at the time, 'the spectre of economic imperialism does not seem to worry North Vietnam's officials'. Government spokesmen were confident that sovereignty could be maintained by carefully controlling the conditions of foreign involvement. 'Besides', one official quipped, 'if half a million GIs couldn't subjugate us, a few dozen foreign companies won't be able to do so'.[4] The new policy initiative was followed in 1977 by the publication of a foreign investment law with liberal provisions for western capital involvement quite unprecedented among socialist countries and a precursor of later Chinese initiatives. Soon after the end of the war, Vietnam became one of the first countries ruled by a communist party to join the World Bank, the IMF and the Asian Development Bank.

An executive letter from President Nixon at the time of the Paris Agreement made the offer of a virtual Marshall Plan for post-war reconstruction. Far from rejecting this as American imperialist interference in another form – 'sugar-coated bullets' in Mao's phrase – the Vietnamese government repeatedly pressed for it, and was most disappointed not to receive this aid.

Subsequent events have shown that Vietnam's unexpected overtures to the West were prompted by increasing preoccupation with China, which was seen as an increasingly significant threat to the maintenance of Vietnamese independence. In January 1974, not quite a year after the Paris Agreement, Chinese air and naval forces seized the Paracel Islands off the eastern coast of Vietnam from Saigon government troops. With this act China translated into military action for the first time its longstanding claim to the oil-rich 'South China Sea' ('Eastern Sea' in Vietnamese geography!).[5] By the end of the war, the main obstacle to Vietnam's prospects for taking over the Mekong Delta off-shore area where oil had already. been discovered was no longer the United States or the foreign oil companies which had bought concessions from the Saigon government, but rather the Chinese government, which claimed the entire area off Vietnam's coast as Chinese territorial waters. This claim had more than territorial and military implications. Given the crucial role of oil for both industrial and agricultural modernisation (mechanisation, chemical insecticides and fertiliser) it had major implications for Vietnam's prospects for economic development.

In the South, following the collapse of the Thieu government, the major foreign threat to the unification and consolidation of Vietnam came from the Khmer Rouge led by Pol Pot which voiced claims to the Mekong Delta region with its significant Khmer minority population. The area had been seized from the Khmer empire by the Vietnamese empire centuries before. Pol Pot's broadcasts referred to Saigon and Mekong Delta provinces by their ancient Khmer name. In short, western military withdrawal from the area led to the calling into question of boundaries frozen under French colonial rule. With Chinese military aid, Khmer Rouge revanchist rhetoric escalated into destabilising military forays attacking Vietnamese villages across the border. In the first two years after the end of the war many overseas Vietnamese had applied to return to their country. In the new context of escalating tension and conflict with Kampuchea and China, however, the tide turned, and waves of ethnic Chinese (*Hoa* minority in Vietnamese terminology) as well as Vietnamese fled the country from which the hope of post-war peace and economic recovery had vanished.[6]

The territorial dispute with China, which echoes the

millenial history of Chinese military attempts to re-establish control over the area once ruled as China's southernmost province, along with attacks on the southern border from the Chinese-backed Khmer Rouge, weighed heavily in Vietnam's eventual decision in favour of alignment with the Soviet Union. But the government had hoped to be able to balance or even forestal this with an opening to the West; as a Vietnamese official told American visitors in 1974: 'Our policy is that of independence. So we will not be like China or Korea or the COMECON countries. We will be freer than they are.'[7] Losing the freedom to stand between China and the Soviet Union, Vietnam was aiming for the freedom to stand between the West and the Soviet Union. It seems clear that, under increasing pressure to choose sides as the war drew to a close, most Vietnamese leaders did not relish the loss of flexibility that a single dominant foreign alignment would entail. It was not until doors were closed by the US refusal to normalise relations, Chinese cancellation of all aid projects in 1978, and an escalating military conflict with the Chinese-armed Pol Pot forces that Vietnam finally joined CMEA (Comecon) and concluded a treaty (but not a military alliance) with the Soviet Union.

During the war, US policy-makers had justified their actions in Vietnam as stopping Chinese expansion and treated the DRV as a Chinese pawn. US Secretary of State Dean Rusk accused China of 'fighting to the last Vietnamese' against the US. Now that the Soviet Union rather than China is viewed in the West as the major threat, a US-Chinese alliance and joint economic aid embargo have had the result of pressuring Vietnam into a close alliance with the Soviet Union and the other CMEA countries in its attempt to both have some military security and gain some assistance in restoring the war-torn economy. Like a self-fulfilling prophecy, the justification for continuing to treat Vietnam as a pariah country is now based on the claim that Vietnam is not independent, but a Soviet pawn. Any indication of Vietnam's continued desire to pursue an independent foreign policy tends to be ignored. For example, Vietnam has remained a member of the World Bank and the IMF, and thus has the highly unusual status of formally belonging to both major world economic systems. However, the influential Brandt report ignores Vietnam's World Bank and IMF membership, mentioning only its adherence to the CMEA. On the other hand, the same report welcomes China's interest in joining the World Bank and IMF, which at the time of the report had not yet been translated into actual membership.[8] China has managed to pull off the feat of remaining a communist-ruled country while wooing and winning western aid and investment. Meanwhile, there has been relatively little aid and no post-war economic settlement for Vietnam after forty years of nearly continual warfare.

Changes in Vietnamese Development Thinking in Comparative Perspective

In recent years there have been changes in internal conditions as well as in the international context which have had a deep impact on Vietnamese thinking about development policy. In the early post-colonial years, DRV leaders hoped that a combination of political will, revolutionary structural changes, socialist bloc aid to build up industry, plus 'mass mobilisation' of peasant labour power for basic construction and agricultural production would lead to the swift eradication of poverty. It was not only war that defeated these hopes. Economic prosperity, unlike independence, cannot be taken by storm. It is now increasingly argued in Vietnam that at the present stage balanced development programmes, rather than one-sided sectoral campaigns, are most essential. Development is increasingly seen, in Vietnam as elsewhere, as a very complex, long-term process involving basic economic, social and cultural as well as political determinants and constraints. Many of the development programmes introduced in Vietnam over the course of the last two decades, such as crop intensification and birth control measures, to name just two, are not specific to any socio-political system. In this context of common problems, the exchange of information and experience on development issues with western as well as with non-socialist Third World countries appears increasingly important and has been translated into Vietnamese involvement in a wide range of international organisations.

In the period after the second world war, when many former colonies gained their independence, there was considerable and wide spread optimism about their prospects for rapid development once freed from the constraints of colonial rule. In the cold war context of the time, the possible 'development paths' were seen as rigidly polarised: the 'communist' or socialist v. the 'free world' or capitalist way. During this period of Manichean ideological division between two camps, it was widely assumed that the primary choice for the 'emerging nations' was that of political system and foreign policy alignment. Foreign aid from the appropriate camp, plus 'nation building', 'institutionalisation' and 'political modernisation' on one side; and the 'building and consolidation of socialist institutions' and 'socialist transformation of relations of production' on the other, were seen as the basic preconditions of successful development. Implicitly or explicitly, politics rather than economics tended to be the major problematic for orthodox development thinkers on both sides of the ideological divide.

In the early stages, the DRV looked to the Soviet Union and to China for concrete socialist development policies. Agricultural programmes in the initial years closely followed earlier Chinese experience, particularly in land reform and co-operativisation. Maoism made a deep impact on Vietnam, though many Chinese initiatives (such as the Great Leap Forward and the Cultural Revolution) and institutions (notably large-scale communes) were not adopted, and certain specific policies (for example, close planting of rice) were tried and found inappropriate.[9] In the 1970s there has been much less confidence in Vietnam that a ready-made formula for development exists, or even that foreign socialist policies can provide signposts on a high road to socialist prosperity. A Vietnamese economist in Hanoi summed up Vietnam's economic difficulties as stemming from the fact that 'there is no proven, successful path to prosperity for a poor country; we have had to feel our way by trial and error, correcting mistakes as they became apparent'.[10] This appears to have led to greater attention to non-socialist development experience as well as a return to a study of the basic principles of Marxist economic analysis.

There had been debate over priorities in development

strategy from the beginning. Recent policy changes in the relative priority accorded to industry and agriculture, and the extent of direct political and managerial control of the economy were first suggested in the early 1960s. However, until recently, the availability of socialist bloc aid and the particular political and economic requirements of the war years reinforced the ideological logic of sticking to familiar orthodox socialist development formulae, such as priority to state investment in heavy industry. This is frequently alluded to as an indication of an orthodox Stalinist orientation on the part of the DRV leadership. I would argue, however, that this formulation ignores differences between Soviet and Vietnamese (as well as Chinese) industrialisation policies and similarities between Stalinist and Maoist orientations to heavy industry.

As the only former European colony to have joined the socialist camp in the early cold war era, the DRV benefited from a considerable amount of aid, especially from the Soviet Union and China. This contributed to optimism on the part of the leadership that Vietnam would be able to develop without having to go through the painful rigours of indigenous accumulation that had characterised capitalist development in England or the Soviet Union under Stalin's forced and brutal drive for industrialisation and collectivisation.

In its first five-year plan (1960–5) Vietnam adopted the orthodox socialist priority to heavy industry. Unlike the Soviet Union, the primary source of finance was to come from abroad. For example, the largest single project, the Thai Nguyen iron and steel complex begun in 1960 with Chinese aid, cost the equivalent of one year's entire harvest in Vietnam.[11] Although the cost did not come from indigenous sources, the project did absorb precious resources in skilled cadres and workers for an undertaking which had few forward or backward linkages to the Vietnamese economy. The raw material for the factory was imported from, and the produce exported to China, the donor country.[12] Vietnam's initial industrialisation programme thus did not involve draining agriculture, but neither was its *primary* orientation to provide inputs into agricultural development.

The relationship between agriculture and industry in this initial period of Vietnam's independent development most closely resembled the Chinese pattern: state investment was concentrated on the industrial sector, but there was much less extraction from the countryside than in the early stages of Soviet industrialisation. The state budget came primarily from foreign aid and industrial profits rather than draining agriculture. In this, it should be noted, Vietnam did not differ significantly from the Maoist model, which concentrated on encouraging rural self-reliance while channeling state investment into urban industry. As a recent re-evaluation of Maoist policies in China notes,

Contrary to claims of having put more stress on the peasant and agriculture, in fact, the percentage of investment in the Mao era that went into heavy industries such as steel and electronics for the military actually increased.... Peasants may have been first in Maoist hearts but they were last in the budget.[13]

As applied in Vietnam as well as in China, the Maoist development model in fact minimised rural – urban links: the combination of rural low-level industrialisation financed primarily by the mobilisation of local resources, and local self-sufficiency in grain provided the policy context for local self-reliance and the ideological justification for low levels of state investment in agriculture. This policy made a lot of sense in a situation of war or threat of war, as the nation could concentrate state investment on development of heavy industry for defence requirements, while self-sufficient rural communes would provide the basis for local militia resistance in case of foreign invasion.

In the wake of Nixon's *rapprochement* with China and the ending of over two decades of economic blockade and cold war international hostility to China, the international context which had influenced this development strategy changed dramatically. Economic growth rather than national defence has achieved new salience in Chinese development thinking. Furthermore, years of national self-reliance in building up large-scale industry and rural industrialisation and self-reliance in the countryside now gives China a very strong base for its entry into the world market.

Similar post-war attempts at integration into foreign markets on the part of Vietnam, however, are made from a position of weakness rather than strength. Before the

American bombing, the DRV had benefited from an unusual degree of foreign aid from both the Soviet Union and China due to its unique position. But the factories built with foreign socialist aid between 1955 and 1965 were destroyed or severely damaged during the bombing. After the end of the war in 1975, far from getting increased aid for post-war reconstruction as had been the case following the earlier war against French colonialism, the volume of CMEA nation assistance declined, and the terms stiffened: grant aid was changed to repayable loans. The cut-off of Chinese commodity aid in 1975, and of all aid construction projects in 1978, caused severe hardship and dislocation. There were many more competitors for socialist aid than at the time of the DRV's ambitious and optimistic first five-year plan in 1960. It became clear that the rebuilding of Vietnam's economy could not be effected primarily with aid, but would have to be paid for by trade. Moreover, the attack on Vietnam by Mao's successors ironically strengthened the position of those within the Vietnamese Communist Party who wished to reject certain aspects of the Vietnamese socio-economic system. In this context, a new look at economic policy became necessary, and important disagreements over political-economic strategy emerged. Given the crucial significance of agriculture in this predominantly rural country, and the centrality of agricultural questions in recent debates, I shall focus primarily on agrarian issues. In the next two sections, I shall briefly discuss the agreed ideological context within which policy is debated in Vietnam and the history of debate over agricultural policy. In the last section, I shall turn to the debates of the late 1970s and early 1980s.

The Ideological Framework of Vietnamese Development Policy

As we have seen in preceding sections, Vietnamese development policy has been neither monolithic nor unchanging. However, the ideological world view of Vietnamese government and Communist Party leaders and policy-makers sets the broad framework for discussion of development questions. There are certain questions which have not been open to debate and which form the bedrock points of consensus concerning the definition of 'socialist development'.

(a) To Vietnamese leaders it is axiomatic that 'building socialism' means first and foremost *industrialisation*; this has never been questioned as a primary aim. The concept of a comfortable and cultured agricultural society as the end aim of the development process (such as, for example, William Morris's utopian agrarian vision in *News from Nowhere*) has never been seriously raised or considered. In Vietnamese communist thinking, a developed socialist society is by definition an industrialised society.

(b) Vietnamese leaders define the development task as transforming their agricultural country into an industrial one without following the path of European industrialisation studied by Marx, i.e. capitalism. Capitalist development is rejected as an alternative on the grounds that, as described by Marx in *Capital*, the early stages of capitalist industrialisation include an intolerable depression of the material and moral condition of the working people.

(c) The development of human resources is seen as crucial for raising economic productivity. It is believed that if individual ownership and an unregulated market were allowed to dominate the economic system, then basic social needs crucial for national development, including health and education, would not adequately be provided for. This is seen to necessitate state intervention through economic planning and redistributive measures such as the provision of basic necessities at set prices, and the systematic inclusion of welfare and income distribution considerations in economic decision-making.

(d) It is held that in socialist development, as in the earlier struggle for national independence, the state and the Communist Party must play the leading role.

(e) The crucial difference between capitalism and socialism is seen as lying in ownership of the means of production.

(f) An industrial society is understood as characterised by large-scale production in both agriculture and industry. Socialist development is conceived as transforming small-scale 'handicraft' or petty commodity production into large-scale socialist (state-owned) production. There is therefore a tendency to preoccupation with scale and the view that the larger the productive unit, the more 'socialist' it is.

To date, any case for development policy change has to be seen to satisfy these basic points in order to be acceptable to the Communist Party consensus as to what 'socialist development' means; there can be no question of rejecting industrialisation as an ultimate aim, restoring capitalism, or introducing a multi-party system. Within this agreed framework, however, there have been major policy shifts and debates, and these basic points of principle and long-term aims have been increasingly open to radically differing stresses, interpretations and short-term policies.

There has long been considerable distance between various points of socialist principle and what has been done in practice in a country which, as its leaders state, is not yet socialist. For example, the association of socialism with large-scale production precludes promoting the concept 'small is beautiful', and petty commodity production is officially seen as a major fetter on Vietnamese development. However, Vietnam has been one of the most successful Third World countries in the development and application of intermediate or 'appropriate' technology. Most recently, the new experiments encouraging a greater economic role to small-scale household production and the market, long taboo in both Maoist and orthodox socialist thinking as 'capitalist' measures, have been acceptable so long as the principle of socialist (state or collective) ownership is maintained.

Although there is no question of challenging the principle of the state and Party's vanguard role in setting the broad guidelines of economic policy, the desirable extent of direct political intervention and decision-making in economic administration has long been open to debate. As early as January 1957 (i.e. before the first steps for socialist transformation of the economy were initiated), Prime Minister Pham van Dong warned the National Assembly that

> because our country is still a backward agricultural country where the economy of small-scale producers is predominant, in the matter of economic management we must be cautious and correct bureaucratic management which puts too much weight on administrative measures.

This warning was not heeded at the time, but as we shall see later, re-emerged with renewed vigour in intra-party debates in the 1970s which culminated in the Sixth Plenum of the Party Central Committee in 1979. According to the Sixth

Plenum line there are limits to the ability of the Party and administration to exercise the direct control of the economic system which has been attempted in Vietnam's adoption of the socialist model of planning, procurement and allocation, and the failure to recognise these limits and adjust the system accordingly has led to major irrationalities and inefficiencies. In short, this view attacks formalistic concern with 'socialist' appearances (i.e. economic decision-making by officials of state or co-operative socialist organisations) rather than with (Marxist) 'laws' of economic development.

Stages and Debates in Vietnamese Agricultural Development Policy

Agricultural and rural development policy has undergone several changes in emphasis and approach over the past three decades. Three broad policy periods can be identified, characterised by priority first to class struggle and redistribution in the 1950s, then, in the 1960s, to consolidating co-operative agriculture as a framework for raising rural living standards and introducing basic improvements in agricultural science, technology and infrastructure to increase land productivity, while in the 1970s the emphasis shifted to raising labour productivity, developing crop specialisation and to national and international commercialisation of agriculture. It is not a mere question of stages; none of these periods was free from major policy debates as outlined below.

The 1950s: Beginning in the period of anti-colonial struggle and continuing through the first years of DRV independence, priority was given to structural transformations in the system of landownership through land reform and co-operativisation. Class analysis and class struggle, redistribution, and reorganisation along socialist lines, were considered the keys to solving problems of agricultural development, making this the most overtly 'political' policy period.[14] Vietnam's poverty was blamed directly on the socio-economic structure of the preceding 'feudal' and colonial periods. It was believed to be a 'law of social development' that 'backward relations of production', particularly unequal distribution of land and other means of agricultural production, had stifled economic growth. Land reform (1953–6) was expected to 'liberate the forces of production', mainly labour, from rent and debt bondage. This was expected to provide the impetus for a sharp increase in agricultural productivity since the surplus would be used by the peasantry and the state in productive ways rather than squandered by parasitic classes (landlords, village notables and the royal court) or extracted from the country by French colonialists. The formation of co-operatives which began in 1958 was intended to maintain and strengthen these gains by preventing the re-emergence of class differentiation as well as facilitating rural development through pooled and better organised utilisation of scarce agricultural resources.

The main state investment in agricultural improvement during this period was in irrigation, using traditional labour-intensive construction methods. The technique of mass mobilisation, involving political motivation for the redeployment of labour, played a crucial role in all three major programmes of this period (land reform, co-operativisation and irrigation).

The major policy debate of this period was over the promotion of class struggle in the countryside during the land reform campaign of 1953–6. This policy had involved expulsions from the Party and administration of 'rural exploiters', i.e. landlords, rich peasants and even many middle peasants, who had played a significant role in the preceding anti-colonial struggle. Although important in preventing the anti-colonial leadership from emerging as a new privileged class, there were many mistakes in implementation, and the policy itself harmed the national united front strategy which was the major priority for the Communist Party in the South. Opposition within the Party to the excesses caused by the priority to class struggle during the land reform led to the resignation of Truong Chinh in September 1956 from the post of Party Secretary General. He remained, however, a member of the political bureau and a leading agricultural policy-maker. He played an important role defending the interests of his poor peasant constituency during the period of 'rectification of errors' committed in the land reform, and was the primary architect of the co-operativisation policy begun in 1958.

The 1960s: During the first years of the decade a socialist transformation of agriculture was carried out involving the gradual transfer of landownership from individuals to rural co-operatives (1958-late 1960s). Unlike either the preceding land reform or the forced collectivisation of the Soviet Union, this was done without physical coercion. Initially, peasants who pooled their land for collective cultivation by a small co-operative of peasant members were paid a return for their land and other capital inputs into the co-operative as well as for their labour. Gradually, the amount paid according to original capital and land contribution was reduced and finally eliminated, while the percentage paid for labour proportionally increased. This method of co-operativisation by moving from semi-socialist to socialist agricultural collectives had originated in China, but was applied much more gradually in Vietnam. (China took three years to involve 88 per cent of peasant families in fully socialist co-operatives, whereas in the DRV the same transformation was spread out over nine years, from 1958–66.)[17]

Towards the beginning of this process of transformation the argument was made that continued reforms in relations of production were less crucial than raising the productivity of the forces of production, especially land, through advances in science and technology. Le Duan, who emerged as Secretary General at the Party's Third Congress (September 1960) argued in February 1960 when there were as yet few fully socialist co-operatives in the DRV, that 'the development of the productive forces lags behind that of the new relations of production'.[18] His name is associated with the policy of the 'three revolutions' formulated at the Third Party Congress which remains the official Vietnamese conception of priorities to this day: revolution in relations of production, revolution in culture and ideology, and revolution in science and technology, of which the *revolution in science and technology is key*.

In agricultural policy the primary emphasis was placed on improving the system of co-operative management and popularising agronomic knowledge through a network of trained agricultural technicians at the co-operative level. Significant advances were made, most notably the development and adaptation of new seed varieties with higher yields and faster maturation, making possible a third crop. The principal agricultural campaigns of this period related to increasing land yields through crop multiplication and more efficient use of traditionally available inputs, primarily water and organic fertiliser. The transition from family micro-holdings to co-operative units made possible extensive irrigation and drainage canal works, while educated youth in co-operative technical teams spread the use of azolla, a nitrogen-fixating plant traditionally grown as a fertiliser only in a few areas of the Red River Delta. The invention and adaptation of the two-compartment latrine both improved rural health and provided a traditional fertiliser for the fields in a sanitised form. Thus the technocratic-sounding priority to 'revolution in science and technology' actually involved popularising very low-level 'appropriate technology'.

The earlier intra-party debate over the priority to accord to class struggle continued during this period. The Fifth Plenum of the Party Central Committee in 1961 minimised class struggle, arguing that an undifferentiated 'collective peasant class' was emerging in the countryside. This evaluation was later criticised in 1963 when Maoist views on class struggle were in ascendance in the Central Committee.

A second and closely-related debate concerned the relationship between co-operatives and the family economy of co-operative members. Particularly after the beginning of the bombing of the North, many co-operatives subcontracted steps in agricultural production as well as co-operative land to the households of co-operative members (the so-called 'three contracts' system). This policy was denounced in late 1968 by the guardian of socialist orthodoxy, Truong Chinh as a 'return to the individualistic ways of working' which destroyed the meaning of agricultural production co-operatives turning them into mere formal structures.[19] Truong Chinh's position was adopted as official policy, and for the following ten years subcontracting of land (although not of individual steps in the labour process) was ideologically taboo, a position which closely resembled the Maoist line on the same controversy in China. The debates of the late 1960s were to come to the fore in the period of economic crisis of the late 1970s when the issue of subcontracting land to co-operative families, and the threat to both egalitarianism and communalism which that entailed, became once more the topic of the day.

The basic structure of the socialist co-operative system which emerged in Vietnam during the 1960s was broadly similar to that of China. This included a three-tiered state procurement system (agricultural taxes, an obligatory state delivery quota, and additional sales at an 'incentive' price still below free market prices), a stress on the use of 'moral incentives' by co-operative cadres to urge peasants to produce for social (state and co-operative) rather than narrow household material gain, and a fairly egalitarian balance of social need (number of mouths to feed per household) with work-point labour remuneration in the distribution of the harvest. However, a number of important differences from the Maoist model also emerged, the most important of which were dropping class labels based on pre-or post-land reform holdings of peasant families in favour of the category of 'collective peasants', and the absence of any cultural revolution-type campaign against intellectuals (many of whom inevitably came from families which were well-off before the Revolution). In an interview in September 1979, the agricultural editor of the party newspaper *Nhan Dan*, Nguyen Huu Tho, stated that Mao had been 'displeased' at the Vietnamese divergence from his policy of continuing the pre-revolutionary class struggle in the period of transition to socialism. Tho attributed Vietnamese success in the anti-American war to two major factors: co-operatives, which provided a secure economic base and social assistance for the families of young men mobilised into the army, and the 'enlightened class line' stressing national social harmony: 'rely on the working class, unite with the collective peasant class and have a correct attitude towards the intellectuals'.[20]

The positive DRV policy on intellectuals led to the emergence in the 1960s of a remarkably developed set of research institutes including agronomy and basic physical sciences as well as the social sciences.[21] Foreign visitors are very favourably impressed by the intellectual level of academic work in Vietnam despite the economic poverty of the country, wartime damage and difficulties of contact with the outside world. It was the stress on the importance of the 'revolution in science and technology' as a major socialist task given higher priority than class struggle which provided the political basis for this important institutionalisation of professional development-oriented research in the 1960s. The aspect of China's Cultural Revolution viewed with most abhorrence in Vietnam was the attack on intellectuals, especially on the basis of class of origin or previous contact with the West.

The 1970s: The network of peasant co-operatives which characterised Vietnam during the period of the bombing has been accurately described as crucial to the success of Vietnamese defence. They provided the institutional network for maximum local level economic self-sufficiency along with decentralisation of political decision-making and initiative which are crucial ingredients for the success of a people's war. However, during the 1970s the limitations of the co-operative system as the basis for growth in productivity and especially surplus generation became increasingly apparent. Crop multiplication, after some initial success, levelled off. Crop yields per acre increased, but the nutritional density (population per unit of cultivated land) rose even faster. Increased yields could be attributed in significant measure to intensification of labour inputs. While co-operativisation could be shown to have led to rises in *land* productivity, labour productivity actually declined. Demographic increase and declining labour productivity was the Vietnamese scissors crisis of the 1970s. The egalitarian distribution system of co-operatives showed clear signs of being the basis for what Clifford Geertz has termed 'agricultural involution' (the capacity for wet rice agriculture to support more and more people on the same amount of land through increased labour inputs in a 'shared poverty' context).[23] The urgency of raising agricultural labour productivity and the generation of a surplus became a major theme in the 1970s.

During this period, the attitude towards co-operatives became more ambiguous. As early as 1970 Le Duan pointed to the danger of guild-type collective spirit 'which divorces one's small collective from the unified leadership of the proletarian state and pits the interest of one collective against those of another'.[24] Whereas the priority of the 1960s was to build up co-operatives as basic and self-reliant political economic units in the countryside, by the late 1970s cadres were speaking of the need to 'break the autarky of the co-operatives'.[25] The attempt was made to limit the quite extensive scope of autonomous decision-making by the co-operative. A new policy was introduced in the early 1970s of carrying out surveys to zone agricultural crop areas according to soil type with a view to moving toward crop specialisation on the basis of regional comparative advantage. It proved very difficult, however, to induce villages to give up their self-reliant cropping patterns and rely on the state distribution system; transport difficulties and pricing irrationalities strongly militated against such a move away from local level autarky. The next plan was to build up the district as the key local economic and political unit; this too met with limited success, as it would necessitate surrender of power by well-established provincial and co-operative (village) political and economic institutions. The latest policy initiative of encouraging co-operatives to subcontract their land to co-operative households for cultivation for all but the initial steps of the labour process could well promote increased commercialisation through a new role for market forces and increased economic incentives for heightened productivity. It is not yet clear, however, whether subcontracting is a temporary tactical retreat from orthodox conceptions of socialist organisation or the inauguration of a new and more flexible system. In the context of a re-evaluation of the Maoist approach to co-operative management and an endemic food and procurement crisis, there are now fundamental disagreements over agricultural policy as part of broader debates over economic policy, which will be the topic of a later section.

Post-war Developments: Reunification and Agricultural Policy in the South

Alongside the continuities of development concerns during the 1970s outlined above, there were also a number of major shifts in economic policy and concerns under the impetus of the dramatic changes which took place in the decade.

The victory in the South in 1975, the rapid formal reunification of the country as the Socialist Republic of Vietnam in 1976, and the unexpected and total deterioration of relations with China which culminated in early 1979 with a Chinese military invasion, mark the end of an era. The greatest challenges of the new period were integrating two entirely different politico-economic systems into one nation, solving long deferred economic problems in the aftermath of great wartime destruction, but with reduced outside aid, and facing a new threat from China. The new crisis had to be faced without any resolution of the preceding conflict; there was neither normalisation of relations with the United States, nor time to heal the wounds of war.

In 1975 it was expected that reunification of the Democratic Republic of Vietnam and the Provisional Revolutionary Government (PRG) of South Vietnam would be a slow process going parallel to step-by-step, gradual unification on an economic and social level; a number of PRG and DRV leaders stated as much. The context of continuing US hostility and emerging tension with China and Kampuchea created a complicated internal security situation in the South which must have strengthened the hand of those who wanted a rapid incorporation of the South under essentially the national political structures of the DRV rather than a more gradual evolution. At the time of reunification in 1976, DRV political institutions were transformed with relatively few structural changes into those of the Socialist Republic of Vietnam.

True reunification of the societies, polities and economies of the long divided halves of Vietnam has yet to be achieved. It is, of course, a truism in politics that external threats necessitate stringent internal security measures; it is therefore unlikely that a satisfactory solution will be reached in the context of international hostility in which Vietnam continues to find itself. In the context of threats from the world's most powerful country (the US) and its most populous one (China), Vietnam's own 'hardliners' in the government find justification for rejecting measures for political liberalisation. The complexities of non-PRG opposition to the former Saigon régime are not generally understood by northerners, and activists of the former 'Third Force' are distrusted.

This does not mean, however, that the post-war economic transformations in the South followed the model of post-colonial changes in the DRV nearly two decades earlier. In agricultural policy, only in Central Vietnam was there success in the type of slow but steady and popularly supported co-operativisation which had taken place in the rural DRV in the late 1950s and early 1960s. In that region, revolutionary political traditions and socio-economic conditions closely resembled those which had characterised most of the North before co-operativisation: dense population on tiny land-holdings very vulnerable to frequent natural disasters. Wartime destruction in this area, considered enemy territory and a rural free-fire zone by the American military during the war, left no village or family intact. This made the restoration of agriculture on a family basis particularly difficult, further strengthening the case for social co-operation in production on a hamlet or village rather than a narrow household basis.

In the Mekong Delta in the late 1970s, unlike the Tonkin Delta in the 1950s, the major priority was not land to the tiller (i.e. land redistribution), but rather getting tillers back to the land (population redistribution). The wartime bombing in the Mekong Delta had driven millions of peasants to the relative safety of the cities and towns. Unemployed urban dwellers were urged to leave the cities for New Economic Zones on which the priority was to get production going by any means possible, whether the form was private, co-operative or state farming. Many of these settlers returned to the cities as they were unaccustomed after years of living off US aid to the rigours of making a living from the land, especially in such harsh economic conditions.

In those areas of the fertile Mekong Delta, where agricultural production had continued during the war, farmers (they were no longer pre-capitalist peasants) had enjoyed relative economic prosperity during the war. Successive revolutionary as well as US-sponsored land reforms had given them land, while during the war they did not have to pay taxes (most land records were destroyed)—the Saigon government budget had been paid for by the American rather than the Vietnamese taxpayer. The inflated Saigon market and aid subsidies for agricultural inputs such as fertilisers and tractors, as well as consumer goods, created a relative wealth in material goods for these farmers or middle peasants that owed nothing to the native Vietnamese economy.

Whereas socialist egalitarianism had meant improving the standard of living of DRV peasants, for relatively prosperous Mekong Delta farmers it would necessarily mean a tightening of the belt to assist other areas of the country which are less fertile and more subject to natural disasters. From the point of view of the new government of the reunified Socialist Republic of Vietnam, the Mekong Delta was the traditional surplus-producing ricebowl which should be restored and transformed to serve as the nation's granary. The government campaign to form co-operatives (or 'production collectives') in this area was frankly motivated by the desire to raise procurement dramatically. In one speech, Vo Chi Cong, in charge of the socialist transformation of agriculture in the South, specified that whereas taxation on individual land-holdings was only some 10 per cent of the harvest, with co-operativisation the percentage procured had been raised to 30–40 per cent.[26] (It should be emphasised that this was not the case everywhere in former South Vietnam: the poor co-operatives of southern central Vietnam have little surplus over the needs of their members and often require state aid.) In this context joining co-operatives clearly goes against the economic interests of the farmers, and the attempt to co-operativise the Mekong Delta has made slow progress with frequent reversals.

Post-war Debates in Vietnamese Economic Policy

The primary political debates in post-war Vietnam have not been over political institutions, but rather over economic policy. The urgency of the economic situation, along with rapid changes in the international situation, have opened the realm of economic debate within the Party and government. Disagreements over economic policy which are sufficiently clearly delineated to be considered two schools are not pure theory, but touch the interests of powerful groups within the society. Economic debate has become the forum in which implicitly political issues are discussed.

The authoritative political document for the post-war period is the report of the Central Committee produced at the Fourth National Congress (14–20 December 1976). The text contains a confusing mixture of reiteration of orthodoxy and significant new departures. An article intended to guide Party study-groups discussing the Fourth Party Congress documents admonished that if Party members had not seen what was new in policy, economic structure and administrative organisation, they had not understood the resolutions.[27] However, in fact, the documents included too much of the old along with the new for readers to discern a clear new direction. Perhaps the most significant passage in the resolution was an official admission of an area of uncertainty:

The line for socialist revolution mapped out by the Party is basically correct. However...the fundamental principles of socialist revolution, especially questions concerning the advance from small-scale production to large-scale socialist production, which have the character of laws, are generally speaking not well understood.[28]

How can a 'line' be correct if the 'laws' it is based on are not understood? The first sentence is the voice of orthodoxy, the next a significant green light to innovation in theory and policy by economic reformers within the Party. The passages which follow this statement contain the core of the emerging critique of economic policy: 'Not enough importance has been attached to agriculture and light industry', and 'One of our great shortcomings in economic management is the bureaucratic and administrative method of management.' These two statements in the 1976 resolution were not acted on decisively during the next two years; they were later elaborated more fully, and most forcefully, after the Sixth Plenum of September 1979, whose concrete policy changes concerned encouragement of agricultural and handicraft (light industrial) production outside of the state and co-operative sectors, and whose longer-term (and more debated) programme was a fundamental attack on 'the bureaucratic and administrative method of management' in favour of more attention to basic principles of economic development.[29] Vietnamese supporters of this new economic policy which has been compared to the NEP which followed war communism in the Soviet Union in the 1920s, can insist, with some justification, that the seemingly dramatic Sixth Plenum changes are not new at all, but follow on from the line of the Fourth Congress.

Throughout the 1970s, a number of Vietnamese economists within the Party had become increasingly sceptical of the capacity of the state administrative system to control every aspect of the economy to the extent that it was trying to do through the system of plans, obligatory targets, fixed prices and procurement levels. Any move, however, in the direction of replacing some of the reliance on direct political control with more use of economic levers and untying the unseen hand of the market was a direct threat to the jobs of those central and local administrators and political officials who spent their time communicating plan targets and exhorting the peasants to fulfil them. Cutting of bureaucratic corners by reducing the extensive role of planning and state control would also cut away some lucrative niches that influential local people had built for themselves by their control of politico-administrative links and of the account books.

A systematic critique of the 'administrative style of management' in agriculture and the irrationalities and mismanagement to which it had led appeared very shortly after the end of the war. For example, an article entitled 'Improve Planning in Agricultural Co-operatives' argued that waste and corruption were major problems that could not be solved merely by improving the planning system.[30] Rather, a major portion of blame was laid to

Economic management by bureaucratic administrative means, by a rigid apparatus and style of work that impedes expansion of production and by issuing orders and directives from superior to subordinate heedless of the objective necessities in economic matters (p. 26).

As a result of bureaucratic formalism, the article argued, the production plans of many co-operatives were 'just a collection of subjective hopes' with 'little practical effect'. The poor economic performance of many co-operatives was put down to irrational government price policies. A survey carried out in 1973 had indicated that around 25–30 per cent of co-operatives were suffering a net loss in operations each year because they were pressured into selling rice to the government at prices which failed to cover their costs of production.

The economic arbitrariness of higher levels forced many co-operatives 'to prepare two types of plans: one for presentation to superiors for "approval" and another for organising production'. The existence of many incorrect reports on production results opened the way for corruption by co-operative cadres. (According to another source, many co-operatives had three sets of books: one for co-operative members, one for co-operative cadres, and one for dealing with higher administrative levels. Through their control of the books, some co-operative cadres were able to cheat both co-operative members and the state.) As a result of these unsolved and pervasive contradictions between state and co-operative on the one hand, and the co-operative cadres and members on the other, it was reported that in some areas peasants upset about cadre waste and corruption had asked to leave the co-operatives.

The fact that this article, and others like it, was published is in itself an indication of the openness of debate over economic policy. The position argued was one which had been rejected in no uncertain terms by the Party's Secretary General, Le Duan, just a few months before. In August 1974, at a meeting on agricultural development problems, Le Duan had noted that, 'At this conference you have said that the price problem is one of the causes for the co-operatives' lack of enthusiasm in production', but insisted that although some adjustments would be made, in fact in the peasant-state relationship it was the peasants who were gaining the most already, and that instead of feeling that they should get more recompense for the contribution their children had made to national defence, 'to demand special rights and privileges', the peasants should continue in the wartime spirit of being willing to make great sacrifices for the collective good.[31] His was a continuation of the earlier position insisting on the primacy of moral over material incentives in economic development.

It was not until the Sixth Plenum (1979) that the view that economic laws in peacetime are not the same as those of wartime finally prevailed. A key editorial, entitled 'Plan and Market', in the Party newspaper *Nhan Dan* outlined the new Party line on the important role to be played by the unorganised family economy and the market during the period of transition to socialism, and strongly criticised opponents of this position (*Nhan Dan*, 22 October 1979). The state plan, the editorial stated, could not control small-scale production, but only indicate general directions. Before planning could be extended to include the entire economy, 'there is a long period when planned production and distribution on a large scale coexist with production by relatively small collective units and the dispersed economy of individual family households'. The family economy, argued the editorial, had a great potential for supplying many necessary consumer goods if correctly guided and assisted. However, the family economy had been repressed in the past because 'a number of weak spirited comrades are obsessed with the spectre of the spontaneous development of capitalism inherent in any productive or exchange activity which is not organised'. In fact, this position ascribed to the weak spirited could be called a central tenet of Maoism. Countering this orthodox socialist as well as Maoist view which had held sway up until that time, the editorial argued that 'petty individual production or petty trade can only develop into capitalism through a process of accumulation of capital and its use in capitalist enterprises, creating private ownership of large-scale means of production'. This, the socialist state would not allow to happen. In the transition period socialist ownership and planning of large-scale production could coexist with individual and co-operative ownership of the means of small-scale production.

The simple mentality of wanting all production and distribution to be taken in hand by administrative laws and regulations immediately, and eliminating everything else by not allowing anyone to do anything outside of nationalised industries and co-operatives and forbidding all forms of uncontrolled exchange can only lead to an economic situation of poverty and slow growth.

Another editorial expressing the ideas of the Sixth Plenum entitled 'Objective laws and revolutionary ardour' argued that socialist economic transformation must go through certain steps which could not be leapt over or ignored by revolutionary will (*Nhan Dan* 13 October 1979). The editorial attacked the 'dangerous' view that will could solve everything, and concluded with the resounding sentence: 'Voluntarism is the enemy of Marxism-Leninism and of revolutionary science.' This editorial was not only one side of the perennial philosophical debate over the roles of 'will' and 'determinism' in setting the parameters of the possibilities of human accomplishment and development; it was also an indirect statement on the limits of direct political control of economic decision-making. The 'vanguard party' is the institutionalised embodiment of a belief in the efficacy of human will and political organisation to cause radical change. Within the Party there is a tendency to generalise from the successes of the Party in the political and military sphere to the realm of economic development. The economists' view was that economic laws differ from the dynamics of war and revolution. Will, and the Party and administrative apparatus as direct organiser and mobiliser of efforts to overcome seemingly insurmountable odds, had been crucial in achieving victory against French colonialism and American military might, but were insufficient to the task of overcoming poverty and organising production.

One of the earliest counter-attacks on the Sixth Plenum line appears to have been in a speech by Le Duc Tho (Political Bureau member, and formerly chief DRV negotiator at the Paris talks) commemorating, appropriately enough, the birthday of Lenin, the father of the doctrine of the vanguard party. The speech attacked both left and right extremes in socialist thought, Maoism and 'market socialism', as doctrines which although different in form were similar in denying 'the universal laws of the socialist revolution and socialist construction' and replacing 'Marxism-Leninism by reformist and reactionary theories'. He argued at some length that any deficiencies in the state and Party's management of the economy should be remedied by improving, rather than decreasing, administrative control of the economy. Because of the many years of war in which national defence had been the major priority, he argued, 'economic organisation and management remain a new task in which we still lack experience'. The solution, he maintained, would be to 'concentrate on consolidating and perfecting the organisational apparatus of the party, state and mass organisations', so that they would be more adequately prepared for their tasks of economic management.[32]

For some time there was a stand-off between these two tendencies within the Party: on the one hand the political and administrative personnel who believed that socialism equals economic decision-making by state and Party officials and whose *raison d'être* had long been their role in the planned economy, v. those who held it to be counter-productive to try to plan and control all aspects of economic life.

One can analyse the two positions as two variants of Marxism-Leninism, one stressing the leading role of the Party and state apparatus, the other returning to Marx's analysis of the dynamics of economic processes. The first type cites Lenin; the second quotes Marx's *Capital*.

The Fifth Congress of the Vietnam Communist Party in March 1982 was a victory for the economic reformist tendency since the Central Committee made a long self-criticism blaming 'the system of administrative, bureaucratic management' – by now a familiar phrase – for many of the country's problems.[33] It seems unlikely, however, that this constitutes the end of the debate, for the administrative, bureaucratic apparatus remains basically intact (there has been no Cultural Revolution-style movement to close down government offices). Despite a number of high-level personnel changes, many of those in favour of the continuation of the old system of maximum direct administrative control of the economy remain in office and are in a position to use their power to limit the extent of systemic change.

Present Policy in Socialist Perspective

Does the present policy of an enlarged role for direct and unplanned exchange both between economic producers (whether small-scale individual or larger co-operative and state enterprises) and between these producers and consumers imply a 'restoration of capitalism'? I think not, as there is no question of either totally abandoning economic and social planning nor of turning large-scale means of production over to private ownership. It is important not to fetishise commodity exchange *per se* as constituting capitalism, but rather to examine carefully the social relations involved, particularly since the actually existing socialist alternative to commodity exchange is some form of bureaucratic allocation.

Envisaging an enlarged role for market forces and 'the law of value' within the context of Vietnam's present politico-economic structures is not turning back the clock. In the 1950s and 1960s, when Vietnamese communist leaders embarked on fundamental structural transformations of the economy, 'market forces' were clearly the antithesis of socialism as they were tools in the hands of the enemies of revolutionary change: i.e. the colonialists, landlords and grain speculators, who controlled and knew how to manipulate the various markets in international commodities, land, rice, money, etc. Planning, political mobilisation and administrative controls were used and developed as the best tools for revolutionaries to bring the economy under control and guide its development.

As the 'new system' became progressively consolidated, two important new phenomena emerged. First, a growing number of Party cadres and government civil servants gained either professional training in economics or extensive practical experience in direct economic management of enterprises, and became convinced both that supply-and-demand or market prices (generally referred to under the rubric 'the law of value') could be used as 'economic levers' within a socialist-planned economy and that irrationalities in the price system were interfering with economic growth. According to this argument, the fine tuning involved in the manipulation of economic levers would make socialist planning more effective and socialist units of production more viable.

Secondly, an increasing number of important socioeconomic problems appeared to be the result of problems with the new socialist system itself rather than attributable to the aftermath of feudalism, colonialism, imperialism or wartime destruction. Not only were attempts to raise productivity by means of political exhortation and administrative rewards and penalties ineffective, but the mass of administrative fetters on economic decision-making by households, co-operatives and industrial enterprises were contributing to alienation ('lack of enthusiasm in production', as it was called in the Vietnamese press), economic stagnation, black markets, and corruption on the part of officials in a position to take advantage of their administrative power over economic processes. Revolutionary morality and therefore Party credibility was being seriously undermined.

This is the background to the present consensus in favour of economic liberalisation, and a dramatic change in policy orientation. This is not to say, however, that the new direction holds all of the answers. On the contrary, it can be argued that the new policies will contribute to a number of social problems. For example, agricultural productivity is now up, primarily because the manual agricultural labour force, overwhelmingly female, is given the financial incentives to work harder through the new subcontracting system. However, it is likely that productivity gains are at a high cost in terms of women's health, children's education, and social welfare provisions.[35] Furthermore, the demographic implications of a farming system based on household labour, which has built-in incentives in favour of producing many children, have been well documented.[36] If population growth is not checked, it will quickly negate any short-term improvements in productivity. At the time of the inauguration of the Sixth Plenum policy direction in 1979, it was recognised that there was a significant danger of increasing social inequalities through the increased scope for household organisation of production and for the operation of the market.[37]

Looking to the future, it seems likely that the next set of problems to emerge will be sociological. Just as the emphasis on political and administrative solutions to development problems which characterised the Vietnamese policy approach from the 1950s through the late 1970s exacerbated economic problems, the present stress on encouraging economic productivity above all is likely to contribute to the blossoming of social problems which will eventually bring socio-political questions to the forefront of the policy agenda.

Notes

1 For example, see most of the contributions to William S. Turley (ed.), *Vietnamese Communism in Comparative Perspective*, Boulder, Colorado, Westview Press, 1980.

2 Gareth Porter, 'Vietnam and the socialist camp: center or periphery?', in Turley, *op. cit.*, pp. 225–64.

3 For a more detailed discussion of these issues, see George McT. Kahin and John W. Lewis, *The United States in Vietnam*, New York, Delta, 1969.

4 Frances Fitzgerald, 'A reporter at large: journey to North Vietnam', *The New Yorker*, 28 April 1975. For a report by another member of the same group of American visitors, see David Marr, 'North Vietnam: a personal journal', *Indochina Chronicle*, no. 39, March 1975.

5   For a Vietnamese account of the history of this conflict, see *Vietnam's Sovereignty over the Hoang Sa and Truong Sa Archipelagos*, SRV Ministry of Foreign Affairs, 1979.

6   For a discussion of the issues involved in the China-Vietnam-Kampuchea conflict, see the symposium with articles by Barnett, Summers and Kiernan in the *Bulletin of Concerned Asian Scholars* XI, 4, October–December 1979, pp. 2–25; and Anthony Barnett, 'Interview with Vietnamese Foreign Minister Nguyen Cao Thach', *Far Eastern Economic Review*, 31 October 1980. For Vietnamese and Chinese analyses of the issue of ethnic Chinese leaving Vietnam, see Vietnam Courier (ed.), *The Hoa in Vietnam*, dossiers 1 and 2, Hanoi 1978; and *On Vietnam's Expulsion of Chinese Residents*, Peking, Foreign Language Press, 1978.

7   Fitzgerald, *op. cit.*

8   Willy Brandt, *North–South: A Programme for Survival*, London, Pan, 1980, pp. 37, 46.

9   For a detailed comparison of China and Vietnam on these issues, see David Elliott, *Revolutionary Re-integration: A Comparison of the Foundation of Post-Liberation Political Systems in North Vietnam and China*, Ann Arbor, University Microfilms, 1976; and Christine White, *Agrarian Reform and National Liberation in the Vietnamese Revolution: 1920–1957*, Ann Arbor, University Microfilms, 1981.

10 Interview by author at the Economic Institute, Hanoi, September 1979.

11 See the account by a researcher at the Economics Institute in Hanoi: Le Vinh, 'Problèmes de l'industrialisation', *La Nouvelle Critique*, Paris, no. 135, March 1962, pp. 107–9.

12 Jacques Charrière, 'Socialism in North Vietnam', *Monthly Review*, February 1966, pp. 19–41.

13 Edward Friedman, 'The original Chinese revolution remains in power', *Bulletin of Concerned Asian Scholars*, 13, 3, 1981, p. 44.

14 See C. White, *op. cit.*; Elliott, *op. cit.*, and 'Political integration in North Vietnam: the cooperativization period', in J. Zasloff and M. Brown (eds.), *Communism in Indochina: New Perspectives*, Lexington, Massachusetts, D.C. Heath, 1975; and Alec Gordon, 'North Vietnam's collectivization campaigns: class struggle, production and the "middle peasant" problem', *Journal of Contemporary Asia*, 11, 1, 1981, pp. 19–43.

15 For a detailed discussion of these issues, see White, *op. cit.*.

16 Elliott, *op.. cit.*, 1975; and Gerard Chaliand, *The Peasants of North Vietnam*, Penguin, 1969.

17 Gordon, *op. cit.*, p. 21.

18 Le Duan, February 1960: 'The tasks of socialist revolution in North Vietnam and scientific work', in *On the Socialist Revolution in Vietnam*, vol. III, 1967.

19 Truong Chinh, 'Weaknesses, shortcomings and mistakes in agricultural co-operatives', *Vietnam: Documents and Research Notes*, Document no. 63, Saigon, US Mission in Vietnam, January 1969.

20 Christine White, 'Interview with Nguyen Huu Tho, agricultural editor of *Nhan Dan*', *Journal of Contemporary Asia*, 11, 1, pp. 127–30.

21 For scientific research, see Alan Hooper, *Biology as applied to Agriculture in Vietnam*, 1980 mimeo report on Vietnamese research institutes and personnel available from the author at the Department of Genetics and Cell Biology, University of Minnestota, St Paul, MN 55108, USA; the organisation of social science research is described by David Marr, 'The state of the social sciences in Vietnam', *Bulletin of Concerned Asian Scholars*, 10, 4 October–December 1978, pp. 70–7.

22 Chaliand, *op. cit.*, 1969.

23 Clifford Geertz, *Agricultural Involution*, Berkeley, University of California Press, 1966.

24 Le Duan, *The Vietnamese Revolution: Fundamental Problems: Essential Tasks*, Hanoi, Foreign Languages Publishing House, 1970, p. 99.

25 Interview by the author, Economics Institute, Hanoi, September 1979.

26 Vo Chi Cong, address 5–9 April 1979 to a conference reviewing agricultural transformation in the Mekong Delta provinces, broadcast in Vietnamese, Ho Chi Minh domestic service, 14 May 1979, translated in US Foreign Broadcasts Information Service, 17 May 1979. (FBIS-APA-79-097, p. K14.)

27 *Tap Chi Cong San*, 4, 1978.

28 Communist Party of Vietnam, *Fourth National Congress: Documents* Hanoi, FLPH, 1977, pp. 31–2.

29 For a sophisticated discussion of the issues involved in the Sixth Plenum decision, see Nguyen Huu Dong, '6ᵉ Plenum: adaptions conjoncturelles ou réformes durables? Essais sur la politique economique du socialisme', *Vietnam* no. 2, April 1981, pp. 41–60. See also Tran Ngoc Bich, *De nouvelles mesures pour relancer l'économie vietnamienne*, (Document de Fraternité Vietnam), Sudestasie, Paris, 1980.

30 Le Thu Y, 'Improve planning in agricultural co-operatives', *Nghien Cuu Kinh Te*, no. 87, September–October 1975, pp. 41–53. (Available in English in US, *Joint Publications Research Service* 66638 21 January 1976. Translations on Vietnam 1759.)

31 Le Duan, *Towards a Large-scale Socialist Agriculture*, Hanoi, FLPH, 1975, pp. 11–12.

32 Le Duc Tho, Speech broadcast on 21 April 1980 in FBIS-APA-80-083, 28 April 1980.

33 Nguyen Khac Vien, 'The economic options of the Fifth Congress', *Vietnam Courier*, vol. 18, no. 6, 1982, p. 15.

34 For a detailed description of Byzantine regulations on agricultural work, see 'The management of co-operatives', *Vietnamese Studies* no. 51.

35 For a detailed discussion of this issue, see Christine White, 'Socialist transformation of agriculture and gender relations: the Vietnamese case', in 'Agriculture, the peasantry and socialist development', *Bulletin*, Institute of Development Studies, Sussex, vol. 13, no. 4, 1982.

36 Benjamin White, 'Population, employment and involution in rural Java', *Development and Change*, no. 7, 1976: and 'Child labour and population growth: notes on some recent studies', mimeo, IDS Child Labour Workshop, 6–8 January 1981.

37 Christine White, 'Interview with Nguyen Huu Tho', *op. cit.*

Vietnam: Country Profile

Official name:	Socialist Republic of Vietnam, established on 2 July 1976.
Population:	52.7 million (1979 census).
Capital:	Hanoi 2.6 million (1979 census); (largest city Ho Chi Minh City, formerly Saigon, 3.4 million).
Land area:	329,400 sq km, of which 38 per cent woodland and forest, 17 per cent arable land, 15 per cent pastures (1978).
Official language:	Vietnamese.
Membership of international organisations:	UN since 1977, IBRD and IMF since 1976, CMEA (from observer status to full membership in 1978)
Political structure	
Constitution:	As of December 1980
Highest legislative body:	National Assembly of 496 members. 7th legislature elected in April 1981
Highest executive body:	Government Council
Prime Minister:	Pham Van Dong, assumed office 2 July 1976 (Prime Minister for DRV since 1955).
President:	Vacant since the death of Ton Duc Thang in March 1980
Irrigated area:	1.5 million ha or 25 per cent of arable land (in terms of cropped area higher because of multiple cropping; 1978).
Food self-sufficiency:	Shortage of rice since the war. Total food production in 1980 is estimated by FAO to have been 25 per cent below consumption needs.[d] (1978).
Energy balance –	
commercial consumption:	125 kg coal equivalent per capita.
liquid fuels (%):	15.
imports (%):	1.
primary production by type of energy (%):	Solid fuels 99, hydroelectric 1.

Growth indicators[II](% p.a.) –	(1976)[e]	(1977–9)[e]
national income[i]:	14.6	1.3
industry:	12.6	3.4
heavy:	15.1	1.4
consumer:	11.1	4.5
agriculture:	10.2	0.5
food production per capita:	7.1[6]	0.9[6]

Foreign trade and economic integration
(numerical data, from the 1977 Plan)[i]

Trade balance –

exports:	US$ 446.
imports:	US$ − 1045.
	Grants and loans and in recent years emigrants' remittances make substantial contributions to foreign exchange earnings.
Exports as % of GNP:	6.
Main exports:	Fishery products, coal, rubber, mining products (anthracite), forestry and farm products, handicrafts and other manufactures.
Main imports (%):	Food grain 9, other consumer goods 8, intermediate goods (fuel, raw materials, spare parts and fertilisers) 53, machinery and equipment 32.
Destination of exports (%):	Socialist countries 63. Non-socialist countries 37.
Main trading partners:	USSR, eastern European countries, Japan, south-east Asian countries.
Foreign aid:	Contribution of external grants and loans to state budget revenue 20 per cent. External capital inflows: socialist countries US$ 200m[IV], other 399m.
Foreign debt:	US$ 200 million disbursed and outstanding by the former government of South Vietnam at the end of 1975 to non-socialist countries; no debts to socialist countries at the time of unification.
Foreign investment:	A foreign investment code was adopted in April 1977; investment has so far been initiated in off-shore oil exploration.
Ruling party:	Vietnam Communist Party, founded in 1930 as the Indochinese Communist Party, named Vietnam Workers' Party 1951–76.
Secretary General of the Party:	Le Duan, assumed office in 1960.
Party membership:	1.53 million (c. 5 per cent of adult population) in 1976;[g] membership reduced since the reissue of party cards in 1980.
Armed forces:	Regular army 1 million (c.3.5 per cent of working-age population, 1980) plus regional forces and a people's militia.

Population
  Population density: 160 per sq km.
  Population growth (% p.a.):   3.1 (1976–79).[e]
  Population of working age   52 (1978).
  (15–64, %):
  Urban population (%):   23 (1980).
  Ethnic groups: 84 per cent Vietnamese (Kinh); ethnic minorities include Chinese, Tay-Nung, Khmer, Thai, Muong, Meo, Zao, Cham (1977).[b]

Education and health
  School system: Ten years (7–17) of 1st–3rd level general education universally available.
  Primary school enrolment   122; males 128, females 116 (1977).
  (gross ratios, %):
  Secondary school enrolment   51; males 56, females 47 (1977).
  (gross ratios, %):
  Higher education   2.9; males 3.9, females 1.8 (1977).
  enrolment (gross ratios, %):
  Adult literacy rate (%):   87 (1975).
  Life expectancy: 62 (1978).
  Child death rate (per 1000):   6 (1977).
  Population per hospital bed: 270 (1978).[e]
  Population per physician: 5170 (1976)[l]; 1300 including assistant doctors (1978).[e]

Economy
  GNP: US$ 8.5 billion (1979).[16]
  GNP per capita: US$ 160.
  Domestic investment as   19 (1977 plan).[i]
  % of national income[l]:
  State budget (expenditure)   35 (1977 plan).[i]
  as % of GNP:
  Structure of production: Industry including rural handicrafts: 59 per cent of total value of industrial and agricultural production (1978).[e]
  Structure of industry (%):   Heavy industry 37, consumer goods industry 63 (1978).[e]
  Total labour force   25.5 million (1979)[16]; agriculture 73,
  by sector (%):   industry 8, service 9 (1978).
  Structure of ownership (1971)[a]:   The North – Industry: nationalised, with state-owned enterprises representing 64 per cent and co-operatives[II] 30 per cent of total output values. Agriculture: all land nationalised, with 5 per cent used by state farms, 81 per cent by co-operatives, 8 per cent as family plots

by co-op members, and 6 per cent by individual farmers (1978).[c] 96 per cent of peasant families belonged to a co-operative by 1971.[f]

The South – Industry: includes state-owned enterprises (70 per cent of industrial output value in 1976)[I], joint state-private enterprise, co-operatives and some private small industry. Agriculture: under re-organisation of small peasant farms into production groups and ultimately co-operatives; state farms are being set up in the New Economic Zones.

Main crops: Rice (occupying 75 per cent of cropped land in 1977), maize, sweet potatoes, cassava, tea, sugar cane.

Notes

[I]For definition, see appendix.
[II]Mainly handicraft industry.
[III]By total value.
[IV]Estimated as a residual by the World Bank.

Sources

[a]Foreign Language Publishing House, *The Democratic Republic of Viet Nam*, Hanoi, 1975.

[b]Foreign Languages Publishing House, *Viet Nam – Forward to a New Stage*, Hanoi, 1977.

[c]*Giao Trinh Kinh Te Nong Nghiep* (Agricultural Economics Textbook), University Publishing House, Hanoi, 1978.

[d]John Montagu, 'The Enemy Within', *The Guardian*, 17 June 1981.

[e]*Nghien Cuu Kinh Te* (Economic Research) 4, 1980, p. 75–8.

[f]Nguyen Tien Hung, G., *Economic Development of Socialist Vietnam 1955–80*, Praeger, New York, 1977.

[g]Turley, William S. 'Hanoi's domestic dilemmas.' *Problems of Communism*, vol. 29, no. 4, July–August 1980.

[h]*Vietnam Courier*, no. 6, 1980, p. 13.

[i]World Bank Report no. 1718-VN, *The Socialist Republic of Viet Nam. An Introductory Economic Report*, Washington DC, August 1977.

Vietnam: Chronology

1858   French forces seize Da Nang, beginning period of colonial conquest.

1884   All of Vietnam comes under French colonial rule.

1945   September, Declaration of Independence of Vietnam by Ho Chi Minh.

1946   December, outbreak of war between France and the Viet Minh.

1954   July, Geneva Agreements end the Indochina War and divide Vietnam at the 17th Parallel into two temporary military regroupment zones.

1955   U.S. replaces France in southern Vietnam and supports Ngo Dinh Diem as replacement to French-backed Bao Dai.

1960   Third Party Congress inaugurates first Five-Year Plan in North; formation of National Liberation Front of South Vietnam; beginning of guerrilla war in South.

1964   US escalation: large troop landings in South and first bombings of the North.

1968   Tet offensive defeats US hopes of military victory; bombing halt and opening of peace talks in Paris.

1969   September, death of DRV President Ho Chi Minh.

1972   February, Shanghai Communiqué: China-US détente; March, Spring Offensive shakes US strategy of 'Vietnamisation' of the war; bombing of DRV resumed.

1973   January, Paris Agreement signed: all US military forces to withdraw from Vietnam; recognition of two administrations and military zones of control in the South.

1974   January, China takes Paracel Islands from Saigon government forces.

1975   April, Military collapse of Saigon government.

1976   July, country unified as the Socialist Republic of Vietnam; December, Fourth Party Congress outlines economic policy.

1977   Escalating conflict with Kampuchea; Pol Pot forces attack Vietnamese settlements across the border.

1978   Crisis in Sino-Vietnamese relations: exodus of Chinese (Hoa) residents in Vietnam; cut-off of all Chinese aid projects;
June: Vietnam joins CMEA;
November: Vietnam signs Treaty of Friendship and Co-operation with the USSR;
December: exiled Kampucheans in Vietnam form Kampuchean National Front for National Salvation and join Vietnamese army in overthrowing Pol Pot; Vietnamese occupation of Kampuchea begins.

1979   February: Chinese military attack on Vietnam;
September: Sixth Plenum begins move toward economic liberalisation.

1982   March: Fifth Congress of Vietnam Communist Party confirms policy of economic liberalisation.

GENERAL BIBLIOGRAPHY
FOR THE COUNTRY
PROFILES

Appendix A:

1 Banks, Arthur and William Overstreet, *Political Handbook of the World 1980*, London, 1980.
2 Day, Alan J. and H.W. Degenhart, *Political Parties of the World*, Harlow, 1980.
3 Europa Publications, *Africa South of Sahara 1979–80*, London, 1980.
4 Europa Publications, *The Far East and Australasia 1980–81*, London, 1980.
5 Economist Intelligence Unit, *Quarterly Economic Reviews* (annual supplements 1980) of: China, Hong Kong and North Korea; Indochina; Tanzania; Mozambique; Uganda, Ethiopia, Somalia, Djibouti, London, 1980.
6 Food and Agricultural Organisation (FAO), *Production Yearbook, 1979*, Geneva, 1980.
7 Food and Agricultural Organisation (FAO), *Trade Yearbook 1979*, Geneva, 1980.
8 The International Institute for Strategic Studies, *The Military Balance* (annual), 1978/79–1980/81 issues, London.
9 International Monetary Fund, *Balance of Payments Statistics* (monthly), various issues, Washington, DC.
10 International Monetary Fund, *Government Finance Statistics Yearbook 1980*, Washington, DC, 1980.
11 United Nations, *Monthly Bulletin of Statistics*, New York, March 1981.
12 United Nations, *World Statistics in Brief. UN's statistical pocket book*, New York, 1979.
13 United Nations, *Yearbook of International Trade Statistics 1979*, vols I and II, New York, 1980.
14 UNCTAD, *Handbook of International Trade and*

Development Statistics, supplement 1980, New York, 1980.
15 UNESCO, *Statistical Yearbook 1980*, Paris, 1980.
16 US, CIA, *Handbook of Economic Statistics 1980*, Washington, DC, 1980.
17 US, CIA, *National Basic Intelligence Factbook*, Washington DC, January 1980.
18 World Bank, *World Development Report 1980*, Washington, August 1980 (and earlier issues).

Appendix B: Clarification of Data Categories

The following definitions and sources apply to data given in the profiles when not otherwise clarified. The source references refer to the bibliography in Appendix A. Note that for the countries covered in this volume, a large proportion of the data from international sources, as well as from other sources, are based on incomplete information and represent merely estimates.

Population: Mid-year estimates, UN.[11]

Capital: Population estimates from political or area year books.[1,3,4]

Land area: Arable land – land under temporary crops, temporary meadows for mowing or pasture, land under market or kitchen gardens, land temporary fallow or lying idle (potentially productive land is not included), FAO.[6]

Party membership: Day and Degenhart.[2]

Armed forces: International Institute for Strategic Studies.[8]

Population growth: Based mainly of UN estimates. World Bank.[18]

Population of working age: As above.

Urban population: Estimates are based on national definitions of 'urban', and may therefore not be appropriate for cross-country comparisons. World Bank.[18]

School enrolment gross ratios: Enrolment of all ages at the indicated level as percentage of respective school-age population (the latter normally 6–11 for primary, 12–17 for secondary, and 18–22 for higher education). The gross ratio therefore includes the enrolment of over-aged pupils and can exceed 100 per cent. UNESCO.[15]

Literacy rate: Percentage of persons aged fifteen and over who can read and write. World Bank.[18]

Life expectancy: Average numbers of life remaining at birth. World Bank.[18]

Infant death rate: Annual deaths of infants under one year of age per 1000 live births.

Child death rate: Annual deaths of children aged 1–4 per 1000 children in the same age group. World Bank.[18]

Population per hospital bed: UN.[12]

Population per physician: World Bank.[18]

Gross Domestic Product, Gross National Product and National Income: The western concept of GNP measures the total domestic and foreign output claimed by residents of a country. GDP measures the total final output of goods and services produced within a country's territory by residents and non-residents. The *Marxist concept of national income* (which is used by most of the countries represented in this volume) represents the net value added in the production of material goods and in providing the services directly required to bring the goods to their final sales point (i.e. transportation, communication services for the material production sphere, agricultural procurement and the wholesale and retail networks). The main branches of material production are industry, agriculture, construction and the group of branches providing the mentioned services, but a large part of the service sector as defined in the western GNP is not included in the Marxist method: these are services from the non-material sphere which comprises government administration, free public services, and services sold to households and to the public sector.

The figures quoted for GNP per capita are from the World Bank,[18] and calculated according to the World Bank Atlas method; these have been multiplied by population estimates in the same source to achieve the total GNP estimates. Note that the lack of exchange rates suitable for conversion into US $, as well as the difference in definitions causes a considerable margin of error in the estimates.

Gross domestic investment: represents outlays for additions to fixed assets plus net value of inventory changes. World Bank.[18]

GDP by sector: Calculated from current price series factor cost (without taxes and subsidies) when data permit. Agriculture: agriculture, forestry, hunting and fishing, Industry: mining, manufacturing, construction, electricity, water and gas. Service: all other branches of economic activity. World Bank.[18]

Total labour force: Comprises here economically active persons, i.e. includes the armed forces, unemployed seeking work and unpaid family workers assisting in a family farm or business. Since definitions vary between countries the estimates may lack in comparability. FAO.[6]

Labour force by sector: Sectors are defined as for GDP by sector. Most estimates are geometric extrapolations of ILO labour force estimates for 1970 published in 1977.

Irrigated area: FAO.[6]

Energy balance: Liquid fuels include natural gas liquids. UNCTAD.[14]

Growth indicators: Growth of gross value added calculated from constant price series. World Bank.[18] The growth rates for agricultural production and food production per capita are based on FAO's quantum index series calculated from the sum of price-weighted quantities with the three-year average 1969–71 as base.[6]

Real growth of exports: World Bank.[18]

Destination of exports: The source defines the country groups as follows: Industrialised countries – OECD members except Greece, Portugal, Spain and Turkey which are included among developing countries. Socialist countries ('centrally-planned market economies') – the USSR, eastern Europe, Albania, China, Mongolia, North Korea. Capital surplus oil exporters – Iran, Iraq, Kuwait, Libya, Oman, Qatar, Saudi Arabia, United Arab Emirates. All other countries, including Cuba and the Asian socialist countries not mentioned above, are included among developing countries. World Bank.[18]

Foreign debt: Refers to external public debt outstanding and disbursed as of end of year stated and comprises public and publicly guaranteed loans net of cancelled loan commitments and repayments of principal. World Bank.[18]

Foreign aid: (generally) includes net disbursements of loans and grants made at concessionary financial terms by official agencies of assisting countries.

INDEX